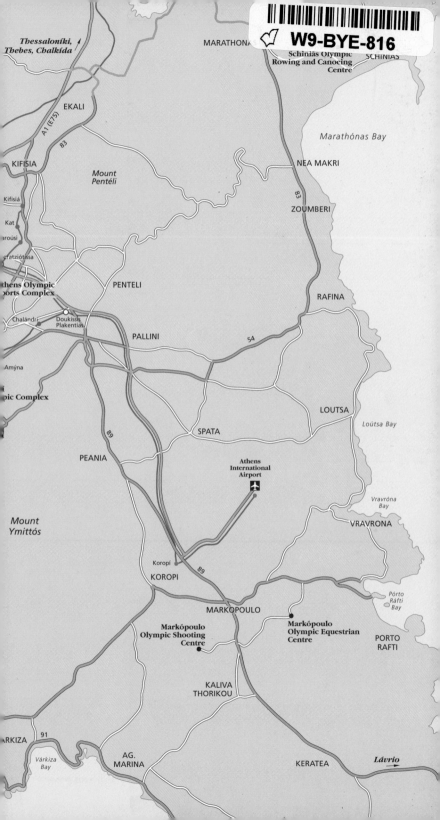

EYEWITNESS TRAVEL GUIDES

ATHENS

EYEWITNESS TRAVEL GUIDES

ATHENS

Main Consultant: MARC DUBIN

LONDON, NEW YORK,
MELBOURNE, MUNICH AND DELHI
www.dk.com

PROJECT EDITOR Jane Simmonds
ART EDITOR Stephen Bere
EDITORS Isabel Carlisle, Michael Ellis, Simon Farbrother,
Claire Folkard, Marianne Petrou, Andrew Szudek
DESIGNERS Tessa Bindloss, Jo Doran, Paul Jackson,
Elly King, Marisa Renzullo
MAP CO-ORDINATORS Emily Green, Dave Pugh
VISUALIZER Joy Fitzsimmons
PICTURE RESEARCH Ellen Root, Brigitte Arora
LANGUAGE CONSULTANT Georgia Gotsi

CONTRIBUTORS AND CONSULTANTS
Rosemary Barron, Marc Dubin, Jane Foster, Mike Gerrard, Andy
Harris, Lynette Mitchell, Colin Nicholson, Robin Osborne,
Barnaby Rogerson, Paul Sterry

MAPS
Gary Bowes, Fiona Casey, Christine Purcell (ERA-Maptec Ltd)

PHOTOGRAPHERS
Joe Cornish, Rob Reichenfeld, Peter Wilson

ILLUSTRATORS
Stephen Conlin, Paul Guest, Steve Gyapay, Maltings Partnership,
Chris Orr & Associates, Paul Weston, John Woodcock

Reproduced by Colourscan (Singapore)
Printed and bound by L. Rex Printing Company Limited, China

First published in Great Britain in 2004
by Dorling Kindersley Limited
80 Strand, London WC2R 0RL

A CIP CATALOGUE RECORD IS AVAILABLE FROM THE BRITISH LIBRARY.

ISBN 1-4053-0608-4

CONTENTS

View of the Acropolis and Parthenon fro

◁ **View of the Acropolis at sunset**

thwest

HOW TO USE THIS GUIDE

THIS GUIDE helps you to get the most from your stay in Athens, before, during and after the Olympics. It provides expert recommendations and practical information. *The History of the Olympic Games* charts the progress of the Games from their origins to modern times. *Athens at a Glance* gives an overview of the city's highlights. The main sightseeing section of the book is *Athens Area by Area*. It describes all the main sights with maps, photographs and illustrations. Restaurant and hotel listings can be found in *Travellers' Needs*. The *Survival Guide* has tips on everything from using a telephone to transport.

ATHENS

Athens has been divided into two sightseeing areas. Each has its own chapter, opening with a list of the sights described. All sights are numbered on an area map, and are described in detail on the following pages.

Sights at a Glance
gives a categorized list of the chapter's sights: Museums and Galleries; Squares, Parks and Gardens; Churches and Historic Buildings.

All pages relating to Athens have red thumb tabs.

A locator map shows you where you are in relation to the rest of Athens.

1 Area Map
The sights are numbered and located on a map. Sights in the city centre are also shown on the Athens Street Finder *on pages 140–153.*

2 Street-by-Street Map
This gives an overhead view of the key areas in central Athens. The numbering on the map ties in with the area map and the fuller descriptions that follow.

Stars indicate the sights that no visitor should miss.

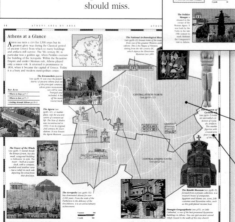

A suggested route for a walk around a particular area of the city is shown in red.

Each sightseeing area is clearly defined by a boundary line and labelled.

3 Athens at a glance
All the main sights to visit are located on the map, given a short description and cross-referenced to their main catalogue entry.

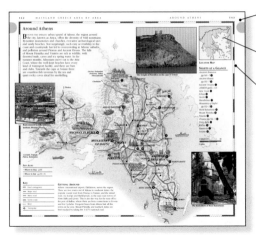

Each region can be identified by its colour coding, shown on the inside front cover.

A locator map shows you where you are in relation to the rest of the country.

4 Pictorial map
This shows the region covered in the chapter. The main sights are numbered on the map. The major roads are marked and there are useful tips about the best ways of getting around the area.

PRACTICAL INFORMATION

Each entry provides all the information needed to plan a visit to the sight. The key to the symbols used is on the inside back cover.

5 Detailed Information on each sight
All important sights in each area are described in depth in this section. They are listed in order, following the numbering on the Area Map. Practical information is also provided.

Telephone number

Nearest metro station

Sight number

Mitrópoli ⑫
Μητρόπολη

Plateía Mitropóleos, Pláka. **Map** 6 E1.
📞 210 322 1308. **M** Monastiráki.
⏰ 6:30am–7pm daily.

ADDRESS

Opening hours

Map reference to *Street Finder* at back of book

Story boxes highlight special aspects of a particular sight.

A Visitors' Checklist provides the practical information you will need to plan your visit.

6 Athens' major sights
These are given one or more full pages. Historic buildings are dissected to reveal their interiors. Many of the ancient sites are reconstructed to supplement information about the site as it is seen today.

THE HISTORY OF THE OLYMPIC GAMES

THE HISTORY OF THE OLYMPIC GAMES *has its roots steeped in legend and pagan rituals. Originally a one-day festival limited to the city states of ancient Greece, today it is the most prestigious sporting event on earth, attracting competitors from 201 countries worlwide and entertaining millions across the globe.*

ANCIENT OLYMPICS

Although the Olympics probably began as far back as the 11th century BC, the first recorded games were held on the plains of Olympia in 776 BC. They lasted one day, with the sole event being the men's sprint over a distance of about 200m (650 ft), one lap of the ancient stadium. The games were dedicated to the gods and were held every four years in late summer. Over the centuries that followed, events such as the Pentathlon (sprinting, wrestling, javelin, discus and long jump), wrestling, boxing, the Pankration (a brutal form of hand-to-hand combat) and equestrian sports (horse racing and chariot racing) were added, and the duration of the games was extended first to three, then to five days.

Only free-born male Greeks were entitled to compete and since they competed naked, women were banned from spectating. At the end of the games winning athletes were awarded with a palm tree branch and showered with flowers thrown

Flame lighting ceremony, Sydney 2000 Olympic Games

by spectators. As of 752 BC, under the advice of the Oracle at Delphi, each victor was also crowned with an olive wreath at the closing ceremony.

The stadium at Olympia could seat 20,000 and as a prestigious sporting event, the games were attended by the leaders of various city states. As well as entertainment, the games provided leaders with an ideal opportunity to promote diplomacy and seal agreements. They were also a place where merchants would strike new deals, and artists would perform and find new patrons.

Under the Romans the games were opened up to male competitors from the entire Greek and Roman world. Large sums of money were offered as prizes, and the event became more professional, and more corrupt. In 67 BC, Emperor Nero rescheduled the games so he could compete. He carried off most the prizes, despite having fallen from his chariot. In AD 393, with the rise in Christianity, the Olympics were banned by Emperor Theodosius I for being too pagan.

TIMELINE

776 BC First recorded games held at Olympia

Wrestlers, 510 BC relief detail

393 AD Christian Emperor Theodosius I bans games for being too pagan

| 800 BC | 600 BC | 400 BC | 200 BC | 0 | 200 AD | 400 AD |

720 BC Women banned from attending Olympics

67 BC Roman Emperor Nero competes, unfairly rescheduling the games, and 'wins' most prizes

Saints, 3rd century lime-stone relief

◁ **Detail of a runner from an Etruscan fresco, 480–470 BC**

MODERN OLYMPICS

The Olympic Games were revived in 1896 by a French Baron, Pierre de Coubertin. Under the Olympic values of 'Participation, Brotherhood and Peace', the first modern Olympics was held in Kallimármaro stadium, in Athens. Built in the 4th century BC for the Panathenaic Games, it had long lain in ruin, but was restored using marble for the 1896 event.

Approximately 300 athletes from 13 countries participated in a total of nine sports: Track and field events (including the marathon), swimming, cycling, fencing, gymnastics, shooting, lawn tennis, wrestling and weightlifting. The winner of each event received a silver medal, a certificate and an olive wreath, while the runner up took a bronze medal. The athlete who came in third went away empty handed.

De Coubertin was instrumental in defining the identity of the modern Olympics. He conceived the Olympic symbol of five interlocking rings, symbolising the unity of the five continents, and lay down the Olympic Creed, which states, "The most important thing in the Olympic Games is not to win but to take part, just as the most important thing in life is not the triumph but the struggle. The essential thing is not to have won but to have fought well".

Four years later, in 1900, the games were held in Paris, despite Greece's wish that they should remain in their homeland. 28 nations took part in 75 events. Women competed for the first time, albeit representing only 20 of the 1000 athletes present.

Illustrated view of Panathinaikó stadium during the 1896 Olympic Games, Athens

The 1908 games in London saw the first opening procession, with athletes marching into the stadium behind their respective national flags. As of 1928, when the games were held in Amsterdam, the procession has traditionally been led by Greece, followed by other countries in alphabetical order, usually with the host nation taking up the rear.

The question of professional status arose for the first time at the Stockholm games in 1912. America's Jim Thorpe won the pentathlon and decathlon, but his medals were taken back when it was discovered that he had earnt money from playing baseball as a teenager. Thorpe was the first athlete to be disqualified for being a 'professional', though he was pardoned in 1982, 29 years after his death.

The 1916 games were cancelled due to the atrocities of World War I, then resumed at Antwerp in 1920. As a symbol of peace between the nations, doves were released at the opening ceremony, and the Olympic flag, bearing the five interlocking

Vⁿ OLYMPIADE STOCKHOLM 1912

Poster of the 1912 Stockholm Olympics

TIMELINE

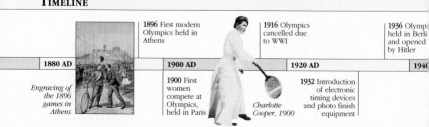

1896 First modern Olympics held in Athens

1916 Olympics cancelled due to WWI

1936 Olymp held in Berli and opened by Hitler

1880 AD   1900 AD   1920 AD   194(

Engraving of the 1896 games in Athens

1900 First women compete at Olympics, held in Paris

Charlotte Cooper, 1900

1932 Introduction of electronic timing devices and photo finish equipment rings, was flown for the first time. The Olympic Oath was also introduced: Traditionally made by an athlete from the host country, it promises sportsmanship, fair play and honour.

The 1924 games in Paris saw the introduction of the Olympic motto, 'Citius, Altius, Fortius' (Faster, Higher, Stronger). In the same year, three golds were taken by US swimmer Johnny Weissmuller, who later became better known for his role as Tarzan in early cinema.

Gymnast, Olga Korbett

Pierre de Coubertin passed away in 1932, and upon his request his heart was placed in a commemorative 'stele' at the ancient site of Olympia. That same year, at Los Angeles, electronic timing devices and photo finish equipment were used at the games for the first time, though it was not until the 1960 event in Rome that the Olympics enjoyed live television coverage and worldwide transmission.

As World War II loomed, the 1936 Games were held in Berlin and opened by Adolf Hitler. The ancient tradition of lighting the Olympic flame from the sun's rays at an altar at Olympia was reintroduced, after which it travelled hand to hand from Olympia to Berlin as part of the Olympic torch relay.

The 1972 Olympics in Munich witnessed the most tragic event in the games' history when a terrorist attack on the Israeli team left 11 athletes, five terrorists and one policeman dead. The games were suspended for one day and a memorial service held. With the consent of Israeli officials, the event was resumed the following day.

Political tensions in the 1980s saw the US, West Germany and Japan boycott the 1980 Moscow games. The USSR went on to boycott the 1984 Los Angeles games. By the 1992 games, held in Barcelona, tensions had cooled and not a single nation declined entry. Germany took part as a single nation, and with the end of apartheid, South Africa was allowed to compete.

2004 is the year that will finally see the Olympics return to their homeland. In the run up to the games, the Olympic torch will travel the entire globe in 78 days, visiting all former Olympic cities and passing through all five continents, marking its first trip to Africa and Latin America. Its return to the Athens Olympic stadium on 13 August will signal the beginning of the 2004 event, which will be attended by some 16,000 athletes and a staggering 45,000 security personnel.

Part of the spectacular opening ceremony, Sydney 2000 Olympic Games

ATHENS
AREA BY AREA

Athens at a Glance

ATHENS HAS BEEN A CITY for 3,500 years but its greatest glory was during the Classical period of ancient Greece from which so many buildings and artifacts still survive. The 5th century BC in particular was a golden age, when Perikles oversaw the building of the Acropolis. Within the Byzantine Empire and under Ottoman rule, Athens played only a minor role. It returned to prominence in 1834, when it became the capital of Greece. Today it is a busy and modern metropolitan centre.

The Kerameikós quarter (see pp38–9) *was once the potters' district of ancient Athens and site of the principal cemetery, whose grave monuments can still be seen. Tranquil and secluded, it lies off the main tourist track.*

SEE ALSO

- *Where to Stay* pp86–90
- *Where to Eat* pp100–104
- *Getting Around Athens* pp136–9

The Agora (see pp40–41), *or market place, was the ancient centre of commercial life. The Stoa of Attalos was reconstructed in 1953–6 on its original, 2nd-century BC foundations. It now houses the Agora Museum.*

The Tower of the Winds (see pp36–7) *stands beside the Roman forum, but this small, octagonal building is Hellenistic in style. The tower – built as a water clock, with a compass, sundials and weather vane – has a relief on each side depicting the wind from that direction.*

The Acropolis (see pp44–51) *has dominated Athens for over 2,000 years. From the scale of the Parthenon to the delicacy of the Erechtheion, it is an extraordinary achievement.*

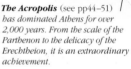

| 0 metres | 500 |
| 0 yards | 500 |

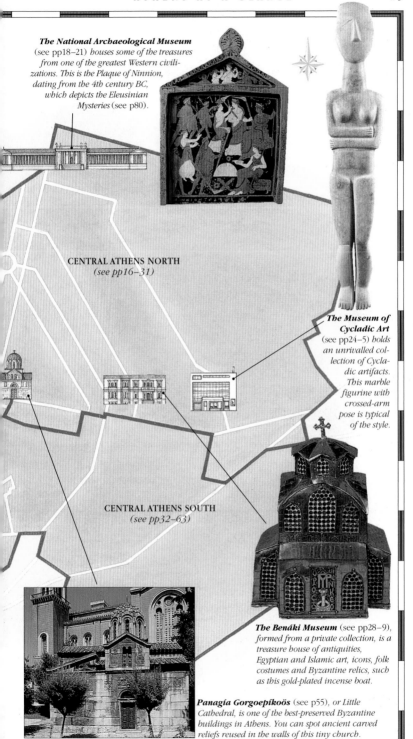

The National Archaeological Museum (see pp18–21) *houses some of the treasures from one of the greatest Western civilizations. This is the Plaque of Ninnion, dating from the 4th century BC, which depicts the Eleusinian Mysteries* (see p80).

CENTRAL ATHENS NORTH *(see pp16–31)*

The Museum of Cycladic Art (see pp24–5) *holds an unrivalled collection of Cycladic artifacts. This marble figurine with crossed-arm pose is typical of the style.*

CENTRAL ATHENS SOUTH *(see pp32–63)*

The Benáki Museum (see pp28–9), *formed from a private collection, is a treasure house of antiquities, Egyptian and Islamic art, icons, folk costumes and Byzantine relics, such as this gold-plated incense boat.*

Panagía Gorgoepíkoös (see p55), *or Little Cathedral, is one of the best-preserved Byzantine buildings in Athens. You can spot ancient carved reliefs reused in the walls of this tiny church.*

CENTRAL ATHENS NORTH

INHABITED FOR 7,000 YEARS, Athens was the birthplace of European civilization. It flourished in the 5th century BC when the Athenians controlled much of the eastern Mediterranean. The buildings from this era, including those in the ancient Agora and on the Acropolis, lie largely in the southern part of the city. The northern half has grown since the early 1800s when King Otto made Athens the new capital of Greece. When the king's architects planned the new, European-style city, they included wide, tree-lined avenues, such as Panepistimíou and Akadimías, that were soon home to many grand

Icon of the Archangel Michael, from the Byzantine Museum

Neo-Classical public buildings and mansion houses. Today, these edifices still provide elegant homes for all the major banks, embassies and public institutions, such as the University and the Library.

The chic residential area of Kolonáki is located in the north of the city centre, as is the cosmopolitan area around Patriárchou Ioakeím and Irodótou. These streets have excellent shopping and entertainment venues. Most of Athens' best museums, including the National Archaeological Museum, are also found in this area of the city. For information on getting around Athens, see pages 136–9.

SIGHTS AT A GLANCE

Museums and Galleries
Benáki Museum pp28–9 ❿
Byzantine Museum ❼
City of Athens Museum ⓬
Museum of Cycladic Art pp24–5 ❽
National Archaeological Museum pp18–21 ❶
National Gallery of Art ❺
National Historical Museum ⓭
Theatrical Museum ⓫
War Museum ❻

Squares, Parks and Gardens
Exárcheia and Stréfi Hill ❷
Lykavittós Hill ❸
Plateía Kolonakíou ❾

Churches
Kapnikaréa ⓮

Historic Buildings
Gennádeion ❹

KEY

Ⓜ Metro station

Ⓟ Parking

ℹ Tourist Information

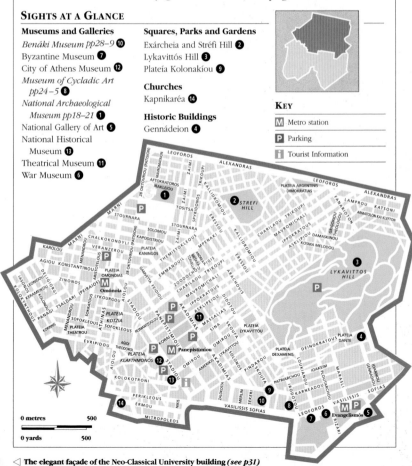

◁ **The elegant façade of the Neo-Classical University building** *(see p31)*

National Archaeological Museum ❶
Εθνικό Αρχαιολογικό Μουσείο

Hellenistic bronze head from Delos

O PENED IN 1891, this superb museum, often known simply as the National Museum, brought together a collection that had previously been stored all over the city. New wings were added in 1939. The priceless collection was then dispersed and buried underground during World War II to protect it from possible damage. The museum reopened in 1946, but it took a further 50 years of renovation and reorganization finally to do justice to its formidable collection. With the combination of such unique exhibits as the Mycenaean gold, along with the unrivalled amount of sculpture, pottery and jewellery on display, this is without doubt one of the world's finest museums.

Neo-Classical entrance to the National Archaeological Museum on Patission

GALLERY GUIDE

On the ground floor, Mycenaean, Neolithic and Cycladic finds are followed by Geometric, Archaic, Classical, Roman and Hellenistic sculpture. Smaller collections of bronzes, Egyptian artifacts, the Eléni Stathátou jewellery collection and the Karapános collection are also on the ground floor. The first floor houses a collection of pottery.

Bronze collection

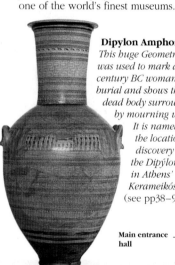

Dipylon Amphora
This huge Geometric vase was used to mark an 8th-century BC woman's burial and shows the dead body surrounded by mourning women. It is named after the location of its discovery near the Dipylon Gate in Athens' Kerameikós (see pp38–9).

Sculpture garden

Main entrance hall

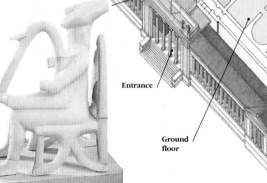

Entrance

Ground floor

Harp Player
The minimalist Cycladic style of sculpture flourished in the 3rd millennium BC and originated in the Cyclades. The simple lines and bold forms of the marble figurines influenced many early 20th-century artists, including the British sculptor Henry Moore.

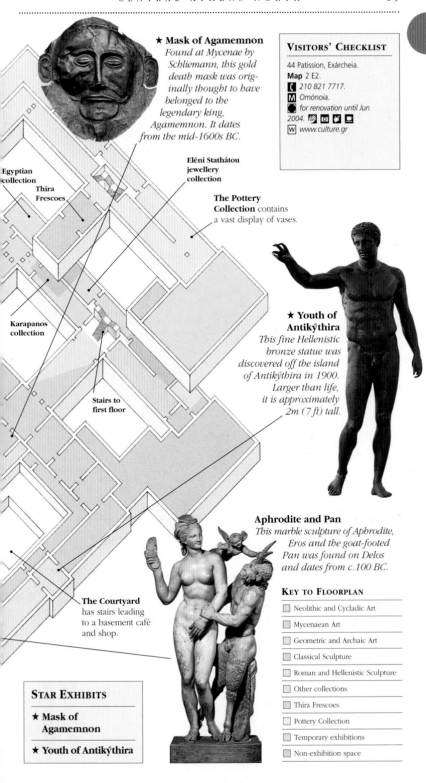

★ Mask of Agamemnon
Found at Mycenae by Schliemann, this gold death mask was originally thought to have belonged to the legendary king, Agamemnon. It dates from the mid-1600s BC.

Eléni Stathátou jewellery collection

The Pottery Collection contains a vast display of vases.

Egyptian collection

Thíra Frescoes

Karapanos collection

Stairs to first floor

★ Youth of Antikýthira
This fine Hellenistic bronze statue was discovered off the island of Antikýthira in 1900. Larger than life, it is approximately 2m (7 ft) tall.

Aphrodite and Pan
This marble sculpture of Aphrodite, Eros and the goat-footed Pan was found on Delos and dates from c.100 BC.

The Courtyard has stairs leading to a basement café and shop.

KEY TO FLOORPLAN

- Neolithic and Cycladic Art
- Mycenaean Art
- Geometric and Archaic Art
- Classical Sculpture
- Roman and Hellenistic Sculpture
- Other collections
- Thíra Frescoes
- Pottery Collection
- Temporary exhibitions
- Non-exhibition space

STAR EXHIBITS

- **★ Mask of Agamemnon**
- **★ Youth of Antikýthira**

Exploring the National Archaeological Museum's Collection

DISPLAYING ITS TREASURES in chronological order, the museum presents an impressive and thorough overview of Greek art through the centuries. Beginning with early Cycladic figurines and continuing through the Greek Bronze Age, the exhibits end with the glories of Hellenistic period bronzes and a collection of busts of Roman emperors. High points in between include the numerous gold artifacts found at Mycenae, the elegant Archaic *koúroi* statues and the many examples of fine Classical sculpture.

Mycenaean head of a sphinx

NEOLITHIC AND CYCLADIC ART

THE DAWNING of Greek civilization (3500–2900 BC) saw primitive decorative vases and figures. This collection also contains terracotta figurines, jewellery and a selection of weapons.

The vibrant fertility gods and goddesses, such as the *kourotrópbos* (nursing mother) with child, are particularly well preserved. Of exceptional importance are the largest known Cycladic marble figurine, from Amorgós, and the earliest known figures of musicians – the *Flute Player* and *Harp Player* both from Kéros. Later finds from Mílos, such as the painted vase with fishermen, reveal the changes in pot shapes and colour that took place in the late Cycladic Bronze Age.

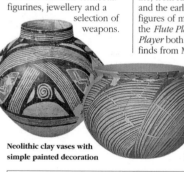

Neolithic clay vases with simple painted decoration

MYCENAEAN ART

IT IS NOT DIFFICULT to understand the allure of the museum's most popular attraction, the Hall of Mycenaean Antiquities, with its dazzling array of 16th-century BC gold treasures. Other exhibits in the collection include frescoes, ivory sculptures and seal rings made out of precious stones.

From the shaft graves of Mycenae's nobles came a procession of daggers, cups, seals and rings as well as a number of regal death masks, including the justly famous *Mask of Agamemnon*. Two superb *rhytons*, or wine jugs, are also on display: one in the shape of a bull's head, made in silver with gold horns, and one in gold shaped like a lion's head. Equally rich finds from sites other than Mycenae have since been made. These include two gold bull cups found at Vafeió, in Crete, a gold phial entwined with dolphins and octopuses (excavated from a royal tomb at Déntra), clay tablets with the early Linear B script from the Palace of Nestor in the Peloponnese and a magnificent sword from the Tomb of Stáfylos on the island of Skópelos.

Mycenaean bronze dagger, inlaid with gold

THE DEVELOPMENT OF GREEK SCULPTURE

Sculpture was one of the most sophisticated forms of Greek art. We are able to trace its development from the early *koúroi* to the great works of named sculptors such as Pheidias and Praxiteles in Classical times. Portraiture only began in the 5th century BC; even then most Greek sculptures were of gods and goddesses, heroes and athletes and idealized men and women. These have had an enormous influence on Western art down the centuries.

The Volomándra Koúros was discovered in Attica and dates from the mid-6th century BC. The highly stylized koúroi (statues of naked youths) first appear in the mid-7th century BC. Derived from Egyptian art, these figures share a common pose and proportions. Clothed kórai are the female counterpart.

The Marathon Boy (340 BC), like many other Greek bronzes, was found on the sea floor. The dreamy expression and easy pose of the figure are characteristic of the works of Praxiteles, the leading late Classical sculptor. An example of the "heroic nude", it shows a great naturalism and perfect balance.

**Hellenistic bronze known
as the *Horse with the
Little Jockey***

GEOMETRIC AND ARCHAIC ART

FAMED FOR ITS monumental burial vases, such as the *Dipylon Amphora*, the Geometric period developed a more ornate style in the 7th century BC with the introduction of mythological and plant and animal motifs. By the 6th century BC the full artistry of the black-figure vases had developed. Two rare examples from this period are a *lekythos* depicting Peleus, Achilles and the centaur, Cheiron, and the sculptured heads known as *aryballoi*.

**Warrior from Boiotia,
early 7th century BC**

CLASSICAL SCULPTURE

THE COLLECTION OF Classical sculpture contains both fine statues and a selection of grave monuments, mostly from the Kerameikós. These include the beautiful *stele* (c.410 BC) of Hegeso *(see p38).* Classical votive sculpture on display includes parts of a statue of the goddess

This "valedictory stele" *(mid-4th century BC) shows a seated woman bidding farewell to her family. The figures express a dignified suffering found in many Greek funerary reliefs.*

Hera, from the Argive Heraion in the Peloponnese, and many statues of the goddess Athena, including the *Varvakeion Athena*, a reduced copy of the original ivory and gold statue from the Parthenon *(see p49).*

ROMAN AND HELLENISTIC SCULPTURE

ALTHOUGH A LARGE number of Greek bronzes were lost in antiquity, as metal was melted down in times of emergency for making weapons, the museum has some excellent pieces on display. These include the famous bronzes *Poseidon* and the *Horse with the Little Jockey*, both found at Cape Artemísion on Evvoia, and the *Youth of Antikýthira*, found in the sea off that island. Another of the best known sculptures is the *Marathon Boy*.

OTHER COLLECTIONS

THE MUSEUM also houses several collections donated by private individuals. Among these is the glittering **Eléni Stathátou jewellery collection**, which covers the Bronze Age through to the Byzantine period. The **Karapános collection**, which is composed mainly from discoveries made at the site at Dodóni in Central Greece, contains many fine bronzes, including *Zeus Hurling a Thunderbolt*. Also on display are small decorative and votive pieces, and strips of lead inscribed with questions for the oracle at Dodóni.

Other collections include the recently opened **Egyptian collection** and the **Bronze collection** which comprises many small pieces of statuary and decorative items discovered on the Acropolis.

THIRA FRESCOES

THREE OF THE FAMOUS frescoes discovered at Akrotíri on the island of Thíra (Santoríni) in 1967, and originally thought to be from the mythical city of Atlantis, are displayed in the museum. The rest remain on Santoríni. Dating from 1500 BC, they confirm the sophistication of late Minoan civilization. The colourful, restored images depict a naval expedition, elegant women, children, naked fishermen, animals and flowers.

POTTERY COLLECTION

THE STRENGTH of this vast collection lies not only in its size, but in the quality of specific works, representing the flowering of Greek ceramic art. The real gems belong to the 5th century BC when red-figure vases and white-ground *lekythoi* (funerary vases) became the established style and were produced in vast numbers. Expressive painting styles and new designs characterize this period. The most poignant pieces are by the "Bosanquet Painter" and the "Achilles Painter" who portrayed men by their graves.

**Gold Hellenistic ring
from the Eléni
Stathátou collection**

View northeast to Lykavittós Hill from the Acropolis

Exarcheía and Stréfi Hill ❷

Εξάρχεια
Λόφος Στρέφη

Map 2 F2 & 3 A2. **M** *Omónoia.*

UNTIL RECENTLY, the area around Plateía Exarcheíon was renowned as a hotbed of anarchist activity. Prior to the invasion of students, Exárcheia was a very attractive area and the 19th-century Neo-Classical buildings still stand as testament to this. Today, the area is picking up again and although parts of it are still rather run-down, an influx of new gentrification has brought many fashionable cafés, bars and *ouzerí* to the area. Themistokléous, which leads off the square down to Omónoia, is pleasant to wander along; the local food stores and small boutiques make a refreshing change from the noisy bars. Plateía Exarcheíon is especially lively at night when the outdoor tavernas and the open-air cinema, the Riviera, in the streets that climb towards Stréfi, attract many visitors.

Every year a demonstration takes place on 17 November, marking the date in 1973 when many students were killed by the military Junta during a sit-in.

The nearby park of Stréfi Hill, with its intriguing maze of paths, is quiet and peaceful by day but comes to life at night when its cafés are full. Stréfi Hill is one of the many green areas in Athens that provide welcome relief from the noise and grime of the city, particularly in the oppressive heat of summer.

The restaurant on Lykavittós Hill, overlooking Athens

Lykavittós Hill ❸

Λόφος Λυκαβηττού

Map 3 C3. **Funicular:** *from Ploutárchou, 8:45am–12:45pm Mon–Wed & Fri–Sun, 10:30am–12:45pm Thu.*

THE PEAK of Lykavittós (also known as Lycabettus) reaches 277 m (910 ft) above the city, and is its highest hill. It can be climbed on foot by various paths or by the easier, albeit vertiginous, ride in the funicular from the corner of Ploutárchou. On foot, it should take about 45 minutes. The hill may derive its name from a combination of the words *lýki* and *vaino*, meaning "path of light". The ancient belief was that this was the rock once destined to be the Acropolis citadel, accidentally dropped by the city's patron goddess, Athena. Although it is without doubt the most prominent hill in Athens, surprisingly little mention is made of Lykavittós in Classical literature; the exceptions are passing references in Aristophanes's *Frogs* and Plato's *Kritías.* This landmark is a favourite haunt for many Athenians, who come for the panoramic views of the city from the observation decks that rim the summit.

The small whitewashed chapel of **Agios Geórgios** crowns the top of the hill. It was built in the 19th century on the site of an older Byzantine church, dedicated to Profítis Ilías (the Prophet Elijah). Both saints are celebrated on their name days (Profítis Ilías on 20 July and Agios Geórgios on 23 April). On the eve of Easter Sunday, a spectacular candlelit procession winds down the peak's wooded slopes.

Lykavittós Hill is also home to a summit restaurant, some cafés and the open-air **Lykavittós Theatre**, where contemporary jazz, pop and dance performances are held annually during the Athens Festival *(mid-Jun to mid-Sep).*

Gennádeion
Γεννάδειον

American School of Classical Studies,
Souidías 61, Kolonáki. **Map** 3 C4.
🎫 *210 721 0536.* Ⓜ *Evangelismos.*
🚌 *3, 7, 8, 13.* 🕐 *9am–5pm
Mon– Fri (to 8pm Thu), 9am–2pm
Sat.* ⬤ *Aug, main public hols.*

THE GREEK DIPLOMAT and
bibliophile, Ioánnis
Gennádios (1844–1932),
spent a lifetime accumulat-
ing rare first editions and
illuminated manuscripts. In
1923, he donated his collection to the American School
of Classical Studies. The
Gennádeion building, named
after him, was designed and
built between 1923 and 1925
by the New York firm Van
Pelt and Thompson to house
the collection. Above its
façade of Ionic columns is an
inscription which translates as
"They are called Greeks who
share in our culture" – from
Gennádios's dedication speech
at the opening in 1926.

Researchers need special
permission to gain access to
over 70,000 rare books and
manuscripts and no items are
allowed to be removed from
the library. Casual visitors
may look at selected exhibits
that are on show, and books,
posters and postcards are for
sale at the souvenir stall.

Exhibits in the main reading
room include 192 Edward
Lear sketches purchased in
1929. There is also an eclectic
mix of Byron memorabilia,
including the last known
portrait of the poet made
before his death in Greece
in 1824 *(see p73).*

**The imposing Neo-Classical
façade of the Gennádeion**

National Gallery of Art
Εθνική Πινακοθήκη

Vasiléos Konstantínou 50, Ilísia.
Map 7 C1. 🎫 *210 723 5937.*
Ⓜ *Evangelismos.* 🚌 *3, 13.*
🕐 *9am–3pm Mon, Wed–Sat (also
6–9pm Mon & Wed), 10am–2pm Sun.*
⬤ *main public hols.* 🔲 ♿

OPENED IN 1976, the National
Gallery of Art is housed
in a modern low-rise building
which contains a permanent
collection of European and
Greek art. The ground floor
stages travelling exhibitions
and opens out on to a sculpture garden. The first floor,
with the exception of five
impressive works by El Greco
(1541–1614), is devoted to a
minor collection of non-Greek,
European art. Alongside
works of the Dutch, Italian
and Flemish schools, there
are studies, engravings and
paintings by Rembrandt,
Dürer, Brueghel, Van Dyck,
Watteau, Utrillo, Cézanne and
Braque, among others. These
include Caravaggio's *Singer*
(1620), Eugène Delacroix's
Greek Warrior (1856) and
Picasso's Cubist-period *Woman
in a White Dress* (1939).

A changing display of Greek
modern art from the 18th to
the 20th century is featured
on the second floor. The 19th
century is represented mainly
by numerous depictions of
the War of Independence and
seascapes, enlivened by portraits such as Nikólaos Gýzis's
The Loser of the Bet (1878),
Waiting (1900) by Nikifóros
Lýtras and *The Straw Hat* (1925)
by Nikólaos Lýtras. There are
many fine works by major
Greek artists including Chatzimichaïl, Chatzikyriákos-Gkíkas,
Móralis and Tsaroúchis.

War Museum
Πολεμικό Μουσείο

Corner of Vasilíssis Sofías & Rizári,
Ilísia. **Map** 7 C1. 🎫 *210 725 2975.*
Ⓜ *Evangelismos.* 🚌 *3, 7, 8, 13.*
🕐 *9am–2pm Tue–Fri, 9:30am–2pm
Sat & Sun.* ⬤ *main public hols.* ♿

THE WAR MUSEUM was
opened in 1975
after the fall of
the military
dictatorship
(1967–1974).
The first nine
galleries are
chronologi-
cally ordered,
and contain
battle scenes,
armour and
plans from as far
back as ancient
Mycenaean

**Spartan
bronze
helmet**

times through to the more
recent German occupation of
1941. Other galleries contain
a miscellany of items
including a selection of
different uniforms and
Turkish weapons.

There is a fine display of
paintings and prints of leaders
from the Greek War of Independence, such as General
Theódoros Kolokotrónis (1770–
1843). His death mask can also
be seen in the museum. A
sizeable collection of fine oils
and sketches by the artists
Floras-Karavías and Argyrós
vividly captures the hardships
of the two world wars.

Modern sculpture outside the National Gallery of Art

Museum of Cycladic Art ❽
Μουσείο Κυκλαδικής Τέχνης

OPENED IN 1986, this modern museum offers the world's finest collection of Cycladic art. It was initially assembled by Nikólas and Dolly Goulandrí and has expanded with donations from other Greek collectors. The museum now has an excellent selection of ancient Greek art, the earliest from about 5,000 years ago.

The Cycladic figurines, dating from the 3rd

Cycladic marble head

millennium BC, have never enjoyed quite the same level of popularity as Classical sculpture. However, the haunting simplicity of these marble statues has inspired many 20th-century artists and sculptors, including Picasso, Modigliani and Henry Moore.

LOCATOR MAP

The third floor houses temporary exhibitions.

Second floor

Red-Figure Kylix
This 5th-century BC drinking cup depicts a boxing match between two young male athletes, supervised by their instructor.

First floor

Main entrance

Ground floor

Violin-Shaped Figurine
This 13-cm (5-in) high, Cycladic, white marble statuette is thought to be a stylized human figure. Most figurines of this shape come from Páros and Antíparos.

Stairs to toilets and café

Walkway leading to Stathátos Mansion

GALLERY GUIDE
In the main building, the Cycladic collection is on the first floor. Ancient Greek art is on the second, and the third shows temporary exhibitions. The fourth floor houses the Charles Polítis collection. In the Stathátos Mansion is the Greek art collection of the Athens Academy.

STAR EXHIBITS

★ Cycladic Figurine

★ White Lekythos

★ **Cycladic Figurine**
This "Folded Arm" type statue of a woman is 39 cm (15 in) tall. It has only four toes on each foot and a swollen abdomen, indicating pregnancy.

Terracotta Figurine
This elegant figure of a woman is one of many that were thought to have been produced at Tanágra, in Boiotia, Central Greece. It dates from 330–320 BC.

VISITORS' CHECKLIST

Neofýtou Doúka 4, Kolonáki (entrance to Stathátos Mansion at Irodótou 1). **Map** 7 B1.
🕿 210 722 8321. 🚌 3, 7, 8, 13. 🕐 10am–4pm Mon, Wed–Fri, 10am–3pm Sat. 🔴 main public hols. 🎫 📷 ♿ limited.
📧 Ⓦ www.cycladic.gr

KEY

☐ Shop and ticket office

☐ Cycladic art

☐ Ancient Greek art

☐ Temporary exhibitions

☐ Charles Polítis collection

Fourth floor

Stairs and lifts connecting all floors

★ White Lekythos
This fine clay lekythos (funerary vase) is an example of white-ground vase painting and was used to contain embalming oil. It depicts a mourning woman taking offerings to a grave, and dates from c.450 BC.

Bronze Askos
This elegant Hellenistic bronze wine jar dates from the 2nd century BC. The jar is so named because of its resemblance to the shape of a goat skin, or askos.

Entrance to main building via walkway

The first floor houses temporary exhibitions.

The original porch is the entrance to the Stathátos Mansion.

The ground floor is home to the Greek art collection of the Athens Academy. The glass conservatory-style roof at the back makes this a very light and airy floor.

STATHATOS MANSION
The "new" wing of the Museum of Cycladic Art was opened in 1992. It is housed in this elegant Neo-Classical building, once the home of Otto and Athína Stathátos. It was designed and built by the architect Ernst Ziller in 1895.

The lower ground floor has a café in the courtyard between the two buildings.

A 14th-century icon of St Michael in the Byzantine Museum

Byzantine Museum **❼**
Βυζαντινό Μουσείο

Vasilíssis Sofías 22, Plateía Rigílis, Kolonáki. **Map** 7 B1. **C** 210 723 1570. **M** Evangelismós. **🚊** 3, 8, 7, 13. **🕐** 8:30 am – 3pm Tue –Sun. **●** main public hols. **📷** **♿** ground floor only.

ORIGINALLY CALLED the Villa Ilissia, this elegant Florentine-style mansion was built between 1840 and 1848 by Stamátis Kleánthis for the Duchesse de Plaisance (1785–1854). This eccentric woman, wife of one of Napoleon's generals, was a key figure in Athens society during the mid-19th century and a dedicated philhellene.

Collector Geórgios Sotiríou converted the house into a museum in the 1930s with the help of architect Aristotélis Záchos. They transformed the entrance into a monastic court, incorporating a copy of a fountain from a 4th-century mosaic in Dafní (see pp 76–7). A modern annexe has enabled the whole collection of icons and mosaics, sculptures and frescoes, and ecclesiastical silverware to be on permanent display in the museum.

Spanning over 1,500 years of Byzantine art and architecture from the Greek diaspora, the ground floor exhibits run in chronological order. Three rooms have been cleverly created from fragments of now lost Byzantine churches. They are of three different periods: an early 5th-century three-aisled basilica, an 11th-century domed cruciform structure and a post-Byzantine church. Icons are on display in these rooms. Elsewhere on the ground floor, the exhibits

Funerary stele showing Orpheus with his lyre

range from early Christian 4th-century basilica fragments from the Acropolis to ornate 15th-century sculptures from the Frankish occupation of Greece. Fine pieces to watch out for include a 4th–5th-century BC funerary stele from Aígina, depicting Orpheus surrounded by wild animals, and an unusual 10th–11th-century marble plaque of three apostles from Thessaloníki.

The first floor is devoted to ecclesiastical objets d'art, including the Epitaphios of Salonika, an intricate 14th-century gold-threaded embroidery. There are also some magnificent frescoes that have been rescued from churches in Náxos, Oropós and Delphi. In addition, the first floor houses an unsurpassed collection of icons from the Greek diaspora. Two of the most stunning icons are the Galaktotrophousa (Virgin Nursing the Child), painted in 1784 by Makários of Galatísta, a monk from Mount Athos, and the famous 14th-century mosaic icon, the Episkepsis, from Bithynia.

The Episkepsis, from the Byzantine Museum, depicting the Virgin and Child

ICONS IN THE ORTHODOX CHURCH

The word icon simply means "image" and has come to signify a holy image through association with its religious use. Subjects range from popular saints such as St Andrew and St Nicholas to lesser known martyrs, prophets and archangels. The image of the Virgin and Child is easily the most popular and exalted. Icons are a prominent feature in the Greek Orthodox religion and appear in many areas of Greek life. You will see them in taxis and buses, on boats and in restaurants, as well as in homes and churches. An icon can be in fresco, a mosaic, or made from bone or metal. The most common form is a portable painting, in wax-based paints applied to wooden boards treated with gesso. The figures are arranged so that the eyes are clearly depicted and appear to be looking directly at the viewer of the icon. These works, often of great artistic skill, are unsigned, undated and share a rigid conformity, right down to details of colour, dress, gesture and expression The icon painter is careful to catch every detail of a tradition that stretches back hundreds of years.

Puppet Theatre from the Theatrical Museum

Museum of Cycladic Art ❽

See pp24–5.

Plateía Kolonakíou ❾
Πλατεία Κολωνακίου

Kolonáki. **Map** 3 B5. 🚌 *3, 7, 8,13.*

KOLONAKI SQUARE and its neighbouring side streets are the most chic and sophisticated part of Athens. The area is often missed by those who restrict themselves to the ancient sites and the popular flea markets of Monastiráki. Also known as Plateía Filikís Etaireías, the square is named after a small ancient column (*kolonáki*) found in the area. Celebrated for its designer boutiques and fashionable bars and cafés, smart antique shops and art galleries, sumptuous *zacharoplastéia* (pastry shops) and *ouzerí*, it revels in its status as the city's most fashionable quarter (*see p108*). The lively pavement cafés around the square each attract a particular devoted clientele. At one there may be rich kids drinking *frappé* (iced coffee) perched on their Harley Davidson motorbikes. Another, such as the *Lykóvrissi*, will be full of an older crowd of intellectuals sipping coffee and discussing the ever-popular subject of politics.

Benáki Museum ❿

See pp28–9.

Theatrical Museum ⓫
Μουσείο και Κέντρο Μελέτης του Ελληνικού Θεάτρου

Akadamías 50, Kéntro. **Map** 2 F4.
📞 *210 362 9430.* Ⓜ *Panepistimio.*
🚌 *3, 8, 13.* ⏰ *9am–2pm Mon–Fri.*
⦿ *Aug, 17 Nov, main public hols.*
🚫 & *limited.* 🎫

HOUSED IN THE BASEMENT of a fine Neo-Classical building, this small museum traces Greek theatrical history from Classical times to present day. There are displays of original posters, programmes, costumes and designs from productions by influential directors such as Károlos Koun. There is also a colourful puppet theatre. The dressing rooms of famous Greek actresses such as Eléni Papadáki and Elli Lampéti have been recreated to give an insight into their lives.

Perikles, from the Theatrical Museum

City of Athens Museum ⓬
Μουσείο της Πόλεως των Αθηνών

Paparrigopoúlou 7, Plateía Klafthmónos, Syntágma. **Map** 2 E5.
📞 *210 324 6164.* Ⓜ *Panepistimio.*
🚌 *1, 2, 4, 5, 9, 11, 12, 15, 18.*
⏰ *10am–2pm Mon, Wed, Fri–Sun.*
⦿ *main public hols.* 🚫

KING OTTO, Greece's first monarch, and Queen Amalía lived here from 1831, until their new palace, today's Voulí parliament building (*see p62*), was completed in 1838. It was joined to the neighbouring house to create what was known as the Old Palace.

The palace was restored in 1980 as a museum devoted to royal memorabilia, furniture and family portraits, maps and prints. It offers a delightful look at life during the early years of King Otto's reign.

Exhibits include the manuscript of the 1843 Constitution, coats of arms from the Frankish (1205–1311) and Catalan (1311–88) rulers of Athens, and a scale model of the city as it was in 1842, made by architect Giánnis Travlós (1908–1985).

The museum also has a fine art collection, including Nikólaos Gýzis's *The Carnival in Athens* (1892) and a selection of water-colours by the English artists Edward Dodwell (1767–1832), Edward Lear (1812–88) and Thomas Hartley Cromek (1809–73).

Upstairs sitting room recreated in the City of Athens Museum

Benáki Museum ⑩
Μουσείο Μπενάκη

THIS OUTSTANDING MUSEUM was founded in 1931 by Antónis Benákis (1873–1954), the son of Emmanouïl, a wealthy Greek who made his fortune in Egypt. Housed in an elegant Neo-Classical mansion, which was once the home of the Benákis family, the collection contains a diverse array of Greek arts and crafts, paintings and jewellery, local costumes and political memorabilia that spans over 5,000 years, from the Neolithic era to the 20th century.

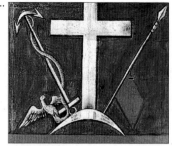

Flag of Hydra
The imagery symbolizes the island of Hydra's supremacy in sea warfare as it was Greece's most powerful naval community.

Lecture hall

Bridal Cushion
This ornate embroidered cushion comes from Epirus and dates from the 18th century. It depicts a bridal procession, with ornamental flowers in the background.

Second floor

Roof garden

Auditorium

★ Detail of Wood Decoration
This intricately painted and carved piece of wooden panelling comes from a mansion in Kozáni, in western Macedonia. It dates from the 18th century.

Atrium

Silver Ciborium
Used to contain consecrated bread, this elegant piece of ecclesiatical silverware is dated 1667 and comes from Edirne, in Turkey.

KEY TO FLOORPLAN

☐	Ground floor
☐	First floor
☐	Second floor
☐	Third floor
☐	Non-exhibition space

Entrance

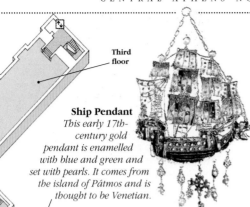

Third floor

Ship Pendant
This early 17th-century gold pendant is enamelled with blue and green and set with pearls. It comes from the island of Pátmos and is thought to be Venetian.

VISITORS' CHECKLIST

Corner of Koumpári & Vassilísis Sofías, Sýntagma.
Map 7 A1.
210 367 1000.
Sýntagma. 3, 7, 8, 13.
9am–5pm Mon, Wed, Fri & Sat, 9am–midnight Thu, 9am–3pm Sun.
1 Jan, 25 Mar, Good Fri am, Easter Sun, 1 May, 25, 26 Dec.
(free Thu)

GALLERY GUIDE

The ground floor collection is arranged into different periods and ranges from Neolithic to late-Byzantine art and Cretan icon painting. The first floor exhibits are organized geographically and are from Asia Minor, mainland Greece and the Greek islands. There is also a collection of ecclesiastical silverware and jewellery. The second floor displays items relating to Greek spiritual, economic and social life, and the third floor concentrates on the Greek War of Independence and modern political and cultural life.

First floor

Ground floor

★ Icon of St Anne
The icon of St Anne was painted in the 15th century. She is carrying the Virgin Mary as a child, who is holding a white lily, symbol of purity.

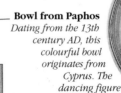

Bowl from Paphos
Dating from the 13th century AD, this colourful bowl originates from Cyprus. The dancing figure is holding rattles.

★ El Faiyûm Portrait
This Hellenistic portrait of a man, painted on linen, dates from the 3rd century AD.

STAR EXHIBITS

★ El Faiyûm Portrait

★ Icon of St Anne

★ Detail of Wood Decoration

Neo-Classical façade of the National Historical Museum

National Historical Museum **⑬**
Εθνικό Ιστορικό Μουσείο

Stadíou 11, Sýntagma. **Map** 2 F5. 210 323 7617. M Sýntagma. 1, 2, 4, 5, 9, 10, 11, 18. 9am–2pm Tue–Sun. main public hols. free Sun.

DESIGNED BY French architect François Boulanger (1807–75), this museum was originally built as the first home of the Greek parliament. Queen Amalía laid the foundation stone in 1858, but it was 13 years later that it became the first permanent site of the Greek parliament. The country's most famous prime ministers have sat in the imposing chamber of the Old Parliament of the Hellenes, including Chárilaos Trikoúpis and Theódoros Deligiánnis, who were assassinated on the steps at the front of the building in 1905. The parliament moved to its present-day site in the Voulí building on Plateía Syntágmatos *(see p62)* after the Voulí was renovated in 1935.

In 1961, the building was opened as the National Historical Museum, owned by the Historical and Ethnological Society of Greece. Founded in 1882, the purpose of the society is to collect objects that illuminate the history of modern Greece. The museum

Statue of General Theódoros Kolokotrónis

covers all the major events of Greek history from the Byzantine period to the 20th century in a chronological display. Venetian armour, traditional regional costumes and jewellery and figureheads from the warships used during the Revolution in 1821 are just some examples of the many exhibits on show.

The collection also focuses on major parliamentary figures, philhellenes and leaders in the War of Independence, displaying such items as Byron's sword, the weapons of Theódoros Kolokotrónis (1770–1843), King Otto's throne and the pen that was used by Elefthérios Venizélos to sign the Treaty of Sèvres in 1920. The revolutionary memoirs of General Makrigiánnis (1797–1864) can also be seen. Among the numerous paintings on view is a fine rare woodcut of the Battle of Lepanto (1571), the work of Bonastro.

Outside the building is a copy of Lázaros Sóchos's statue of Kolokotrónis on horseback, made in 1900, the original of which is in Náfplio, the former capital of Greece. There is a dedication on the statue in Greek, which reads "Theódoros Kolokotrónis 1821. Ride on, noble commander, through the centuries, showing the nations how slaves may become free men."

Kapnikaréa **⑭**
Καπνικαρέα

Corner of Ermoú & Kalamiótou, Monastiráki. **Map** 6 D1. 210 322 4462. M Monastiráki. 8am–1pm Mon–Sat (also 5–7pm Fri), 8–11:30am Sun. main public hols.

THIS CHARMING 11th-century Byzantine church was rescued from demolition in 1834, thanks to the timely intervention of King Ludwig of Bavaria. Stranded in the middle of a square between Ermoú and Kapnikaréa streets, it is surrounded by the modern office blocks and shops of Athens' busy garment district.

Traditionally called the Church of the Princess, its foundation is attributed to Empress Irene, who ruled the Byzantine Empire from AD 797 to 802. She is revered as a saint in the Greek church for her efforts in restoring icons to the Empire's churches.

The true origins of the name "Kapnikaréa" are unknown, although according to some sources, the church was named after its founder, a "hearth-tax gatherer" *(kapnikaréas)*. Hearth tax was imposed on buildings by the Byzantines.

Restored in the 1950s, the dome of the church is supported by four Roman columns. Frescoes by Fótis Kóntoglou (1895–1965) were painted during the restoration, including one of the Virgin and Child. Much of Kóntoglou's work is also on display in the National Gallery of Art *(see p23)*.

The dome and main entrance of the Byzantine Kapnikaréa

Athenian Neo-Classical Architecture

NEO-CLASSICISM flourished in the 19th century, when the architects who were commissioned by King Otto to build the capital in the 1830s turned to this popular European style. Among those commissioned were the Hansen brothers, Christian and Theophil, and also Ernst Ziller. As a result of their planning, within 50 years a modern city had emerged, with elegant administrative

National Bank, built in the 1890s

buildings, squares and tree-lined avenues. In its early days Neo-Classicism had imitated the grace of the buildings of ancient Greece, using marble columns, sculptures and decorative detailing. In later years, it evolved into an original Greek style. Grand Neo-Classicism is seen at its best in the public buildings along Panepistimíou; its domestic adaptation can be seen in the houses of Pláka.

Schliemann's House *(also known as Ilíou Mélathron, the Palace of Ilium, or Troy) was built in 1878 by Ziller. The interior is decorated with frescoes and mosaics of mythological subjects. It is now home to the Numismatic Museum (****Map*** *2 F5).*

The National Library *was designed by Danish architect Theophil Hansen in 1887 in the form of a Doric temple with two side wings. Built of Pentelic marble, it houses over half a million books, including many illuminated manuscripts and rare first editions (****Map*** *2 F4).*

The National Theatre *was built between 1882 and 1890. Ernst Ziller used a Renaissance-style exterior with arches and Doric columns for George I's Royal Theatre. Inspired by the Public Theatre of Vienna, its interior was very modern for its time (****Map*** *2 D3).*

Athens Academy *was designed by Theophil Hansen and built between 1859 and 1887. Statues of Apollo and Athena, and seated figures of Socrates and Plato, convey a Classical style, as do the Ionic capitals and columns. Inside the building, the Academy hall has beautiful frescoes that depict scenes from the myth of Prometheus (****Map*** *2 F4).*

The University of Athens *was designed by Christian Hansen. This fine building, completed in 1864, has an Ionic colonnade and a portico frieze depicting the resurgence of arts and sciences under the reign of King Otto. A symbol of wisdom, the Sphinx is connected with Athens through the Oedipus legend. Oedipus, who solved the riddle of the Sphinx, later found sanctuary in enlightened Athens. Other statues on the façade include Patriarch Gregory V, a martyr of the War of Independence (****Map*** *2 F4).*

CENTRAL ATHENS SOUTH

SOUTHERN ATHENS is dominated by the Acropolis and is home to the buildings that were at the heart of ancient Athens. Pláka and Monastiráki still revel in their historical roots as the oldest inhabited areas of the city, and are full of Byzantine churches and museums. Nestling among the restored Neo-Classical houses are grocery stores,

Relief from Panagía Gorgoepíkoös

icon painters and open-air tavernas. In the busy streets of Monastiráki's flea market, food vendors, gypsies and street musicians provide the atmosphere of a Middle Eastern bazaar. Southeast of Plateía Syntágmatos are the National Gardens, the city centre's tree-filled park. For information on getting around Athens, see pages 136–9.

SIGHTS AT A GLANCE

KEY

Street-by-Street: Monastiráki *pp34–5*

Street-by-Street: Central Pláka *pp52–3*

M Metro

P Parking

0 metres 500
0 yards 500

◁ **The remaining columns of the ancient Temple of Olympian Zeus**

Street-by-Street: Monastiráki

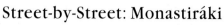

THIS OLD AREA OF THE CITY takes its name from the little sunken monastery in Plateía Monastirakíou. The former heart of Ottoman Athens, Monastiráki is still home to the bazaar and market stalls selling everything from junk to jewellery. The Fethiye Mosque and the Tzistarákis Mosque, home of the Kyriazópoulos Museum, stand as reminders of the area's eastern past. Roman influences are also strong in Monastiráki. The area borders the Roman Agora and includes the remains of Emperor Hadrian's library and the unique Tower of the Winds, a Hellenistic water clock. Monastiráki mixes the atmospheric surroundings of ancient ruins with the excitement of bargaining in the bazaar.

Flea Market
Plateía Avissynías is the heart of the flea market, which extends through the surrounding streets. It is particularly popular on Sundays ❸

KEY

– – – Suggested route

STAR SIGHT

★ **Tower of the Winds**

0 metres   50

0 yards   50

Ifaístou is named after Hephaistos, the god of fire and metal craftsmanship. Areos is named after Ares, the war god.

Monastiráki metro station

The Fethiye Mosque is situated in the corner of the Roman Agora. It was built by the Turks in the late 15th century to mark Mehmet the Conqueror's visit to Athens.

Ancient Agora *(see pp40–41)*

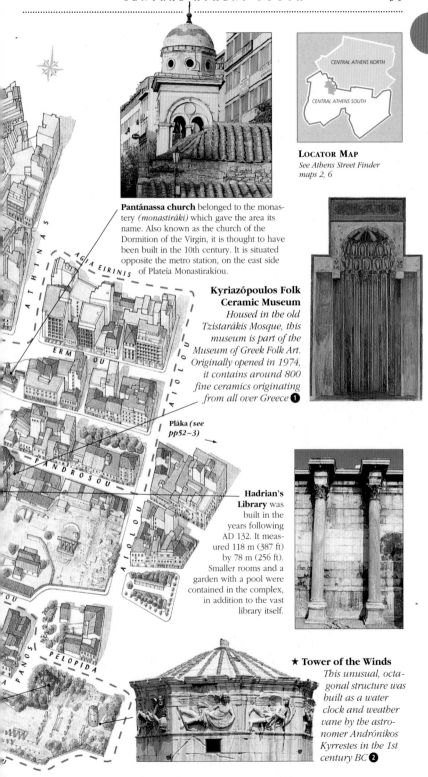

LOCATOR MAP
See Athens Street Finder maps 2, 6

Pantánassa church belonged to the monastery *(monastiráki)* which gave the area its name. Also known as the church of the Dormition of the Virgin, it is thought to have been built in the 10th century. It is situated opposite the metro station, on the east side of Plateía Monastirakíou.

Kyriazópoulos Folk Ceramic Museum
Housed in the old Tzistarákis Mosque, this museum is part of the Museum of Greek Folk Art. Originally opened in 1974, it contains around 800 fine ceramics originating from all over Greece ❶

Pláka *(see pp52–3)* →

Hadrian's Library was built in the years following AD 132. It measured 118 m (387 ft) by 78 m (256 ft). Smaller rooms and a garden with a pool were contained in the complex, in addition to the vast library itself.

★ **Tower of the Winds**
This unusual, octagonal structure was built as a water clock and weather vane by the astronomer Andrónikos Kyrrestes in the 1st century BC ❷

Kyriazópoulos Folk Ceramic Museum ❶

Μουσείο Ελληνικής Λαϊκής Τέχνης, Συλλογή Κεραμικών Β. Κυριαζοπούλου

Tzistarákis Mosque, Areos 1, Monastiráki. **Map** 6 D1. 📞 *210 324 2066.* Ⓜ *Monastiráki.* ⏰ *9am–2:30pm Mon & Wed–Sun.* ⚫ *main public hols.* 📷

THIS COLOURFUL COLLECTION of ceramics was donated to the Greek Folk Art Museum in 1974 by Professor Vasíleios Kyriazópoulos. Now an annexe of the Folk Art Museum, the Kyriazópoulos Folk Ceramic Museum is housed in the imposing Tzistarákis Mosque (or the Mosque of the Lower Fountain). Of the hundreds of pieces on display, many are of the type still used today in a traditional Greek kitchen, such as terracotta water jugs from Aígina, earthenware oven dishes from Sífnos and storage jars from Thessaly and Chíos. There are also some ceramic figures and plates, based on mythological and folk stories, crafted by Minás Avramídis and Dimítrios Mygdalinós who came from Asia Minor in the 1920s.

The mosque itself is of as much interest as its contents. It was built in 1759 by the newly appointed Turkish *voivode* Tzistarákis. The *voivode* was the civil

Ceramic of a young girl from Asia Minor

governor who possessed complete powers over the law courts and the police. He collected taxes for his own account, but also had to pay for the sultan's harem and the treasury. His workmen dynamited the 17th column of the Temple of Olympian Zeus (*see p61*) in order to make lime to be used for the stucco work on the mosque. Destruction of ancient monuments was forbidden by Turkish law and this act of vandalism was the downfall of Tzistarákis. He was exiled the same year. The mosque has now been well restored after earthquake damage in 1981.

Tower of the Winds ❷

Αέρηδες

Within Roman Agora ruins, Pláka. **Map** 6 D1. 📞 *210 324 5220.* Ⓜ *Monastiráki.* ⏰ *8am–3pm daily.* ⚫ *main public hols.* 📷 ♿

THE REMARKABLE Tower of the Winds is set within the ruins of the Roman Agora. Constructed from marble in the 2nd century BC by the Syrian astronomer Andrónikos Kyrrestes, it was built as a combined weather vane and water clock. The name comes from the external friezes, personifying the eight winds. Sundials are etched into the walls beneath each relief.

The tower is well preserved, standing today at over 12 m (40 ft) high with a diameter of 8 m (26 ft). Still simply called Aérides ("the winds") by Greeks today, in the Middle Ages it was thought to be either the school or prison of Socrates, or even the tomb of King Philip II of Macedon. It was at last correctly identified as the Horologion (water clock) of Andronikos in the 17th century. All that remains today of its elaborate water clock are the origins of a complex system of water pipes and a circular channel cut into the floor which can be seen inside the tower.

The west and southwest faces of the Tower of the Winds

The west- and north-facing sides each contain a hole which lets light into the otherwise dark interior of the tower.

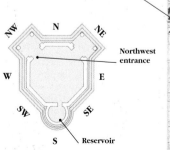

This interior floorplan of the tower shows the compass direction of the building's eight sides. External friezes personify each of the eight winds.

Northwest entrance

Reservoir

NW   N   NE   W   E   SW   SE   S

NORTH

Boreas blows the cold north wind through a large conch shell.

NORTHWEST

Skiron scatters glowing ashes from a bronze vessel.

WEST

Zephyros is a semi-naked youth scattering flowers.

Flea Market ❸
Παζάρι

From Plateía Monastirakíou to
Plateía Avyssinías, Pláka. **Map** 5 C1.
M Thiseío. ☐ 8am–2pm Sun.

A BANNER WELCOMES visitors
to Athens' famous flea
market, past the ubiquitous
tourist trinket shops of
Adrianoú and Pandrósou
streets. For the locals, the true
heart of the market lies just
west of Plateía Monastirakíou,
in Plateía Avyssinías and its
warren of surrounding streets.

On Sunday mornings when
the shops are closed, the
market itself bursts into
action. Traders set out their
bric-a-brac on stalls and the
pavement and many bargains

Shoppers browsing in Athens' lively flea market

can be found, especially the
colourful handwoven woollen
cloths and the many bangles
and beads sold by hippies.
More expensive items are also
on sale, including brassware,
leatherware and silverware.

During the week the shops
in the surrounding area are

open and filled with much
the same as the Sunday stalls.
Individual shops each have
their own specialities, so hunt
around before making a
purchase. You can buy almost
anything, from antiques and
old books to taverna chairs
and army surplus gear.

The southwest wind, *Lips, heralds
a swift voyage. The reliefs show that each
wind was given a personality according
to its characteristics, and each promises
different conditions. Gentle Zephyros
and chilly Boreas, mentioned in Western
literature and represented in art and
sculpture, are the best known of these.*

Whirling dervishes
*used the tower as a
monastery in the
mid-18th century.
The dervishes were
a Muslim order of
ascetics. The tower's
occupants became a
popular attraction for
Grand Tour visitors
who came to witness
the weekly ritual of
a frenzied dance,
which is known
as the* sema.

**Relief carving
of mythological
figure**

**Metal rod
casting
shadow**

**Lines of sundial
carved into
wall of tower**

| SOUTHWEST | SOUTH | SOUTHEAST | EAST | NORTHEAST |

Lips holds the
aphlaston (or
stern ornament) of
a ship as he steers.

Notos is the
bearer of rain,
emptying a
pitcher of water.

Euros is a
bearded old man,
warmly wrapped
in a cloak.

Apeliotes is
a young man
bringing fruits
and corn.

Kaïkias empties
a shield full of icy
hailstones on those
below.

Miss T K, by Giánnis Mitarákis, in the Municipal Art Gallery

Municipal Art Gallery ❹

Πινακοθήκη του Δήμου Αθηναίων

Pireos 51, Plateía Koumoundoúrou, Omónoia. **Map** 1 C4. 📞 210 324 3023. Ⓜ Omónoia. 🕐 9am–1pm & 5–9pm Mon–Fri, 9am–1pm Sat & Sun. ● 3 Oct, main public hols. ✎

THIS LITTLE-VISITED museum has one of the finest archive collections of modern Greek art. Designed by architect Panagiótis Kálkos in 1872, the home of the museum is the old Neo-Classical Foundling Hospital. It was built to cope with the city's population explosion towards the end of the 19th century; unwanted babies were left outside the main entrance to be cared for by hospital staff.

The Municipality of Athens has been amassing the collection since 1923. It now offers a fine introduction to the diverse styles of modern Greek artists. Many paintings are passionate reflections on the Greek landscape, such as Dímos Mpraésas's (1878–1967) landscapes of the Cyclades, or Konstantínos Parthénis's (1882–1964) paintings of olive and cypress trees.

There are also portraits by Giánnis Mitarákis and still lifes by Theófrastos Triantafyllídis. Paintings such as Nikólaos Kartsonákis's *Street Market* (1939) also reveal the folk roots that are at the heart of much modern Greek art.

Kerameikós ❺

Κεραμεικός

THIS ANCIENT CEMETERY has been a burial ground since the 12th century BC. The Sacred Way led from Eleusis *(see pp80–81)* to Kerameikós and the Panathenaic Way set out from the Dípylon Gate here to the Acropolis *(see pp44–7)*. Most of the graves remaining today are along the Street of the Tombs. The sculptures excavated in the early 1900s are in the National Archaeological Museum *(see pp18–21)* and the Oberlander Museum; however, plaster copies of the originals can be seen *in situ*.

Grave *Stele* of Hegeso
This is from the family burial plot belonging to Koroibos of Melite. It shows his wife, Hegeso, admiring her jewels with a servant and dates from the late 5th century BC.

Precinct of Aristion

The Precinct of Lysimachides contains a marble dog, originally one of a pair.

STREET OF THE TOMBS

The Sanctuary of Hekate was sacred to the ancient goddess of the underworld. It contained an altar and votive offerings.

South terrace

Oberlander Museum

★ **Tomb of Dionysios of Kollytos**
This fine tomb belongs to a rich treasurer. A bull often represents the god Dionysos.

STAR MONUMENTS

- ★ **Tomb of Dionysios of Kollytos**

- ★ ***Stele* of Demetria and Pamphile**

STREET OF THE TOMBS

Most of the monuments in the Street of the Tombs date from the 4th century BC. The different styles, from the lavish *stelae* (relief sculptures) to the simple *kioniskoi* (small columns), all reveal the dignity that is typical of Greek funerary art.

LOCATOR MAP

This tumulus was the burial place of an old Attic family dating from the 6th century BC.

Tomb of Hipparete

River Eridanos

The Sacred Way led from the Sacred Gate to Ancient Eleusis *(see pp80–81).*

Sacred Gate, Acropolis

South Hill

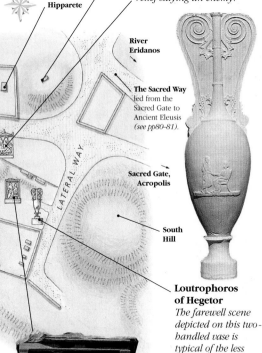

Stele of Dexileos
Dexileos was a young man killed in 394 BC during the Corinthian War. The son of Lysanias, he is seen on the relief slaying an enemy.

Loutrophoros of Hegetor
The farewell scene depicted on this two-handled vase is typical of the less ornate style of commemorative funerary art.

★ **Stele of Demetria and Pamphile**
This moving sculpture shows the seated Pamphile with her sister Demetria behind her. This was one of the last ornate stelae to be made in the late 4th century BC.

VISITORS' CHECKLIST

Ermoú 148, Thiseío. **Map** 1 B5.
📞 210 346 3552. Ⓜ *Thiseío.*
⬤ *closed until May 2004.*

Oberlander Museum
This museum is named after Gustav Oberlander (1867–1936), a German-American industrialist whose donations helped fund its construction in the 1930s. In Gallery 1, some large fragments from grave *stelae* found incorporated into the Dipylon and Sacred Gates are exhibited. These include a marble sphinx (c.550 BC) that once crowned a grave *stele.* Galleries 2 and 3 offer an array of huge Proto-geometric and Geometric amphorae and black-figure *lekythoi* (funerary vases). The most moving exhibits come from children's graves and include pottery toy horses and terracotta dolls. There are also examples of some of the 7,000 *ostraka* (voting tablets) *(see p41)* found in the bed of the river Eridanos. Among the superb painted pottery, there is a red-figure *hydria* (water vase) of Helen of Troy and a *lekythos* of Dionysos with satyrs.

Winged sphinx from grave stele

Geometric funerary amphora from the Oberlander Museum

Ancient Agora ❻
Αρχαία Αγορά

Voting lot

T HE AGORA, or market-place, formed the political heart of ancient Athens from 600 BC. Democracy was practised in the *Bouleuterion* (Council) and the law courts, and in open meetings. Socrates was indicted and executed in the state prison here in 399 BC. The theatres, schools and stoas filled with shops also made this the centre of social and commercial life. Even the city mint that produced Athens' silver coins was here. The American School of Classical Studies began excavations of the Ancient Agora in the 1930s, and since then the vast remains of a complex array of public buildings have been revealed.

View across the Agora from the south showing the reconstructed Stoa of Attalos on the right

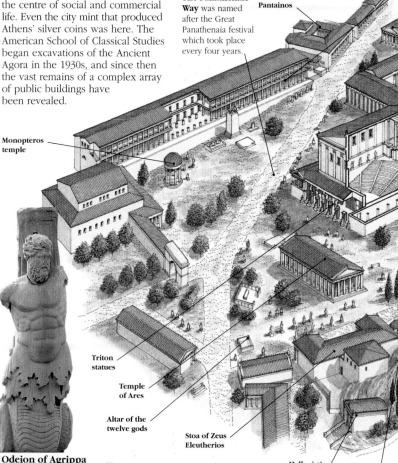

The Panathenaic Way was named after the Great Panathenaia festival which took place every four years.

Library of Pantainos

Monopteros temple

Triton statues

Temple of Ares

Altar of the twelve gods

Stoa of Zeus Eleutherios

Hellenistic temple

Temple of Apollo Patroös

Odeion of Agrippa
This statue of a triton (half-god, half-fish) once adorned the façade of the Odeion of Agrippa. It dates from AD 150 and is now in the Agora museum.

RECONSTRUCTION OF THE ANCIENT AGORA
This shows the Agora as it was in c.AD 200, viewed from the northwest. The main entrance to the Agora at this time was via the Panathenaic Way, which ran across the site from the Acropolis in the southeast to the Kerameikós in the northwest.

0 metres   50
0 yards   50

Stoa of Attalos
This colonnaded building was reconstructed in the mid-20th century as a museum to house finds from the Ancient Agora site.

Statue of Hadrian
Hadrian was Emperor of Rome from AD 117–38. Athens was under his authority. The statue dates from the 2nd century AD.

***Ostrakon** condemning a man named Hippokrates to exile*

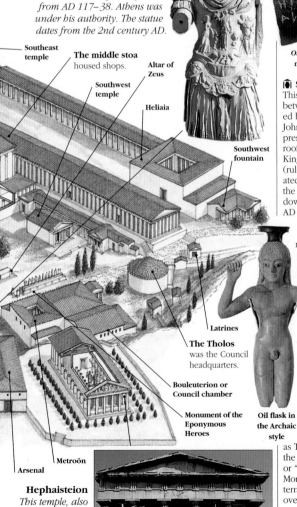

Southeast temple

The middle stoa housed shops.

Altar of Zeus

Southwest temple

Heliaia

Southwest fountain

Latrines

The Tholos was the Council headquarters.

Bouleuterion or Council chamber

Monument of the Eponymous Heroes

Oil flask in the Archaic style

Metroön

Arsenal

Hephaisteion
This temple, also known as the Theseion, is the best-preserved building on the site. It was built c.449–440 BC.

Stoa of Attalos

This fine building was rebuilt between 1953 and 1956, helped by a huge donation from John D Rockefeller, Jr. An impressive two-storey stoa, or roofed arcade, founded by King Attalos of Pergamon (ruled 159–138 BC), it dominated the eastern quarter of the Agora until it was burnt down by the Heruli tribe in AD 267. Reconstructed using the original foundations and ancient materials, it now contains a museum whose exhibits reveal the great diversity and sophistication of ancient life. Artifacts include rules from the 2nd-century AD Library of Pantainos, the text of a law against tyranny from 337 BC, bronze and stone lots used for voting and a *klepsýdra* (water clock) used for timing speeches. *Ostraka* (voting tablets on which names were inscribed) bear such famous names as Themistokles and Aristeides the Just, the latter banished, or "ostracized", in 482 BC. More everyday items, such as terracotta toys and portable ovens, and hobnails and sandals found in a shoemaker's shop, are equally fascinating. Also on display are some beautiful black-figure vases and an unusual oil flask moulded into the shape of a kneeling boy.

Acropolis ⓐ
Ακρόπολη

I N THE MID-5TH CENTURY BC, Perikles persuaded
the Athenians to begin a grand programme of
new building work in Athens that has come to
represent the political and cultural achievements
of Greece. The work transformed the Acropolis
with three contrasting temples and a monumental
gateway. The Theatre of Dionysos on the south
slope was developed further in the 4th century
BC, and the Theatre of Herodes Atticus was
added in the 2nd century AD.

LOCATOR MAP

**★ Porch of the
Caryatids**
*These statues of
women were used
in place of columns
on the south porch
of the Erechtheion.
The originals, four
of which can be
seen in the Acropolis
Museum, have been
replaced by casts.*

An olive tree now
grows where Athena
first planted her tree
in a competition
against Poseidon.

The Propylaia was built
in 437–432 BC to form a
new entrance to the
Acropolis *(see p46).*

★ Temple of Athena Nike
*This temple to Athena of
Victory is on the west side of
the Propylaia. It was built in
426–421 BC (see p46).*

The Beulé Gate
was the first
entrance to
the Acropolis
(see p46).

**Pathway to
Acropolis
from ticket
office**

STAR SIGHTS
★ Parthenon
**★ Porch of the
Caryatids**
**★ Temple of
Athena Nike**

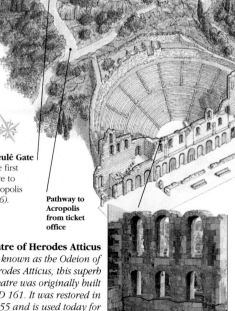

Theatre of Herodes Atticus
*Also known as the Odeion of
Herodes Atticus, this superb
theatre was originally built
in AD 161. It was restored in
1955 and is used today for
outdoor concerts (see p50).*

◁ **The Porch of the Caryatids on the Erechtheion**

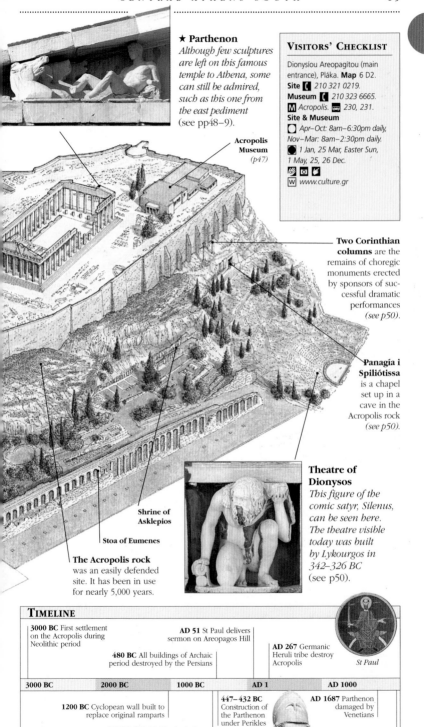

★ **Parthenon**
Although few sculptures are left on this famous temple to Athena, some can still be admired, such as this one from the east pediment (see pp48–9).

Acropolis Museum
(p47)

Two Corinthian columns are the remains of choregic monuments erected by sponsors of successful dramatic performances *(see p50)*.

Panagía i Spiliótissa is a chapel set up in a cave in the Acropolis rock *(see p50)*.

Theatre of Dionysos
This figure of the comic satyr, Silenus, can be seen here. The theatre visible today was built by Lykourgos in 342–326 BC (see p50).

Shrine of Asklepios

Stoa of Eumenes

The Acropolis rock was an easily defended site. It has been in use for nearly 5,000 years.

TIMELINE

3000 BC First settlement on the Acropolis during Neolithic period

AD 51 St Paul delivers sermon on Areopagos Hill

480 BC All buildings of Archaic period destroyed by the Persians

AD 267 Germanic Heruli tribe destroy Acropolis

St Paul

3000 BC	2000 BC	1000 BC	AD 1	AD 1000

1200 BC Cyclopean wall built to replace original ramparts

510 BC Delphic Oracle declares Acropolis a holy place of the gods, banning habitation by mortals

447–432 BC Construction of the Parthenon under Perikles

Perikles (495–429 BC)

AD 1687 Parthenon damaged by the Venetians

AD 1987 Restoration of the Erechtheion completed

Exploring the Acropolis

Relief of Mourning Athena

O NCE THROUGH the first entrance, the Beulé Gate, straight ahead is the Propylaia, the grand entrance to the temple complex. Before going through here, it is worth exploring the Temple of Athena Nike, on the right. Beyond the Propylaia are the Erechtheion and the Parthenon *(see pp48–9)* which dominate the top of the rock. There are also stunning views of Athens itself from the Acropolis. Since 1975, access to all the temple precincts has been banned to prevent further damage. Buildings located at the foot of the Acropolis and the hills immediately to the west are covered on pages 50–51.

View of the Acropolis from the southwest

♭ Beulé Gate

The gate is named after the French archaeologist Ernest Beulé who discovered it in 1852. It was built in AD 267 after the raid of the Heruli, a Germanic people, as part of the Roman Acropolis fortifications. It incorporates stones from the *choregic* monument *(see p59)* of Nikias that was situated near the Stoa of Eumenes. Parts of the original monument's dedication are still visible over the architrave. There is also an inscription identifying a Roman, Flavius Septimius Marcellinus, as

donor of the gateway. In 1686, when the Turks destroyed the Temple of Athena Nike, they used the marble to build a bastion for artillery over the gate.

♭ Temple of Athena Nike

This small temple was built in 426–421 BC to commemorate the Athenians' victories over the Persians. The temple frieze has representative scenes from the Battle of Plataiaí (479 BC). Designed by Kallikrates, the temple stands on a 9.5-m (31-ft) bastion. It has been used as both observation post and an ancient shrine to the goddess of Victory, Athena Nike, of whom there is a remarkable sculpture situated on the balustrade. Legend records the temple site as the place from which King Aegeus threw himself into the sea, believing that his son Theseus had been killed in Crete by the Minotaur. Built

of Pentelic marble, the temple has four Ionic columns 4 m (13 ft) high at each portico end. It was reconstructed in 1834–8, after being destroyed in 1686 by the Turks. On the point of collapse in 1935, it was again dismantled and reconstructed according to information resulting from more recent research.

♭ Propylaia

Work began on this enormous entrance to the Acropolis in 437 BC. Although the outbreak of the Peloponnesian War in 432 BC curtailed its completion, its architect Mnesikles created a building admired throughout the ancient world. The Propylaia comprises a rectangular central building divided by a wall into two porticoes. These were punctuated by five entrance doors, rows of Ionic and Doric columns and a vestibule with a blue-coffered ceiling decorated with gold stars. Two wings flank the main building. The north wing was home to the *pinakothíki*, an art gallery.

During its chequered history – later as archbishop's residence, Frankish palace, and Turkish fortress and armoury – parts of the building have been accidentally destroyed; it even suffered the misfortune of being struck by lightning in 1645, and later the explosion of the Turkish gunpowder store *(see p48)*.

♭ Erechtheion

Built between 421 and 406 BC, the Erechtheion is situated on the most sacred site of the Acropolis. It is said to be where Poseidon left his trident marks in a rock, and Athena's olive tree sprouted, in their battle for possession of the city. Named after Erechtheus, one of the mythical kings of Athens, the temple was a sanctuary to both Athena Polias and Erechtheus-Poseidon.

Famed for its elegant and extremely ornate Ionic architecture and caryatid columns in the shape of women, this extraordinary monument is built on different levels. The large rectangular cella was divided into three

The eastern end of the Erechtheion

rooms. One contained the holy olive wood statue of Athena Polias. The cella was bounded by north, east and south porticoes. The south is the Porch of the Caryatids, the maiden statues which are now in the Acropolis Museum.

The Erechtheion complex has been used for a range of purposes, including a harem for the wives of the Turkish *disdar* (commander) in 1463. It was almost completely destroyed by a Turkish shell in 1827 during the War of Independence. Recent restoration has caused heated disputes: holes have been filled with new marble, and copies have been made to replace original features that have been removed to the safety of the museum.

A youth leading a cow to sacrifice, from the Parthenon's north frieze

🏛 Acropolis Museum

Built below the level of the Parthenon, this museum is located in the southeast corner of the site. Opened in 1878, it was reconstructed after World War II to accommodate a collection devoted

to finds from the Acropolis. Treasures include fine statues from the 5th century BC and well-preserved segments of the Parthenon frieze.

The collection begins chronologically in **Rooms I, II** and **III** with 6th-century BC works. Fragments of painted pedimental statues include mythological scenes of Herakles grappling with various monsters, ferocious lions devouring calves, and the more peaceful votive statue of the *Moschophoros,* or Calf-Bearer, portraying a young man carrying a calf on his shoulders (c.570 BC).

Room V houses a pediment from the old Temple of Athena showing part of a battle where the figures of Athena and Zeus against the giants represent the Greek triumph over primitive forces.

Room IV has recently restored sculptures dating from c.550 BC and **Rooms IV** and **VI** also contain a unique collection of *korai* from c.550–500 BC. These were votive statues of maidens offered to Athena. They represent the development of ancient Greek art – moving from the formal bearing of the *Peplos Kore* to the more natural body movement of the *Kore of Euthydikos* and *Almond-Eyed Kore*. Other representative statues of this later period are the *Mourning Athena*, head of the *Blond Boy* and the *Kritios Boy*.

Rooms VII and **VIII** contain, among other exhibits, a well-preserved *metope* from the south side of the Parthenon

The *Moschophoros* (Calf-Bearer), a sculpture from the Archaic period

showing the battle between the Lapiths and centaurs. The remaining parts of the Parthenon frieze depict the Panathenaic procession, including the chariot and *apobates* (slaves riding the chariot horses), the *thallophoroi* (bearers of olive branches), and a sacrificial cow being led by youths.

Room IX ends the collection with four caryatids from the Erechtheion south porch. They are the only ones on display in Athens and are carefully kept in a temperature-controlled environment.

THE ELGIN MARBLES

These famous sculptures, also called the Parthenon Marbles, are held in the British Museum in London. They were acquired by Lord Elgin in 1801–3 from the occupying Turkish authorities. He sold them to the British nation for £35,000 in 1816. There is great controversy surrounding the Marbles. While some argue that they are more carefully preserved in the British Museum, the Greek government does not accept the legality of the sale and many believe they belong in Athens. A famous supporter of this cause was the Greek actress and politician, Melína Merkoúri, who died in 1994.

The newly arrived Elgin Marbles at the British Museum, in a painting by A Archer

The Parthenon
Ο Παρθενώνας

ONE OF THE WORLD'S most famous buildings, this temple was begun in 447 BC. It was designed by the architects Kallikrates and Iktinos, primarily to house the 12 m (40 ft) high statue of Athena Parthenos (Maiden), sculpted by Pheidias. Taking nine years to complete, the temple was dedicated to the goddess in 438 BC. Over the centuries, it has been used as a church, a mosque and an arsenal, and has suffered severe damage. Built as an expression of the glory of ancient Athens, it remains the city's emblem to this day.

View of the Parthenon today, from the west

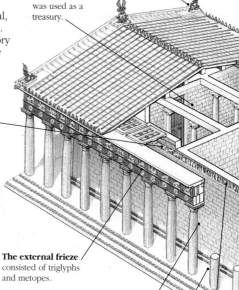

The west cella was used as a treasury.

Akroterion

The external frieze consisted of triglyphs and metopes.

Marble walls concealed the cellas, or inner rooms.

Each column was constructed from fluted drums of marble. The fluting was added once the columns were in place.

The Elgin Marbles (see p47) were taken largely from the internal frieze.

Parthenon Frieze
The frieze, designed by Pheidias, ran around the inner wall of the Parthenon. The metopes (sections of the frieze) depicted the Great Panathenaia festival, honouring Athena.

RECONSTRUCTION OF THE PARTHENON
This reconstruction, from the southeast, shows the Parthenon as it was in the 5th century BC. It was 70 m (230 ft) long and 30 m (100 ft) wide. The entablature of this peripteral temple (with a single row of columns around the edge) was painted in blue, red and gold.

VEDUTA DEL CAST: D'ACROPOLIS DALLA PARTE DI TRAMONTANA

Explosion of 1687
During the Venetian siege of the Acropolis, General Francesco Morosini bombarded the Parthenon with cannon-fire. The Turks were using the temple as an arsenal at the time and the ensuing explosion demolished much of it, including the roof, the inner structure and 14 of the outer columns.

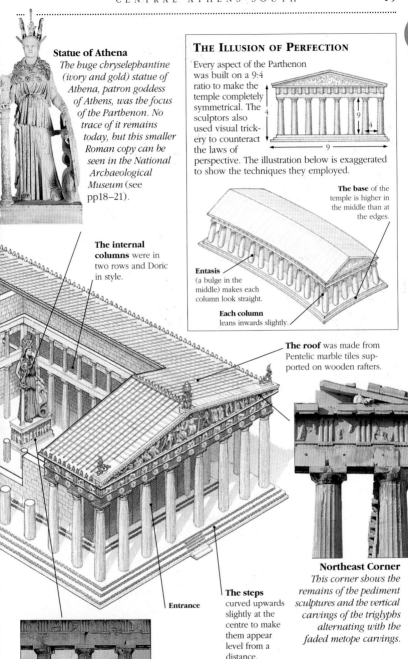

Statue of Athena
The huge chryselephantine (ivory and gold) statue of Athena, patron goddess of Athens, was the focus of the Parthenon. No trace of it remains today, but this smaller Roman copy can be seen in the National Archaeological Museum (see pp18–21).

THE ILLUSION OF PERFECTION

Every aspect of the Parthenon was built on a 9:4 ratio to make the temple completely symmetrical. The sculptors also used visual trickery to counteract the laws of perspective. The illustration below is exaggerated to show the techniques they employed.

The base of the temple is higher in the middle than at the edges.

Entasis (a bulge in the middle) makes each column look straight.

Each column leans inwards slightly.

The internal columns were in two rows and Doric in style.

The roof was made from Pentelic marble tiles supported on wooden rafters.

Entrance

The steps curved upwards slightly at the centre to make them appear level from a distance.

Northeast Corner
This corner shows the remains of the pediment sculptures and the vertical carvings of the triglyphs alternating with the faded metope carvings.

View of the East Cella
The cella was the inner room of the temple. In the case of the Parthenon, there were two – east and west. The east cella contained the enormous cult statue of Athena and the offerings bestowed upon it. The west cella was the back room, reserved for the priestess.

Around the Acropolis

Throne from the Theatre of Dionysos

THE AREA AROUND THE ACROPOLIS was the centre of public life in Athens. In addition to the Agora in the north *(see pp40–41)*, there were the two theatres on the south slope, used for drama festivals in honour of the god Dionysos. Political life was largely centred on the Pnyx and the Areopagos, the hills lying to the west of the Acropolis: the Assembly met on the former and murder trials were heard by a council of ex-magistrates on the latter. Other ancient remains and the Acropolis Study Centre provide a fascinating insight into daily life in ancient Athens.

The remains of the Theatre of Dionysos

⋔ Theatre of Herodes Atticus

This small Roman theatre seats 5,000 spectators and is still in use today. Built by the Roman consul Herodes Atticus between AD 161 and 174, in memory of his wife, the shape was hollowed out of the rocks on the southern slope of the Acropolis. The semicircular orchestra in front of the stage was repaved with alternating blue and white marble slabs in the 1950s. Behind the stage, its distinctive colonnade once contained statues of the nine Muses. The whole theatre was originally enclosed by a cedarwood roof that gave better acoustics and allowed for all-weather performances. Today it is used for a range of entertainment, including plays and concerts, both classical and popular *(see p111)*.

⋔ Theatre of Dionysos

Cut into the southern cliff face of the Acropolis, the Theatre of Dionysos is the birthplace of Greek tragedy, and was the first theatre built of stone. Aeschylus, Sophocles,

Euripides and Aristophanes all had their plays performed here, during the dramatic contests of the annual City Dionysia festival, when it was little more than a humble wood-and-earth affair. The theatre was rebuilt in stone by the Athenian statesman Lykourgos between 342–326 BC, but the ruins that can be seen today are in part those of a much bigger structure, built by the Romans, which could seat 17,000. They used it as a gladiatorial arena, and

added a marble balustrade with metal railings to protect spectators. In the 1st century AD, during Emperor Nero's reign, the orchestra was given its marble flooring, and in the 2nd century AD the front of the stage was decorated with reliefs showing Dionysos's life.

Above the theatre there is a cave sacred to the goddess Artemis. This was converted into a chapel in the Byzantine era, dedicated to **Panagía i Spiliótissa** (Our Lady of the Cave), and was the place where mothers brought their sick children. Two large Corinthian columns nearby are the remains of choregic monuments erected to celebrate the benefactor's team winning a drama festival. The Sanctuary of Asklepios to the west, founded in 420 BC, was dedicated to the god of healing. Worshippers seeking a cure had to take part in purification rites before they could enter the temple precincts.

🏛 Acropolis Study Centre

Makrygiánni 2–4, Makrygiánni.
⌖ *210 923 9186 or 924 9333.*
This handsome Neo-Classical building has suffered considerable earthquake damage and has recently undergone restoration. The building is home to a research centre and storehouse of historical information on the Acropolis. Displays include a scale model of the Parthenon, a complete plaster-cast representation of its frieze and a fascinating account of the quarrying of the famous white Pentelic marble and of how it was brought to Athens.

Interior of the Panagía Spiliótissa chapel, above the Theatre of Dionysos

⌂ Areopagos Hill

There is little left to see on this low hill today, apart from the rough-hewn, slippery steps and what are thought to be seats on its summit. The Areopagos was used by the Persians and Turks during their attacks on the Acropolis citadel, and played an important role as the home of the Supreme Judicial Court in the Classical period. It takes its name, meaning the "Hill of Ares", from a mythological trial that took place here when the god Ares was acquitted of murdering the son of Poseidon. The nearby **Cave of the Furies** inspired the playwright Aeschylus to set Orestes trial here in his play *Eumenides* (The Furies). The hill also achieved renown in AD 51, when St Paul delivered his sermon "On an unknown God" and gained his first convert, Dionysios the Areopagite, who subsequently became the patron saint of Athens.

⌂ Pnyx Hill

Today's role for the Pnyx, as outdoor theatre for multilingual son et lumière performances, seems a sad fate for the home of 4th- and 5th-century BC democracy. This is where the *Ekklesia* (citizens' assembly) met to discuss and vote upon all but the most important matters of state, until it lost its powers during Roman rule. In its heyday, 6,000 Athenians gathered 40 times a year to listen to speeches and take vital political decisions. Themistokles, Perikles and Demosthenes all spoke from the *bema* (speaker's platform) that is still visible today. Carved out of the rock face, it formed the top step of a platform that doubled as a primitive altar to the god Zeus. There are also the remains of the huge retaining

wall which was built to support the semicircular terraces that placed citizens on a level with the speakers. It completely surrounded the auditorium which was 110 m (358 ft) high.

🔒 Agios Dimítrios

Dionysíou Areopagítou, south slope of Acropolis. ⬭ daily. 📷 except Sun.

This Byzantine church is often called Agios Dimítrios Loumpardiáris, after an incident in 1656. The Turkish *disdar* (commander) at the time, Yusuf Aga, laid plans to fire a huge cannon called Loumpárda, situated by the Propylaia *(see p46)*, at worshippers in the church as they celebrated the feast day of Agios Dimítrios. However, the night before the feast, lightning struck the Propylaia, miraculously killing the commander and his family.

Cross from Agios Dimítrios church

⌂ Filopáppos Hill

The highest summit in the south of Athens, at 147 m (482 ft), offers spectacular views of the Acropolis. It has always played a decisive defensive role in Athens' history – the general Demetrios Poliorketes built an important fort here overlooking the strategic Piraeus road in 294 BC, and Francesco Morosini bombarded the Acropolis from here in 1687. Popularly called

The Asteroskopeíon on the Hill of the Nymphs

Filopáppos Hill after a monument still on its summit, it was also known to the ancient Greeks as the Hill of Muses or the Mouseion, because the tomb of Musaeus, a disciple of Orpheus, was traditionally held to be located here.

Built between AD 114–16, the Monument of Philopappus was raised by the Athenians in honour of Caius Julius Antiochus Philopappus, a Roman consul and philhellene. Its unusual concave marble façade, 12 m (40 ft) high, contains niches with statues of Philopappus and his grandfather, Antiochus IV. A frieze around the monument depicts the arrival of Philopappus by chariot for his inauguration as Roman consul in AD 100.

🏛 Hill of the Nymphs

This 103-m (340-ft) high tree-clad hill takes its name from dedications found carved on rocks in today's Observatory Garden. The Asteroskopeíon (Observatory), built in 1842 by the Danish architect Theophil Hansen, with funds from philanthropist Baron Sína, occupies the site of a sanctuary to nymphs associated with childbirth. The modern church of Agía Marína nearby has similar associations of childbirth; pregnant women used to slide effortlessly down a smooth rock near the church, in the hope of an equally easy labour.

The Monument of Philopappus AD 114–116

Street-by-Street: Central Pláka

PLAKA IS THE HISTORIC HEART of Athens. Even though only a few houses date back further than the Ottoman period, it remains the oldest continuously inhabited area of the city. One explanation of its name comes from the word *pliaka* (old), which was used to describe the area by Albanian soldiers in the service of the Turks who settled here in the 16th century. Despite the crowds of tourists and the many Athenians, who come to eat in the tavernas or browse in antique shops, it still retains the feel of a residential neighbourhood.

Mitrópoli
Athens' cathedral was built in the second half of the 19th century ⑫

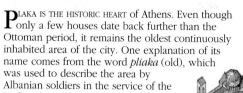

THOUKYDID

APOLLONOS

ADRIANOU

Thoukydídou
is named after the historian Thucydides (c.460–400 BC).

FLESSA

MNISIKLEOUS

LYSIOU

★ **Panagía Gorgoepíkoös**
This tiny 12th-century church, also known as the Little Cathedral, has some beautiful carvings ⑪

Museum of Greek Popular Musical Instruments
A range of folk instruments is displayed in this museum which was opened in 1991 ⑩

Monastiráki
(see pp34–5)

THEORIAS

Acropolis
(see pp44–51)

University of Athens Museum
Occupying the university's original home, this museum has memorabilia from the university's early days, including these old medical artifacts ⑨

Ancient Agora
(see pp40–41)

Kanellópoulos Museum
Privately owned, this museum has exquisite works of art from all areas of the Hellenic world ⑧

Greek Folk Art Museum
Offering the best of Greek folk art, this has everything from shadow puppets to terracotta ornaments **16**

LOCATOR MAP
See Street Finder maps 5–6

CENTRAL ATHENS NORTH

CENTRAL ATHENS SOUTH

Plateía
Syntágmatos
(see p62)

NIKODIMOU

YPEREIDOU

KACHOU

THOUKYDIDOU

KEKOPOS

CHATZIMICHALI

SOTIROS

KYDATHINAION

ADRIANOU

TRIPODON

ADRIANOU

THESPIDOS

0 metres   50
0 yards   50

Agios Nikólaos Ragavás
This 11th-century, Byzantine chapel is a popular location for weddings **13**

Plateía Lysikrátous
Named after the monument in its centre, this square was a favourite haunt of the poet Byron **15**

KEY

– – – Suggested route

STAR SIGHT

★ **Panagía Gorgoepíkoös**

Anafiótika
The whitewashed houses and winding streets resembling a Cycladic village were built in the 19th century by settlers from the island of Anáfi **14**

Rempétika musicians, Museum of Greek Popular Musical Instruments

Kanellópoulos Museum 🔟
Μουσείο Κανελλοπούλου

Corner of Theorías & Pános 12, Pláka.
Map 6 D2. 📞 *210 321 2313.*
Ⓜ *Monastiráki.* ⏰ *8:30am–3pm Tue–Sun, noon–3pm Good Fri.*
⬤ *1 Jan, 25 Mar, Easter Sun, 25, 26 Dec.* 📷 ⭕

IN AN IMMACULATELY restored Neo-Classical town house, this museum contains what was the private collection of wealthy collectors Pávlos and Alexándra Kanellópoulos. A varied collection of artifacts from all over the Hellenistic world, the three floors of exhibits include a selection of coins, 6th-century BC helmets, 5th-century BC gold Persian jewellery and Attic vases. There are also Cycladic figurines, some

Sculpture of a triton from the Kanellópoulos Museum

unusual terracotta figures of actors in their theatrical masks and a fine 2nd-century AD El Faiyûm portrait of a woman.
A huge block of stone that fell from the walls of the Acropolis, so heavy that the museum was built around it, can still be seen as an exhibit on the ground floor.

University of Athens Museum 🔟
Μουσείο Ιστορίας του Πανεπιστημίου Αθηνών

Thólou 5, Pláka. **Map** 6 E2.
📞 *210 324 0861.* Ⓜ *Monastiráki.*
⏰ *2pm–7pm Mon & Wed, 9am–2:30pm Tue, Thu & Fri.*
⬤ *main public hols.*

THIS THREE-STOREY house was the first home of the University of Athens. It opened on 3 May 1837 with 52 students and 33 professors in its first year. In November 1841 the University moved to its new quarters and from 1922 the building was home to many immigrant families. While they were there, a taverna

known as the "Old University" was opened on the ground floor.
In 1963 the building was declared a National Monument. Later reacquired by the university, the old building was opened as a museum in 1974. Today, the "Old University", as it is still known, has an eclectic collection of memorabilia such as corporeal body maps, anatomical models, scientific instruments and medicine jars. There is also a display about the university's past professors and students.

Museum of Greek Popular Musical Instruments 🔟
Μουσείο Ελληνικών Λαϊκών Μουσικών Οργάνων

Diogénous 1–3, Aérides Square.
Map 6 D1. 📞 *210 325 0198.*
Ⓜ *Monastiráki.* ⏰ *10am–2pm Tue–Sun, noon–7pm Wed (6pm in winter).* ⬤ *17 Nov, main public hols.*

CRETAN MUSICOLOGIST Phoebus Anogianákis donated over 1,200 musical instruments from his impressive collection to the Greek State in 1978. In 1991 this study centre and museum was opened, devoted to the history of popular Greek music, including Anogianákis's collection. The museum traces the development of different styles of island music and the arrival of *rempétika* (Greek "blues") from Smyrna in 1922.
Instruments from all over Greece are displayed on the three floors, with recordings and headphones available at every exhibit. The basement contains a selection of church and livestock bells, as well as water whistles, wooden clappers and flutes, which are sold during pre-Lenten carnival celebrations. The ground floor has wind instruments on display including *tsampoúna,* bagpipes made from goatskin. On the first floor, there is a selection of string instruments, such as the bouzouki, the *santoúri* and the Cretan *lýra*. There is also a beautiful 19th-century ivory and tortoiseshell lute.

Panagía Gorgoepíkoös ⓫

Παναγία η Γοργοεπήκοός

Bas-relief from south façade

THIS DOMED CRUCIFORM CHURCH is built entirely from Pentelic marble, now weathered to a rich corn-coloured hue. Dating from the 12th century, it measures only 7.5 m (25 ft) long by 12 m (40 ft) wide. The size of the church is in scale with Athens when it was just a village in the 12th century. Adorned with friezes and bas-reliefs taken from earlier buildings, the exterior mixes the Classical and Byzantine styles. Although dedicated to Panagía Gorgoepíkoös (the Madonna who Swiftly Hears) and Agios Elefthérios (the saint who protects women in childbirth), it is often affectionately known as the Mikrí Mitrópoli (Little Cathedral).

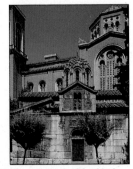

The south façade of the church, dwarfed by the giant Mitrópoli

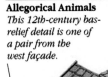

Allegorical Animals
This 12th-century bas-relief detail is one of a pair from the west façade.

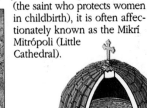

Four brick pillars
replaced the original marble ones in 1834.

The floor
is lower than ground level by about 30 cm (12 in).

Fragments of Classical buildings made from Pentelic marble were combined with new Byzantine sections in the style of a Classical frieze.

Main entrance

Lintel Frieze
This relief depicting the months of the year dates from the 4th century BC. The central cross was added in the 12th century.

Modern mosaics above the main entrance to Athens' cathedral, Mitrópoli

Mitrópoli ⑫
Μητρόπολη

Plateía Mitropóleos, Pláka. **Map** 6 E1.
210 322 1308. Monastiráki.
6:30am–7pm daily.

WORK BEGAN in 1840 on this huge cathedral, using marble from 72 demolished churches for its walls. The cornerstone was laid in a ceremony by King Otto and Queen Amalía on Christmas Day 1842. It took another 20 years to finish the building, using three different architects (François Boulanger, Theophil Hansen and Dimítrios Zézos) which may account for its slightly ungainly appearance. On 21 May 1862, it was formally dedicated to Evangelismós Theotókou (the

Annunciation of the Virgin) by the king and queen. At 40 m (130 ft) long, 20 m (65 ft) wide and 24 m (80 ft) high, it is the largest church in Athens.

The cathedral is the official seat of the Bishop of Athens, and remains a popular city landmark that has been used for ceremonial events from the coronations of kings to the weddings and funerals of the rich and famous.

Inside, there are the tombs of two saints murdered by the Ottoman Turks: Agía Filothéi and Gregory V. The bones of Agía Filothéi, who died in 1589, are still visible in a silver reliquary. Her charitable works included the ransoming of Greek women enslaved in Turkish harems. Gregory V, Patriarch of Constantinople,

was hanged and thrown into the Bosphorus in 1821. His body was rescued by Greek sailors and taken to Odessa. It was eventually returned to Athens by Black Sea (Pontic) Greeks 50 years later.

Agios Nikólaos Ragavás ⑬
Άγιος Νικόλαος ο Ραγυαβάς

Corner of Prytaneíou & Epichármou, Pláka. **Map** 6 E2. 210 322 8193.
Monastiráki. 1, 2, 4, 5, 9, 10, 11, 12, 15, 18. 8am–noon, 5–8pm daily. limited.

THIS TYPICAL 11th-century Byzantine church, rebuilt in the 18th century and restored to some of its former glory in the late 1970s, incorporates marble columns and other remains of ancient buildings in its external walls. It is one of the favourite parish churches of Pláka, frequently used for colourful Greek weddings which spill out on to the street at weekends. It was the first church in Athens to have a bell after the War of Independence (1821), and the first to ring out after the city's liberation from the Germans on 12 October 1944.

Anafiótika ⑭
Αναφιώτικα

Map 6 D2. Monastiráki.

NESTLING BENEATH the northern slopes of the Acropolis, this area is one of the oldest settlements in Athens. Today, its whitewashed houses, cramped streets, lazy cats and pots of

Looking down on Agios Nikólaos Ragavás church from Anafiótika

◁ **View from Anafiótika towards the Ancient Agora**

basil on windowsills still give it the atmosphere of a typical Cycladic village. Its first residents were refugees from the Peloponnesian War (431–404 BC). By 1841, it had been colonized by workmen from Anáfi, in the Cyclades, who eventually gave the area its name. Part of the influx of island craftsmen, who helped to construct the new city following Independence, ignored an 1834 decree declaring the area an archaeological zone, and completed their houses overnight, installing their families by morning. By Ottoman law, this meant the authorities were powerless to knock the new houses down.

The area is bounded by two 17th-century churches: Agios Geórgios tou Vráchou to the east, which has a tiny courtyard filled with flowers, and Agios Symeón to the west, which contains a copy of a miraculous icon, originally brought from Anáfi.

Akrokérama, or terracotta sphinxes, on a roof in Anafiótika

Plateía Lysikrátous ⓯
Πλατεία Λυσικράτους

Lysikrátous, Sélley & Epimenídou, Pláka. **Map 6** E2. 🚌 *1, 5, 9, 18.*

SITUATED IN THE EAST of the Pláka district, this square is named after the monument of Lysikrates that dominates it. Despite Lord Elgin's attempts to remove it to England, the elegant structure is the city's only intact choregic monument. These monuments were built to commemorate the victors at the annual choral and dramatic festival at the Theatre of Dionysos (*see p50*). They take their name from the rich sponsor (*choregos*) who produced the winning team. Built in 334 BC, this is the earliest known example where Corinthian

capitals are used externally. Six columns rise in a circle to a marble dome, decorated with an elegant finial of acanthus leaves which supported the winner's bronze trophy. It bears the inscription "Lysikrates of Kikynna, son of Lysitheides, was choregos; the tribe of Akamantis won the victory with a chorus of boys; Theon played the flute; Lysiades, an Athenian, trained the chorus; Evainetos was archon". The Athenians elected nine magistrates known as archons each year, and referred to the year by the name of one of them, the "eponymous archon." A frieze above this inscription, probably the theme of the winners' performance, depicts a battle between Dionysos, the god of theatre, and Tyrrhenian pirates. Surrounded by satyrs, the god transforms them into dolphins and their ship's mast into a sea serpent.

Capuchin friars converted the monument into a library. Grand tour travellers, such as Chateaubriand (1768–1848) and Byron (*see p73*), stayed at their convent, which was founded on the site in 1669.

The monument of Lysikrates, named after the *choregos* of the winning team of actors

Byron was inspired while staying there and wrote some of his poem, *Childe Harold*, sitting in the monument during his final visit to Athens in 1810.

Not far from the monument is the beautifully restored 11th-century Byzantine church of Agía Aikateríni (St Catherine). In 1767 it was given to the monastery of St Catherine of Mount Sinai. It was renovated but in 1882 the monastery was forced to exchange it for land elsewhere and it became a local parish church.

ICON PAINTERS IN PLAKA

Pláka is littered with small artists' studios where icons are still painted using traditional methods. The best are situated just south of Plateía Mitropóleos, among the ecclesiastical shops selling vestments and liturgical objects, on Agías Filothéis and Apóllonos streets. In some workshops, painters still use the Byzantine method of painting in egg-based tempera on specially treated wood. Customers of all religions can order the saint of their choice in a variety of different sizes. A medium-sized icon depicting a single saint, 25 cm by 15 cm (10 in by 6 in) and copied from a photograph, takes about one day to complete.

Ornate embroidery from Ioánnina, Epirus, on display in the Greek Folk Art Museum

Greek Folk Art Museum 🔟

Μουσείο Ελληνικής Λαϊκής Τέχνης

Kydathinaíon 17, Pláka. **Map** 6 E2.
📞 210 321 3018. 🚌 *2, 4, 9, 10, 11, 12, 15.* 🚋 *1, 5.* 🕐 *10am–2pm Tue–Sun.* ⬤ *main public hols.* 📷
♿ *limited.* 📷

Greek folk art, including some unrivalled regional embroidery and costumes from the mainland and Aegean islands, fills five floors in this fascinating museum. The collection also covers the renaissance of decorative crafts in the 18th and 19th centuries, to reveal a rich heritage of traditional techniques in skills such as weaving, woodcarving and metalwork.

The ground floor has an extensive collection of fine embroidery work, showing a wide range of techniques.

Displays on the mezzanine floor include ceramics, metalwork and woodcarving. The ceramics range from architectural works, such as chimneys, to decorative or practical pieces such as household pots. Made from terracotta

Decorative plate from Rhodes

and faïence, they include both glazed and unglazed pieces. The metalwork on view includes examples made from copper, bronze, iron, steel and pewter. Many are covered with intricate decoration. The woodcarving products are equally impressive in their decoration, often being inlaid with mother-of-pearl, ivory or silver. The wood used varies widely, from walnut to fragrant cedar and wild olive. Also on the mezzanine are disguise costumes. Their origin is thought to be in the ancient Greek drama festivals in honour of Dionysos which made use of overtly expressive masks. The puppets from the Karagkiózis theatre *(see p75)* amused the audience by satirizing topical political and social life.

The first floor houses popular paintings, including works by artist Theófilos Chatzimichaïl (1873–1934). There is an excellent collection of silverware on the second floor of the museum, with displays of various ecclesiastical items such as chalices and crosses, as well as secular pieces, such as ornate weaponry and delicate jewellery. Examples of traditional weaving and stonecarving can be found on the third floor. The range of materials used for weaving includes lamb's wool, goat's hair, silk and plant fibres. Traditional costumes are also on show on this floor. The decorations and design, which are frequently elaborate, vary according to the geographical region. Costumes from many different areas are on display.

Jewish Museum of Greece 🔟

Εβραϊκό Μουσείο της Ελλάδας

Nikis 39, Sýntagma. **Map** 6 F2.
📞 210 322 5582. Ⓜ *Sýntagma.* 🚌 *1, 2, 4, 5, 9, 10, 11, 12, 15, 18.* 🕐 *9am–2:30pm Mon–Fri, 10am–2pm Sun.* ⬤ *Main public hols & Jewish festivals.* ♿ 📷

This small museum moved in 1996 to improved quarters. It traces the history of Greece's Jewish communities which date back to the 3rd century BC. The exhibits present a revealing portrait of the Sephardic Jews, who fled Spain and Portugal in the 15th century, to settle throughout Greece in the religiously tolerant years of the Ottoman Empire.

Among the examples of traditional costumes and religious ceremonial instruments, one item of particular interest is the reconstruction of the *ehal.* This is the ark containing the Torah from the Pátra synagogue, which dates from the 1920s. It was rescued by Nikólaos Stavroulákis, founder of the museum, who has also written several books about the Greek Jews, on sale in the museum bookshop.

Moving displays of documentation record the German occupation of Greece during World War II when 87 per cent of the Jewish population here was wiped out. Over 45,000 Greeks from Thessaloníki alone were sent to Auschwitz and other concentration camps during a period of five months in 1943.

Reconstruction of the ark from Pátra

Hadrian's Arch, next to the Temple of Olympian Zeus

Temple of Olympian Zeus ⑱
Ναός του Ολυμπίου Διός

Corner of Amalías & Vasilíssis Olgas, Pláka. **Map** 6 F3. 210 922 6330. 2, 4, 11. 8:30am–3pm daily. main public hols. limited.

THE TEMPLE of Olympian Zeus is the largest in Greece, exceeding even the Parthenon in size. Work began on this vast edifice in the 6th century BC, in the reign of the tyrant Peisistratos, who allegedly initiated the building work to gain public favour. Although there were several attempts over many years to finish the temple, it was not completed until 650 years later.

The Roman Emperor Hadrian dedicated the temple to Zeus Olympios during the Panhellenic festival of AD 132, on his second visit to Athens. He also set up a gold and ivory inlaid statue of the god inside the temple, a copy of the original by Pheidias at Ancient Olympia. Next to it he placed a huge statue of himself. Both these statues have since been lost.

Only 15 of the original 104 Corinthian columns remain, each 17 m (56 ft) high – but enough to give a sense of the enormous size of this temple, which would have been approximately 96 m (315 ft) long and 40 m (130 ft) wide. Corinthian capitals were added to the columns by a Roman architect in 174 BC in place of the original, simple Doric columns. The temple is situated next to Hadrian's Arch, built in AD 131. It was positioned deliberately to mark the boundary between the ancient city and the new Athens of Hadrian.

The Russian Church of the Holy Trinity

Russian Church of the Holy Trinity ⑲
Ρωσική εκκλησία Αγίας Τριάδας

Filellínon 21, Pláka. **Map** 6 F2. 210 323 1090. 1, 2, 4, 5, 9, 10, 11, 12, 15, 18. 7:30–10am Mon–Fri, 7–11am Sat & Sun. main public hols. limited.

STILL IN USE BY THE Russian community, this was once the largest church in the city. Built in 1031 by the Lykodímou family (also called Nikodímou), it was ruined by an earthquake in 1701. In 1780 the Turkish *voivode* (governor), Hadji Ali Haseki, partly demolished the church to use its materials for the defensive wall that he built around the city. During the siege of the city in 1827, it received more damage from Greek shells fired from the Acropolis.

The church remained derelict until the Russian government restored it 20 years later. It was then reconsecrated as the Church of the Holy Trinity.

A large cruciform building, its most unusual feature is a wide dome, 10 m (33 ft) in diameter. Its interior was decorated by the Bavarian painter Ludwig Thiersch. The separate belltower also dates from the 19th century, its bell a gift from Tsar Alexander II.

The remaining Corinthian columns of the Temple of Olympian Zeus

The Tomb of the Unknown Soldier in Plateía Syntágmatos

Plateía Syntágmatos ⓴
Πλατεία Σύνταγματος

Sýntagma. **Map** 6 F1. 🚌 *1, 5, 9, 10, 12, 15, 18.* Ⓜ *Sýntagma.*

THIS SQUARE (also known as Sýntagma Square) is home to the Greek parliament, in the Voulí building, and the Tomb of the Unknown Soldier, decorated with an evocative relief depicting a dying Greek hoplite warrior. Unveiled on 25 March 1932 (National Independence Day), the tomb is flanked by texts from Perikles's famous funeral oration. The other walls that enclose the square are covered in bronze shields celebrating military victories since 1821.

The National Guard (*évzones*) are on continuous patrol in front of the tomb, dressed in their famous uniform of kilt and pom-pom clogs. They are best seen at the changing of the guard, every Sunday at 11am.

National Gardens ㉑
Εθνικός Κήπος

Borders Vasilíssis Sofías, Iródou Attikoú, Vasilíssis Olgas & Vasilíssis Amalías, Sýntagma. **Map** 7 A1. Ⓜ *Sýntagma.* 🚌 *1, 3, 5, 7, 8, 10, 13, 18.* ⬭ *dawn–dusk.* **Botanical Museum, zoo, cafés** ⬭ *7:30am–3pm daily.*

BEHIND THE VOULI parliament building, this 16-ha (40-acre) park, cherished by all Athenians and formerly known as the "Royal Gardens", was renamed the National Gardens by decree in 1923. Queen Amalía ordered the creation of the park in the 1840s; she even issued the fledgling Greek Navy to bring 15,000 seedlings from around the world. The gardens were landscaped by the Prussian horticulturalist Friedrich Schmidt, who travelled the world in search of rare plants.

Although the gardens have lost much of their original grandeur, they remain one of the most peaceful spots in the city. Shady paths meander past small squares, park benches and ponds filled with goldfish. A huge feral cat population is also resident in the park. Remains of Roman mosaics excavated in the park and an old aqueduct add atmosphere. Modern sculptures of writers, such as Dionýsios Solomós, Aristotélis Valaorítis and Jean Moreas, can be found throughout the park. There is also a small **Botanical Museum** to visit, a ramshackle zoo, and cafés.

South of the park lies the **Záppeion**

exhibition hall, an impressive building in use today as a conference centre. It was donated by Evángelos and Konstantínos Záppas, cousins who made their fortunes in Romania. Built by Theophil Hansen, architect of the Athens Academy (*see p31*), between 1874 and 1888, it also has its own gardens. The elegant café next door to the Záppeion is a pleasant place to relax and refresh after a walk around these charming, peaceful gardens.

The tranquil National Gardens

Presidential Palace ㉒
Προεδρικό Μέγαρο

Iródou Attikoú, Sýntagma. **Map** 7 A2. Ⓜ *Sýntagma.* 🚌 *3, 7, 8, 13.* ⬛ *to the public.*

THIS FORMER royal palace was designed and built by Ernst Ziller (*see p31*) in c.1878. It was occupied by the Greek Royal Family from 1890 until the hasty departure of King Constantine in 1967. It is still guarded by the *évzones* whose barracks are at the top of the street. After the abolition of the monarchy, it became the official residence of the President of Greece and he still uses it today when hosting dignitaries. Its well-maintained gardens can just be seen through the iron railings.

Voulí parliament building in Plateía Sýntagmatos, guarded by *évzones*

Kallimármaro Stadium ⓐ
Καλλιμάρμαρο Στάδιο

Archimídous 16, Pagkráti. **Map** 7 B3.
📞 *210 752 6386.* 🚊 *3, 4, 11.*
🕐 *8am–sunset daily.* ♿

Some of the ornate tombs in the First Cemetery of Athens

THIS HUGE marble structure set in a small valley by Ardittós Hill occupies the exact site of the original Panathenaic Stadium built by Lykourgos in 330–329 BC. It was first reconstructed for gladiatorial contests during Hadrian's reign (AD 117–138), then rebuilt in white marble by the wealthy Roman benefactor Herodes Atticus for the Panathenaic Games in AD 144. Neglected for many years, its marble was gradually quarried for use in new buildings or burnt down to make lime.

In 1895 Geórgios Avérof gave four million drachmas in gold for the restoration of the stadium in time for the start of the first modern Olympic Games on 5 April 1896. Designed by Anastásios Metaxás, the present structure is a faithful replica of Herodes Atticus's stadium, as described in the *Guide to Greece* by Greek writer Pausanias. Built in white Pentelic marble, it is 204 m (669 ft) long and 83 m (272 ft) wide and can seat up to 60,000 spectators. Metaxás was also helped by the plans of architect Ernst Ziller, who excavated the site between 1869 and 1879. Among his finds was a double-headed statue of Apollo and Dionysos, one of many that were used to divide the stadium's running track down its length. It is on show in the National Archaeological Museum (*see pp18–21*).

First Cemetery of Athens ⓐ
Πρώτο Νεκροταφείο Αθηνών

Entrance in Anapáfseos, Méts.
Map 7 A4 📞 *210 923 6118.* 🚊 *2, 4.* 🕐 *5:30am–6pm daily.* ♿ *limited.*

ATHENS' MUNICIPAL cemetery, which is not to be confused with the Kerameikós, the ancient cemetery (*see p38–9*), is a peaceful place, filled with pine and olive trees and the scent of incense burning at the well-kept tombs.

Fine examples of 19th-century funerary art range from the flamboyance of some of the marble mausoleums to the simplicity of the belle époque *Kimoméni* or *Sleeping Maiden*. Created by Giannoúlis Chalepás, this beautiful tomb is found to the right of the main cemetery avenue where many of Greece's foremost families are buried.

Among the notable 19th- and 20th-century figures with tombs here are Theódoros Kolokotrónis (*see p30*), British philhellene historian George Finlay (1799–1875), German archaeologist Heinrich Schliemann (1822–90), the Nobel prize-winning poet Giórgos Seféris (1900–71) and the actress and politician Melína Merkoúri (1922–94).

In addition to the large number of tombs for famous people that are buried here, the cemetery contains a moving, single memorial to the 40,000 Athenians who perished through starvation during World War II.

A lone athlete exercising in the vast Kallimármaro Stadium

AROUND ATHENS

ATTICA

THE AREA AROUND ATHENS, *known as Attica, is the spiritual heart-land of ancient and modern Greece. Its archaeological sites have attracted generations of scholars and plunderers alike, and its mountains and coastline have provided important refuge in times of strife. Today the golden beaches along the eastern coast attract those simply wishing to escape the bustle of modern Athens.*

The land of Attica was the basis of Athenian wealth. The fine marble from the quarries on Mount Ymittós and Mount Pentéli was used for the temples and sculptures of ancient Athens. The silver from Lávrio financed their construction, and the produce from the local agricultural areas fed the population.

Waiting for a ferry in Piraeus

Attica has witnessed many significant historical events. The plain of Marathon was the site of one of the greatest battles in Greek history. Piraeus, now Greece's largest and busiest port, was also the port of ancient Athens. The Classical temples at lesser-known archaeological sites around the countryside, such as Eleusis, Ramnoús and Brauron, offer a rural retreat from the overcrowding and pollution of the city. At Soúnio, the majestic, well-preserved Temple of Poseidon on the cape has been a beacon for mariners for centuries.

The Byzantine era also left a great legacy of fine architecture to the region. Two of the best examples of this are the imposing monasteries of Dafní and Kaisarianí, with their ornate mosaics and elegant stonework.

South of Athens, the summer heat of the Attic plain is ideal for growing crops. Grapes are a speciality in the Mesógeia (Midland) region, which produces some of the finest retsina in the country. North of Athens, the pine-forested Mount Párnitha provides interesting walks and offers superb views over the city from the summit.

The peaceful ruins of the Parthenon of the Bear Maidens at Ancient Brauron

◁ **The Christ Pantokrátor figure in the dome of the *katholikón* of the Monastery of Dafní**

Around Athens

BEYOND THE ENDLESS urban sprawl of Athens, the region around the city, known as Attica, offers the diversity of wild mountains, Byzantine monasteries and churches, evocative archaeological sites and sandy beaches. Not surprisingly, such easy accessibility to the coast and countryside has led to overcrowding in Athens' suburbs, and pollution around Piraeus and Ancient Eleusis. The hills of Mount Párnitha and Ymittós are rich in wildlife, with deserted trails, caves and icy spring water. In the summer months, Athenians move out to the Attic Coast, where the well-kept beaches have every kind of watersport facility, and there are bars and clubs. Towards the cape at Soúnio there are countless fish tavernas by the sea and quiet rocky coves ideal for snorkelling.

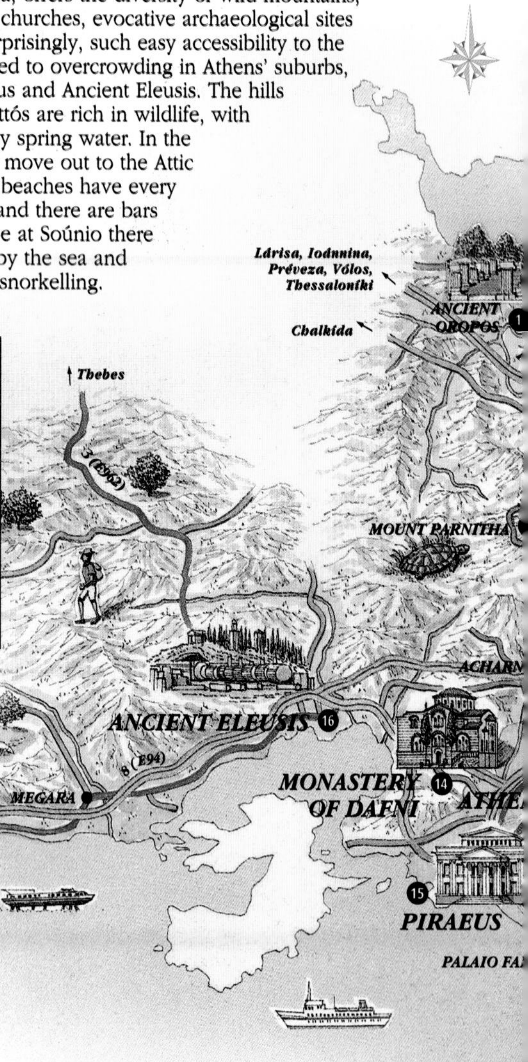

Ldrisa, Iodnnina, Préveza, Vólos, Thessaloniki

Chalkída

ANCIENT OROPOS 1

↑ *Thebes*

MOUNT PARNITHA

ACHARN

ANCIENT ELEUSIS 16

MONASTERY OF DAFNI 14 **ATHE**

MEGARA

15

PIRAEUS

Corinth, Tripoli, Pátra, Kalamáta

PALAIO FA

Boats moored in Mikrolímano harbour, Piraeus

SEE ALSO

- *Where to Stay* pp90–91
- *Where to Eat* pp104–5

Key

▦	Dual carriageway *(Attkí Odos)*
▦	Major road
▦	Minor road
▦	Scenic route
◅▻	River
☼	Viewpoint

GETTING AROUND

Athens' international airport, Elefthérios, serves the region. There are two routes out of Athens to southeast Attica: the popular coastal road from Piraeus to Soúnio, and the inland road, via Korópi and Markópoulo, to the east coast towns of Pórto Ráfti and Lávrio. This is also the way for the turn-off to the port of Rafína, where there are ferry connections to Evvoia and the Cyclades. Frequent buses from Athens link all the towns in the area. Mount Párnitha and northern Attica are best reached by taking the 1 (E75) national road known as Attikí Odos.

The Temple of Poseidon on the cape at Soúnio

0 kilometres _____ 10

0 miles _____ 5

The *katholikón* of Moní Kaïsarianís

View of the Enkoimitírion at Oropós

Ancient Oropós ❶
Ωρωπός

Kálamos, Attica. **Road map** D4.
22950 62144. Kálamos.
daily. main public hols.

THE PEACEFUL SANCTUARY of Oropós nestles on the left bank of the Cheímarros, a small river surrounded by pine trees and wild thyme bushes. It is dedicated to Amphiáraos, a hero credited with healing powers whom, according to mythology, Zeus rescued when he was wounded in battle. It is said that the earth swallowed up Amphiáraos while he was riding his chariot, and that he then miraculously reappeared through the sacred spring at this site. In ancient times visitors would throw coins into the spring in the hope of being granted good health.

The Amphiaraion sanctuary came to prominence as a healing centre in the 4th century BC, when its Doric temple and sacrificial altar were built, attracting the sick from all over Greece. Houses erected during the Roman period, when the area became a popular spa centre, are still visible on the right bank of the river. The Enkoimitírion was the site's most interesting building. It was a long stoa, the remains of which are still visible today, where the patients underwent treatment by *enkoimisis*. This gruesome ritual entailed the sacrifice of a goat in whose bloody hide the patient would then spend the night. The next morning, priests would prescribe medicines based on their interpretations of the dreams of the patient.

Above the Enkoimitírion are the remains of an impressive theatre, which has a well-preserved *proskenion* (stage) and five sculpted marble thrones, once reserved for the use of priests and guests of honour. On the right bank of the valley, opposite the altar, is a water clock dating from the 4th century BC.

Marble throne from the theatre at Oropós

Ramnoús ❷
Ραμνούς

Attica. **Road map** D4. 22940 63477. daily (Sanctuary of Nemesis only). main public hols.

RAMNOUS is a remote but beautiful site, overlooking the gulf of Evvoia. It is home to the only Greek sanctuary dedicated to the goddess of vengeance, Nemesis. The sanctuary was demolished when the Byzantine Emperor Arcadius decreed in AD 399 that all temples left standing should be destroyed. Thus only the remains of this sanctuary can be seen today.

Within its compound, two temples are preserved side by side. The smaller and older Temple of Themis dates from the 6th century BC. Used as a treasury and storehouse in ancient times, its impressive polygonal walls are all that now survive. Within the cella, some important statues of the goddess and her priestess, Aristonoë, were uncovered. They can now be seen in the National Archaeological Museum *(see pp18–21)*.

The larger Temple of Nemesis dates from the mid-5th century BC. It is very similar in design to the Hephaisteion in Athens' Agora *(see pp40–41)* and the Temple of Poseidon at Soúnio *(see p72)*. Built in the Doric

The remains of the Temple of Nemesis at Ramnoús

style, the temple contained a statue of Nemesis by Agorakritos, a disciple of Pheidias *(see p48)*. The statue has been partially reconstructed from fragments, and the head is now in the British Museum.

Marathónas ❸
Μαραθώνας

Attica. **Road map** D4. **C** 22940 55155. **Site & Museum** *Tue–Sun.* ● *main public hols.*

The quayside at the port of Rafína

THE MARATHON PLAIN is the site of the great Battle of Marathon, where the Athenians defeated the Persians. The burial mound of the Athenians lies 4 km (2 miles) from the modern town of Marathónas. This tumulus is 180 m (590 ft) in circumference and 10 m (32 ft) high. It contains the ashes of the 192 Athenian warriors who died in the battle. The spot was marked by a simple *stele* of a fallen warrior, Aristíon, by the sculptor Aristocles. The original is now in the National Archaeological Museum *(see pp18–21)* in Athens. There is a copy at the site, inscribed with an epigram by the ancient poet Simonides: "The Athenians fought at the front of the Greeks at Marathon, defeating the gold-bearing Persians and stealing their power."

In 1970 the burial mound of the Plataians and royal Mycenaean tombs were found nearby in the village of Vraná. The Plataians were the only other Greeks who sent warriors in time to assist the Athenians already at the battle. The **Marathon Museum** displays archaeological finds from these local sites. There are also some beautiful

Plate discovered in the tomb of Plataians

Egyptian-style statues from the 2nd century AD, found on the estate of Herodes Atticus, on the Marathon Plain. This wealthy benefactor was born and bred in this area. He is known for erecting many public buildings in Athens, including the famous theatre located on the southern slope of the Acropolis *(see p50)* that was named in his honour.

ENVIRONS: Just 8 km (5 miles) west of Marathónas is **Lake Marathónas**, which is crossed by a narrow causeway. This vast expanse of water is man-made. The impressive dam, made from white Pentelic marble, was built in 1926. It created an artificial lake that was Athens' sole source of water up until 1956. The lake is fed by the continuous streams of the Charádras and Varnávas which flow down from Mount Párnitha *(see p75)* and makes a good setting for a picnic.

Rafína ❹
Ραφήνα

Attica. **Road map** D4. **8,600**

THE CHARM OF RAFÍNA is its lively fishing port, packed with caïques and ferries. After Piraeus it is the main port in Attica. Frequent buses from Athens bring passengers for the regular hydrofoil and ferry connections to the Cyclades and other Aegean islands.

One of the administrative *demes* (regions) of ancient Athens, Rafína is a long-established settlement. Although there is little of historical or archaeological interest, the town offers a selection of excellent fish restaurants and tavernas. Choose one by the waterside to sit and watch the hustle and bustle of this busy port.

ENVIRONS: North of Rafína, a winding road leads to the more picturesque resort of **Máti**. Once a quiet hamlet, it is packed today with trendy cafés and bars, apartment blocks and summer houses owned by Athenians.

THE BATTLE OF MARATHON

When Darius of Persia arrived at the Bay of Marathon with his warships in 490 BC, it seemed impossible that the Greeks could defeat him. Heavily outnumbered, the 10,000 Greek hoplites had to engage 25,000 Persian warriors. Victory was due to the tactics of the commander Miltiades, who altered the usual battle phalanx by strengthening the wings with more men. The Persians were enclosed on all sides and driven back to the sea. Around 6,000 Persians died and only 192 Athenians. The origins of the marathon run also date from this battle. News of the victory was relayed by a runner who covered the 41 km (26 miles) back to Athens in full armour before dying of exhaustion.

Vase showing Greek hoplites fighting a Persian on horseback

Ancient Brauron ❺
Βραυρώνα

SITUATED NEAR MODERN VRAVRONA, Brauron is one of the most evocative sites near Athens. Although little remains of its former architectural glory, finds in the museum reveal its importance as the centre of worship of Artemis, goddess of childbirth and protectress of animals. Legend relates that it was founded by Orestes and Iphigéneia, the children of Agamemnon, who introduced the cult of Artemis into Greece. Evidence of Neolithic and Mycenaean remains have been found on the hill above the site, but the tyrant Peisistratos brought Brauron its fame in the 6th century BC when he made the worship of Artemis Athens' official state religion.

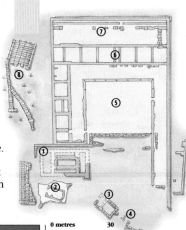

0 metres   30
0 yards   30

KEY TO THE SANCTUARY OF ARTEMIS

① Temple of Artemis
② Chapel of Agios Geórgios
③ Sacred House
④ Tomb of Iphigéneia
⑤ Parthenon of the Bear Maidens
⑥ Dormitories
⑦ Stoa
⑧ Stone Bridge

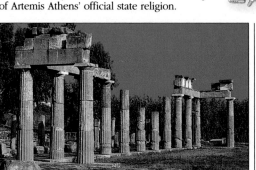

The Parthenon of the Bear Maidens at Brauron

Exploring Ancient Brauron
The centre of this compact site lies just north of the prehistoric acropolis. The 5th-century BC Doric **Temple of Artemis**, of which only the foundations remain, formed the focal point of the sanctuary to the goddess. Beside the temple stands a late Byzantine chapel, dedicated to **Agios Geórgios**.
From here a path leads southeast to the oldest cult site in the sanctuary. This is said to be the **Tomb of Iphigéneia**,

the high priestess of Artemis. Next to it are the foundations of the **Sacred House**, which was used as a home by the cult's priestesses. The most extensive remains at the site are to the northeast, at the **Parthenon of the Bear Maidens**. This courtyard may have been the place where young girls performed the

bear dance. Surrounded by a late 5th-century BC **stoa**, the courtyard had rooms behind that were used as dining areas and **dormitories**. Only the foundations remain, but the stone sleeping couches and bases of statues can still be seen. There is also a 5th-century BC **stone bridge** to the west.

The small Byzantine chapel of Agios Geórgios

BRAURONIA CEREMONY

Held every four years in the spring, the Brauronia festival was celebrated in atonement for the killing of one of Artemis's sacred pet bears. Although little is known about the mysterious rites today, Aristophanes mentions the "bear dance" that initiates had to perform in his play *Lysistrata*. Disguised as bears and adorned with saffron-coloured robes, young girls, aged between 5 and 10, performed a dance honouring this sacred animal.

Relief showing pilgrims approaching the altar of Artemis at the Brauronia ceremony

**Mycenaean vase from the
Brauron Museum, 1200–1100 BC**

⌾ Brauron Museum

This fascinating museum has a wealth of finds from the site. In Room 1, there are cases filled with assorted votive offerings such as miniature vases and jewellery. In Room 2 are the serene statues of *árktoi* ("bear maidens"). Room 3 has a fine votive relief of the gods Zeus, Leto, Apollo and Artemis, and the remains of an altar. Rooms 4 and 5 offer a variety of prehistoric and Mycenaean finds, including some ornate Geometric vases.

**Statue of
a bear
maiden**

RETSINA

Although many Greeks prefer drinking whisky to wine these days, retsina is still favoured by millions of tourists. Around 16 million bottles were drunk in 1994, and 50 per cent of them were exported around the world. The unique, distinctive flavour comes from the Aleppo pine resin which is added in small quantities to the grape juice during fermen-tation. This method has been used since antiquity to preserve and flavour wine in Greece. Since entry into the EEC (now called the EU) in 1981, traditional production areas have had their own appellations. Aficionados agree that some of the best retsina comes from the Mesógeia appellation in Attica, where the Savatiano grape is cultivated. Kourtákis, the largest producers of retsina, have their vineyards in Markópoulo and Koropí.

**Collection
of pine
resin**

Pórto Ráfti ❻
Πόρτο Ράφτη

Attica. **Road map** D4. 🏛 3,300.

PÓRTO RAFTI takes its name from Ráfti island which is visible just off the headland. On the island is a colossal marble statue of a seated female, made in the Roman period, known as "the tailor" *(ráftis)*. It was most likely built to be used as a beacon for shipping and would have lit up the harbour. Pórto Ráfti has one of the best natural harbours in Greece, although the town itself has never developed into an important seafaring port. In April 1941, during World War II, 6,000 New Zealand troops were successfully evacuated from the beach. Today it is primarily a pleasant holiday resort, with tavernas and bars. The area is rich in archaeological history. Many Mycenaean tombs have been found south of the bay of Pórto Ráfti, at Peratí, a port that flourished in the 7th and 6th centuries BC.

ENVIRONS: The remains of a fortress that was built during the Chremonidean War (268–261 BC) between Egypt and Macedon can be seen on the southern **Koróni** headland. The northern coastline of **Peratí** is pockmarked with unexplored caves, and attracts many people who come to swim in the clear water and fish off the craggy rocks.

Markópoulo, a thriving market town and viticultural centre 8 km (5 miles) inland, is famous for its tavernas. Spicy sausages are for sale in the butchers' shops and the bakeries are fragrant with the smell of fresh bread.

Pórto Ráfti harbour with Ráfti island in the background

One of the many 19th-century Neo-Classical buildings in Lávrio

Lávrio **❼**
Λαύριο

Attica. **Road map** D4. 🏛 *8,800.*
🚌 🚆 ⛴ *Thu.*

LAVRIO WAS FAMOUS for its silver mines in ancient times. They were used as a source of revenue for the Athenian state and financed leader Perikles's programme of grand public buildings in Athens in the 5th century BC They also enabled the general Themistokles to construct a fleet capable of beating the Persians at the Battle of Salamis in 480 BC. It was this excellent naval fleet which established Athens as a naval power. Before their final closure in the 20th century, the mines were also exploited by French and Greek companies for other minerals such as manganese and cadmium.

Originally worked by slaves, over 2,000 mine shafts have been discovered in the surrounding hills, and some are now open to visitors as the **Mineralogical Museum**. It is the only such museum in Greece. Traces of ore and minerals in the rock face can be seen on tours of the old mines. Since their closure the area has suffered high unemployment. The old Neo-Classical houses and empty harbourfront warehouses indicate the former prosperity of the town. Makrónisos, the narrow island opposite the port, was used as a prison for political detainees during the Civil War (1946–49).

🏛 **Mineralogical Museum**
Leof Andréa Kordelá. 📞 *22920 26270.* ⏰ *10am–noon Wed, Sat & Sun.* 🚫 ♿

Soúnio **❽**
Σούνιο

9 km (5.5 miles) S of Lávrio, Attica.
Road map D4. 📞 *22920 39363.* 🚌 *to Lávrio.* ⏰ *10am–sunset daily.* 🚫 📷

THE TEMPLE OF POSEIDON, built on a site set back from sheer cliffs tumbling into the Aegean Sea at Soúnio (Cape Sounion), was ideally located for worship of the powerful god of the sea. Its brilliant white marble columns have been a landmark for ancient and modern mariners alike.

The present temple, built in 444 BC, stands on the site of older ruins. An Ionic frieze, made from 13 slabs of Parian marble, is located on the east side of the temple's main approach path. It is very eroded but is known to have depicted scenes from the mythological battle of the Lapiths and centaurs, and also the adventures of the hero Theseus, who was thought to be the son of Poseidon, according to some legends.

The Doric columns of the Temple of Poseidon

Local marble, taken from quarries at nearby Agriléza, was used for the temple's 34 slender Doric columns, of which 15 survive today. The temple also possesses a

The ruins of the Temple of Poseidon on Soúnio

unique design feature which helps combat the effects of sea-spray erosion: the columns were cut with only 16 flutings instead of the usual 20, thus reducing the surface area exposed to the elements.

When Byron carved his name on one of the columns in 1810, he set a dangerous precedent of vandalism at the temple, which is now covered with scrawled signatures.

A waterside restaurant at Várkiza, along the Attic coast

Attic Coast ❾
Παραλία Αττικύς

Attica. **Road map** D4.

THE COASTAL STRIP from Piraeus to Soúnio is often called the "Apollo Coast" after a small Temple of Apollo discovered at Vouliagméni. It is covered with beaches and resort towns that are always very busy at weekends, and particularly so in the summer holiday season.

One of the first places along the coast from Piraeus is the tiny seaside resort of **Palaió Fáliro** which is home to the Phaleron War Cemetery. In this quiet spot is the Athens Memorial, erected in May 1961 to 2,800 British soldiers who died in World War II.

Noisy suburbs near Athens airport, like **Glyfáda** and **Alimos** (famous as the birthplace of the ancient historian Thucydides), are very commercialized with a large number of marinas, hotels and shopping malls.

At chic **Vouliagméni**, with its large yacht marina, luxury

BYRON IN GREECE

The British Romantic poet Lord Byron (1788–1824) first arrived in Greece in 1809 at the tender age of 21, and travelled around Epirus and Attica with his friend John Cam Hobhouse. In Athens he wrote *The Maid of Athens,* inspired by his love for his landlady's daughter, and parts of *Childe Harold.* These publications made him an overnight sensation and, when back in London in 1812, he proclaimed: "If I am a poet it is the air of Greece which has made me one." He was received as a hero on his return to Greece in 1823, because of his desire to help fight the Turks in the War of Independence. However, on Easter Sunday 1824 in Mesolóngi, he died of a fever without seeing Greece liberated. Proving in his case that the pen is mightier than the sword, Byron is still venerated in Greece, where streets and babies are named after him.

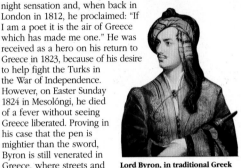

Lord Byron, in traditional Greek costume, by T Phillips (1813)

hotels line the promontory. A short walk northwards away from the coast, beside the main road, is the enchanting Vouliagméni Lake. This unusual freshwater lake lies beneath low, limestone cliffs. The stunning stretch of warm, sulphurous water has been used for years to bring relief to sufferers of rheumatism. There are changing rooms and a café close by.

At **Várkiza**, the wide bay is filled with windsurfers. By the main road there are two massive gin-palace music halls, *On the Rocks* and *Riba's,* where popular Greek singers perform throughout the summer season. From Várkiza, a road snakes inland to **Vári**, renowned for its

restaurants serving meat dishes. The Vári cave is located about 2 km (1 mile) north of the village. Inside is a freshwater spring and some fine stalactites have developed. Some minor Classical ruins remain in the caves, although many have been removed. There is unrestricted access and no admission charge.

From Várkiza to Soúnio, the coastal road is lined with quiet bathing coves, fish tavernas and luxury villas. **Anávysos** is a thriving market town surrounded by vineyards and fields. In its harbour, caïques sell locally caught fish every day, and there is a small street market every Saturday, with stalls piled high with seasonal fruit and vegetables.

Colourful stall of local produce in Anávyssos

Sculpture in the gardens of the Vorrés Museum

Paianía ⑩
Παιανία

Attica. **Road map** D4. 9,700. Tue.

JUST EAST OF ATHENS, Paianía is a town of sleepy streets and cafés. In the main square, the church of **Zoödóchou Pigís** has some fine modern frescoes by the 20th-century artist Fótis Kóntoglou. The birthplace of the orator Demosthenes (384–322 BC), Paianía is more famous today for the **Vorrés Museum**. Set in beautiful gardens, this features private collector Ion Vorrés' eclectic array of ancient and modern art. The museum is divided into two sections, encompassing 3,000 years of Greek history and heritage. The first is housed in what was the collector's private home: two traditional village houses filled with ancient sculptures, folk artifacts, ceramics, Byzantine icons, seascapes and furniture. The second section, housed in a specially built modern building, offers a unique overview of contemporary Greek art since the 1940s, with many excellent works by more than 300 different painters and sculptors, encompassing every major art movement from Photo-Realism to Pop Art.

Vorrés Museum
Diadóchou Konstantínou 1. 210 664 4771. 10am–2pm Sat & Sun. Aug & main public hols.

ENVIRONS: Above Paianía, the **Koutoúki Cave** is hidden in the foothills of Mount Ymittós. It was found in 1926 by a shepherd looking for a goat which had fallen into the 12,200 sq m (130,000 sq ft) cave. There are tours every half hour, with son et lumière effects lighting up the stalagmites and stalactites. The temperature inside is 17˚C (62˚F).

Koutoúki Cave
4 km (2.5 miles) W of Paianía. 210 664 2108. 9am–4:30pm daily.

Moní Kaïsarianís ⑪
Μονή Καισαριανής

5 km (3 miles) E of Athens, Attica. **Road map** D4. 210 723 6619. to Kaisarianís. 8:30am–3pm Tue–Sun. main public hols.

LOCATED IN A WOODED valley of Mount Ymittós, Moní Kaïsarianís was founded in the 11th century. In 1458, when Sultan Mehmet II conquered Athens, the monastery was exempted from taxes in recognition of the abbot's gift to the sultan of the keys of the city. This led to great prosperity until 1792, when it lost these privileges and went into decline. The complex was used briefly as a convent after the War of Independence, until 1855. Its buildings were eventually restored in 1956.

The small *katholikón* is dedicated to the Presentation of the Virgin. All the frescoes date from the 16th and 17th centuries. The finest are those in the narthex, painted by the Peloponnesian artist Ioánnis Ypatos in 1682.

Decorative stonework on Moní Kaïsarianís

The large, peaceful gardens in the monastery are owned by the Athens Friends of the Tree Society, who planted them after all the trees were cut down during World War II. Just above the monastery, the source of the River Ilissós has

Moní Kaïsarianís, hidden in the hills around Mount Ymittós

been visited since antiquity for its sacred Kylloú Péra spring whose water is reputed to cure sterility; water still gushes from an ancient marble ram's-head fountain on the eastern side of the monastery. Before the Marathon dam was built *(see p69)*, the spring was Athens' main source of water.

Kifisiá ⑫
Κηφισιά

12 km (7.5 miles) NE of Athens, Attica.
Road map D4. 🏛 *40,000.* 🚌
Ⓜ *Kifisiá.*

The tiny chapel of Agía Triáda on the hillside of Mount Párnitha

KIFISIA HAS BEEN a favourite summer retreat for many Athenians since Roman times. Once the exclusive domain of rich Greeks, it is congested today with apartment blocks and shopping malls. Traces of its former tranquillity can still be seen by taking a ride in a horse-drawn carriage. These wait by the metro station offering drives down shady streets lined with mansions and villas, built in a bizarre variety of hybrid styles such as Alpine chalet and Gothic Neo-Classicism.

The **Goulándris Natural History Museum**, which opened in 1974, is housed in one of these villas. Its large collection covers all aspects of Greece's varied wildlife and minerals. There are 200,000 varieties of plants in the herbarium, and over 1,300 examples of taxidermy; the stuffed creatures are carefully displayed in their natural habitats.

Clam shell outside the Goulándris Natural History Museum, Kifisiá

🏛 Goulándris Natural History Museum
Levídou 13. 🅲 *210 801 5870.*
🕐 *9am–2:30pm Sat–Thu.*
⬤ *main public hols.* 🈳

ENVIRONS: In Kifisiá's suburb Maroúsi is the small **Spathári Museum of Shadow Theatre**. Opened in 1995, it is devoted to the fascinating history of the Karagkiózis puppet theatre. Shadow theatre originally came to Greece from the Far East, via players who used to travel throughout the Ottoman Empire performing for the aristocracy in the 18th century. It was soon transformed into a popular folk art by entertainers who would travel around Greece with their makeshift theatres. The name Karagkiózis refers to the indomitable and impoverished Greek character who is tormented by the other standard theatrical characters such as the rich Pasha and toughguy Stávrakas. The museum displays the history of two generations of the Spathári family, who were the leading exponents of this dying art, along with the colourful home-made sets and puppets that were used in their past performances.

Puppet from the Museum of Shadow Theatre

🏛 Spathári Museum of Shadow Theatre
Vas Sofias & D. Ralli, Maroussi. 🅲 *210 612 7245.* 🕐 *10am–1:30pm Mon–Fri.*
⬤ *main public hols.*

Mount Párnitha ⑬
Ορος Πάρνηθα

Attica. **Road map** D4. 🚌 *to Acharnés, Thrakomakedónes & Agía Triáda.*

IN ANCIENT TIMES, Mount Párnitha sheltered wild animals. Today, this rugged range, which extends nearly 25 km (16 miles) from east to west, is rich in less dangerous fauna. Tortoises can be seen in the undergrowth and birds of prey circle the summit of Karampóla at 1,413 m (4,635 ft). Wild flowers are abundant, particularly in autumn and spring when cyclamen and crocus carpet the mountain. There are spectacular views of alpine scenery, all within an hour's drive of the city. At the small town of **Acharnés**, a cable car ascends to a casino perched at over 900 m (3,000 ft).

Still little used by hikers, the mountain has plenty of demanding trails. The most popular walk leads from Thrakomakedónes, in the foothills of the mountain, to the Báfi refuge. This uphill march takes about two hours, and offers superb views of the surrounding mountain scenery. Starting with thorny scrub typical of the Mediterranean *maquis*, it follows well-trodden paths to end among alpine firs and clear mountain air. Once at the Báfi refuge, it is worth walking on to the Flampoúri refuge which has some dramatic views.

Monastery of Dafní

Μονή Δαφνίου

THE MONASTERY OF DAFNI was founded in the 5th century AD. Named after the laurels *(dáfnes)* that used to grow here, it was built with the remains of an ancient sanctuary of Apollo, which had occupied this site until it was destroyed in AD 395. In the early 13th century, Otto de la Roche, the first Frankish Duke of Athens, bequeathed it to Cistercian monks in Burgundy. Greek Orthodox monks took the site in the 16th century, erecting the elegant cloisters just south of the church. An earthquake in 2000 means that the beautiful gold-leaf Byzantine mosaics in the *katholikón* (main church) cannot be seen until restoration is completed.

Fresco detail

Aerial view of the monastery complex

The Gothic exonarthex was built almost 30 years after the main church.

Cloisters
This arcade was built in the 16th century. On the other side of the courtyard, above a similar arcade, are the monks' cells.

The symmetry of the design makes Dafní one of the most attractive examples of Byzantine architecture in Attica.

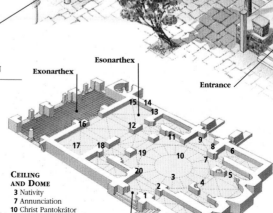

Esonarthex

Exonarthex

Entrance

Entrance

KEY TO MOSAICS IN THE KATHOLIKON

WALLS
1 Resurrection
2 Adoration of the Magi
4 Archangel Gabriel
5 Archangel Michael
6 Nativity of the Virgin
8 St John the Baptist
9 Entry into Jerusalem
12 Dormition of the Virgin
13 Last Supper
14 Washing of the Feet
15 Betrayal by Judas
16 Prayer of Sts Anne and Joachim
17 Blessing of the Priests
18 Presentation of the Virgin
20 St Thomas

CEILING AND DOME
3 Nativity
7 Annunciation
10 Christ Pantokrátor
11 Transfiguration
19 Baptism

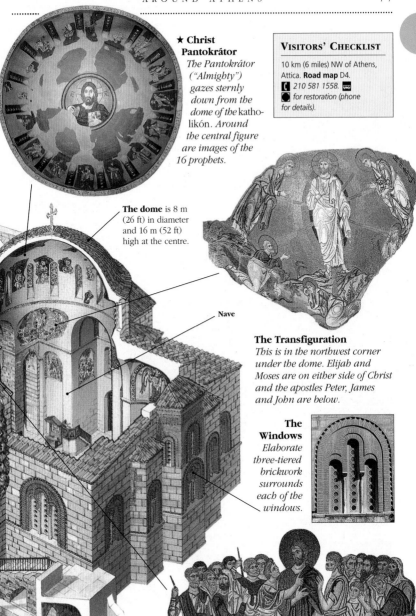

★ Christ Pantokrátor
The Pantokrátor ("Almighty") gazes sternly down from the dome of the katholikón. *Around the central figure are images of the 16 prophets.*

VISITORS' CHECKLIST

10 km (6 miles) NW of Athens, Attica. **Road map** D4.
📞 *210 581 1558.*
⬤ for restoration (phone for details).

The dome is 8 m (26 ft) in diameter and 16 m (52 ft) high at the centre.

Nave

The Transfiguration
This is in the northwest corner under the dome. Elijah and Moses are on either side of Christ and the apostles Peter, James and John are below.

The Windows
Elaborate three-tiered brickwork surrounds each of the windows.

Ticket office and museum

STAR MOSAICS

★ Christ Pantokrátor

★ Esonarthex Mosaics

★ Esonarthex Mosaics
These mosaics include depictions of the Last Supper *and the* Washing of the Feet. *The finest is the* Betrayal *by Judas. Christ stands unmoved as Judas kisses Him.*

Piraeus 🕔
Πειραιάς

Waiting for a ferry

ONE OF THE BIGGEST Mediterranean ports, Piraeus is also one of the largest cities in Greece. It has been the port of Athens since ancient times. The Long Walls between Piraeus and Athens were started in 480 BC by Themistokles. However, Sulla destroyed the walls in 86 BC and by the Middle Ages Piraeus was little more than a fishing village. When Athens became the Greek capital in 1834, Piraeus was once again revitalized, with Neo-Classical buildings and modern factories. In 1923, 100,000 refugees came here from Asia Minor, bringing their culture and contributing to the cosmopolitan feel of this port city.

Small boats moored in peaceful Tourkolímano harbour

View across Kentrikó Limáni with ferries in the foreground

Exploring Piraeus
After the military Junta razed many irreplaceable public buildings in the town centre in the early 1970s, civic pride re-emerged with a vengeance. Beside the Municipal Theatre, there are elegant open-air restaurants and fountains in the shade of Neo-Classical façades. On the streets behind the main banks and ticket offices that rim the **Kentrikó Limáni** (the main ferry port), there are smart restaurants and shops, as well as some fine examples of Neo-Classical architecture, such as the **Town Hall**. For information on ferry departures from Kentrikó Limáni, see page 135.

South of the railway station around Navarínou lies the lively market area, including fishmongers', fruit and vegetable stalls, ships' chandlers and hardware stores. On Sunday mornings there is also a bustling flea market, which

is centred on the antique shops around Plateía Ippodameías, and also on Alipédou and Skylítsi streets.

There are two harbours in Piraeus, situated east of Kentrikó Limáni. **Pasalimáni** (Pasha's Port, also known as Limáni Zéas) was once used to harbour the Ottoman fleet. Today it is filled with luxurious yachts. Once known simply as Zéa, Pasalimáni used to be one of Themistokles's major naval ports, with dry docks for 196 triremes. Marína Zéas, the mouth of Pasalimáni, is a jetty used as a dock for hydrofoils to the Argo-Saronic islands. The second harbour, **Tourkolímano**

(also known as Mikrolímano, or Little Harbour) houses many colourful fishing caïques. It is popular for its waterside fish restaurants and has a more relaxing ambience than the larger harbours.

On the coastal road between Pasalimáni and Tourkolímano, smart bars and clubs inhabit the renovated Neo-Classical mansions in the gentrified Kastélla neighbourhood. Even traditionally working-class areas, such as Drapetsóna (the most important manufacturing centre of the country) are now popular for their late-night restaurants.

🎭 Municipal Theatre
Agíou Konstantínou 2. **C** 210 412 0333. 🕐 Tue–Sun.
The Neo-Classical façade of this imposing building is one of the delights of Piraeus. Designed by Ioánnis Lazarímos (1849–1913), who based his plans on the Opéra Comique in Paris, it has seating for 800, making it one of the largest modern theatres in Greece. It took nearly ten years to complete and was finally

Façade of the Municipal Theatre

inaugurated on 9 April 1895. Today, it is the home of both the **Municipal Art Gallery** and also the **Pános Aravantinoú Museum of Stage Decor**. The Museum of Stage Decor has displays of set designs by the stage designer Pános Aravantinoú (who worked with the Berlin opera in the 1920s), as well as general ephemera from the Greek opera.

Archaeological Museum

Chariláou Trikoúpi 31. **(** *210 452 1598.* **◯** *9am–3pm Tue–Sun.* **●** *main public hols.*

This museum is home to some stunning bronzes. Found by workmen in 1959, these large statues of Artemis with her quiver, Athena with her helmet decorated with owls, and Apollo reveal the great expressiveness of Greek sculpture. The Piraeus *koúros* of Apollo, dating from 520 BC, is the earliest full-size bronze

Statue of Athena in the Archaeological Museum

to be discovered. There is also a seated cult statue of the earth goddess Cybele and a fine collection of Greek and Roman statues and grave stelae. Near the museum are the remains of the 2nd-century BC **Theatre of Zéa**; the remains include a well-preserved orchestra.

Hellenic Maritime Museum

Aktí Themistokléous, Freatýda. **(** *210 451 6264.* **◯** *9am–2pm Tue–Sat.* **●** *main public hols, Aug.*

On the quayside of Marína Zéas, an old submarine marks the entrance to this fascinating museum. Its first room is built around an original section of Themistokles's Long Walls. More than 2,000 exhibits, such as models of triremes, ephemera from naval battleships and paintings of Greek *trechantíri* (fishing caïques), explore the world of Greek seafaring. From early voyages around

VISITORS' CHECKLIST

10 km (6 miles) SW of Athens, Attica. **Road map** D4. **🏛** 200,000. **🚢** Kentrikó Limáni. **🚊** Kékropos (for Peloponnese), Kanári (for Northern Greece). **Ⓜ** Piraeus. **🚌** Plateía Koraï (for Athens), Plateía Karaïskáki (other destinations). **🛈** EOT Athens (210 331 0692). **🎭** Sun (flea market). **🎭** theatre & music festival: May–Jul.

the Black Sea by trireme, to 20th-century emigration to the New World by transatlantic liner, the museum unravels the complexities of Greek maritime history. Exhibits include models of ships, maps, flags, uniforms and pictures. The War of Independence is well documented with information and memorabilia about the generals who served in it. The old naval ship *Averof*, which was the flagship of the Greek fleet up until 1951, has been fully restored and is berthed nearby. As part of the museum, the ship is also open to visitors.

PIRAEUS CITY CENTRE

Archaeological Museum ④
Hellenic Maritime Museum ⑥
Municipal Theatre ②
Pasalimáni ③
Theatre of Zéa ⑤
Town Hall ①

0 metres   150
0 yards   150

KEY

🚢 Ferry service
✝ Church

Ancient Eleusis ⑯
Αρχαία Ελευσίνα

Eleusis was an ancient centre of religious devotion that culminated in the annual Eleusinian Mysteries. These attracted thousands of people from around the Greek-speaking world, for whom the only initial requirement for becoming a *mystes* (or initiate) was to be neither a murderer nor a barbarian. Both men and women were freely admitted. Existing from Mycenaean times, the sanctuary was closed by the Roman Emperor Theodosius in AD 392, and was finally abandoned when Alaric, king of the Goths, invaded Greece in AD 396, bringing Christianity in his wake.

Anaktoron
This small rectangular stone edifice had a single entrance. It was considered the holiest part of the site. Meaning "palace", it existed long before the Telesterion, which was built around it.

Telesterion
Designed by Iktinos, this temple was built in the 5th century BC. It was constructed to hold several thousand people at a time.

4th-century BC shops and bouleuterion (council chamber)

Temple of Kore hewn out of rock

Roman houses

THE ELEUSINIAN MYSTERIES

Perhaps established by 1500 BC and continuing for almost 2,000 years, these rites centred on the myth of the grieving goddess Demeter, who lost her daughter Persephone (or Kore) to Hades, god of the Underworld, for nine months each year. Participants were sworn to secrecy, but some evidence of the details of the ceremony does exist. Sacrifices were made before the procession from the Kerameikós (*see pp38–9*) to Eleusis. Here the priestesses would reveal the vision of the holy night, thought to have been a fire symbolizing life after death for the initiates.

A priestess with a *kiste mystika* (basket)

ANCIENT ELEUSIS

This reconstruction is of Eleusis as it was in Roman times (c.AD 150) when the Mysteries were still flourishing. The view is from the east. Although there is little left today, it is still possible to sense the awe and mystery that the rites of Eleusis inspired.

Ploutonion
This cave is said to be where Persephone was returned to earth. It was a sanctuary to Hades, god of the Underworld and the abductor of Persephone.

Relief from the Telesterion, now in the museum

Greater Propylaia
Built from Pentelic marble in the 2nd century AD by the Roman Emperor Antoninus Pius, this was modelled on the Propylaia of Athens' Acropolis.

One of a pair of triumphal arches

Temple of Artemis Propylaia

Well of Kallichoron
Demeter is believed to have grieved for Persephone here.

Lesser Propylaia
This fragment shows sheaves of grain and poppies, which were used to make kykeon, *the drink of the initiates.*

Eleusis Museum
This small museum, south of the Telesterion, has five rooms. The entrance hall contains a copy of the famous relief from the Telesterion showing Triptólemos receiving grain from Demeter. Also in this room are a large 7th-century BC amphora and a copy of the Ninnion votive painting, one of the few remaining representations of the Eleusinian Mysteries. The other rooms are arranged on the left of the hall. In the first of these there is an elegant 6th-century BC *koúros* and a 2nd-century BC Roman statue of Dionysos. In the second room there are two models of the site. The third room has a Classical period terracotta sarcophagus and a large caryatid from the Lesser Propylaia carrying a *kiste mystika* basket on her head. The last room has a variety of pottery fragments, including examples of unusual terracotta containers that were used to carry foodstuffs in the annual *kernoforía* procession.

Fleeing maiden

TRAVELLERS' NEEDS

WHERE TO STAY

REECE OFFERS the visitor a variety of accommodation that is often good value compared with most other European destinations. Choices range from low-budget, informal *domátia* (rooms) and mid-range chain hotels, to accommodation in restored traditional buildings and luxurious hotels. Centrally-located hotels are the best choice for a stay in Athens and will

Doorman at the Grande Bretagne hotel, Athens

make travelling to the main sights less time consuming. The Hellenic Chamber of Hotels have a complete list of hotels in the city and are able to make reservations. The GNTO website (see p117) also has an extensive list of hotels available. The listings section on the following pages gives detailed descriptions and information on the facilities available at more than 70 hotels in Athens and Attica.

HOTELS

MOST GREEK HOTELS are of standard Mediterranean concrete architecture, though in coastal resorts height limits restrict towering structures. Many surviving hotels date from the 1967–74 Junta era, when massive investment in "modern" tourism was encouraged. A very few Neo-Classical, or older, hotels remain, now benefiting from government preservation orders. Hotels built since the 1980s are generally designed with more imagination and sensitivity to the environment. The more expensive hotels will have a correspondingly higher level of service, offered by trained personnel.

CHAIN HOTELS

GREECE, with its tradition of family business ownership, has not taken to the idea of chain hotels. Among the few that operate on the mainland, the oldest is the formerly

state-run Xenía chain, founded during the 1950s. Though some of their hotels are in need of an uplift, they often provide a decent option in smaller towns. Newer chains, such as **Chandrís** and **Diváni**, are a better bet. They both offer accommodation in the Athens area, and Diváni also has hotels in central Greece.

GRADING

THE EOT grade Greece's hotels. Hotel categories range from E-class up to A-class, plus deluxe. There is supposed to be a direct correlation between amenities and the classification, but there are many local deviations – usually the result of a dispute with local authorities.

E-class hotels, with the most basic facilities and narrow profit margins, are almost extinct. D- class still survive, and these should have at least some rooms *en suite*. In a C-class hotel, all rooms must

Hotel housed in a restored, traditional building

have *en suite* baths, and the hotel must have some sort of common area, if only a small combination bar and breakfast area where a basic continental breakfast can be served.

B-class hotels have extra amenities such as a full-service restaurant, a more substantial breakfast, and at least one sports facility, such as a gym, pool or tennis court. A-class hotels offer all conceivable diversions, as well as aids for the business traveller, such as conference halls and tele-communications facilities.

CHAIN HOTELS

Chandrís Hotels
Syngroú 385, 17564 Paleó
Fáliron, Athens.
📞 210 947 1000.
🖳 www.chandris.gr

**Club Mediterranée
Hellas SA**
Omírou 8, 10564 Athens.
📞 210 937 0341.

Diváni Hotels
Parthenónos 19/25,

11742 Athens.
📞 210 922 9650.

Stathópoulos Hotels
7 Kapnikareas St &
Mitropoleos, 10556 Athens.
📞 210 322 2706.

Xenotel Hotels
Anagnostopoulou 22,
10672 Athens.
📞 210 362 0662.
or
lous 5, Thessaloníki.
📞 2310 224710.

**DISABLED
TRAVELLERS**

Holiday Care Service
2nd Floor, Imperial
Buildings, Victoria Road,
Horley, Surrey RH6 7PZ,
England.
📞 01293-774 535.
@ holiday.care@virgin.net

**FURTHER
INFORMATION**

Greek Travel Pages
Psýlla 6, corner Filellínon,

10557 Athens.
📞 210 324 7511.

**Tourist
Guide of
Greece**
Patission 137,
11251 Athens.
📞 210 864 1688.

**Hellenic Chamber
of Hotels**
Stadiou 24,
10564 Athens.
📞 210 323 7193.

◁ **Fruit and vegetable market on Athínas Street, Athens**

The pool at the Aphrodite Astir Palace Hotel *(see p91)*

Deluxe category hotels are effectively self-contained resort complexes.

PRICES

THE PRICE of hotel rooms should correspond to their official category, though this depends on the season and their location. For 18 euros or under, it is possible to find an E/D-class hotel. C-class hotels charge between 26 and 32 euros. B-class hotels ask 32 to 44 euros per double room; A-class hotels typically cost 44 to 65 euros. Deluxe resorts are exempt from the EOT price control scheme and can run in excess of 88 euros per night.

All of these rate approximations are for high season, including VAT and taxes; prices can drop by almost 50 per cent in early spring or late autumn. Hotel rates include breakfast. Stays of less than three nights can carry a surcharge in high season. In mainland skiing resorts there is often a vast difference in weekend and mid-week rates.

OPENING SEASONS

MOST MAINLAND hotels stay open year-round, except those at seafront resorts, which operate only from May to October. High season runs from early July to late September. The period from April to June, plus the month of October are mid-season,

and low season runs from the beginning of November to the end of March.

BOOKING

THE MOST COMMON and cost-effective way of booking accommodation is through a package holiday agency. If you contact a hotel direct, do so by fax so that the transaction is recorded in writing. You may need to provide a credit card number or send travellers' cheques to the value of the first night's stay. It is also possible to book a hotel via the internet. A useful address to try is www. united-hellas.com

A sign for rooms to rent

DISABLED TRAVELLERS

THE GUIDE *Holidays and Travel Abroad*, published by **RADAR** (Royal Association for Disability and Rehabilitation) – see page 117 for their address – provides details on wheelchair access to the more established hotels in Greece. Write to the **Holiday Care Service** for an information sheet with hotels and useful contact numbers in Greece. In the hotel listings of this guide *(see pp86–91)* we have indicated which

establishments have suitable facilities, such as lifts and ramps, for the disabled.

Greek information sources for disabled travellers tend to be rudimentary; the EOT only publishes a questionnaire, which can be sent to specific accommodation establishments to assess their suitability.

FURTHER INFORMATION

AN INVALUABLE BOOKLET is published yearly by the EOT *(see p117)*. It is called *Guide to Hotels*, and a current copy can be obtained from any EOT office. The booklet covers all officially registered hotels, indicating prices, facilities and their operating season. The EOT also periodically publishes an informative leaflet entitled *Rural Tourism*. Two other hotel manuals, which are both issued by private organizations, are the *Greek Travel Pages* (GTP) and the *Tourist Guide of Greece*. They are not as complete or authoritative as the EOT guides, but are published more frequently. The GTP is monthly, offering only skeletal information unless the hotel concerned has purchased advertising space; this is also true of the quarterly publication *Tourist Guide of Greece*.

Conservatory at Grande Bretagne hotel, Athens *(see p90)*

Choosing a Hotel

THESE HOTELS have been selected across a wide price range for their good value, facilities and location; they are listed by region, starting with Athens. Use the colour-coded thumb tabs, which indicate the areas covered on each page, to guide you to the relevant section of the chart. For Athens map references see pages *128–35*; for road map references see the inside back cover.

	NUMBER OF ROOMS	RESTAURANT	GARDEN OR TERRACE	SWIMMING POOL	AIR-CONDITIONING

ATHENS					
AMPELOKIPOI: *Androméda* W www.andromedaathens.gr €€€€€ Timoléontos Vásou 22, 11521. **Map 6 F4.** 210 641 5000. FAX 210 646 6361. A deluxe hotel with immaculate attention to detail in all the rooms and a reception area featuring work by contemporary designers. 🚌 P 🔥 🖥	30	●			■
AREOS: *Park Hotel Athens* W www.park.hotel.gr €€€€€ Leofóros Alexándras 10, 10682. **Map 3 A1.** 210 883 2711. FAX 210 823 8420. Situated opposite the relaxing Areos Park, this hotel has spacious rooms. There is also a good rooftop bar and a 24-hour coffee shop. 🚌 P 🔥 🖥	143	●	■	●	■
AVEROF: *Zafólia* W www.zafoliahotel.gr €€€€€ Leofóros Alexándras 87–89, 11474. **Map 3 C2.** 210 644 9002. FAX 210 644 2042. This hotel offers bright, modern rooms and is close to the National Archaeo- logical Museum. Rooftop pool and views over Acropolis. 🚌 P 🔥 🖥	192	●	■	●	■
EXARCHEIA: *Exarcheíon* €€€ Themistokléous 55, 10683. **Map 2 F3.** 210 380 0731. FAX 210 380 3296. This hotel is close to the late-night action of Plateía Exarcheíon. Rooms are basic, but there is a roof garden and a good pavement café. 🚌 🔥 🖥	58		■		
EXARCHEIA: *Museum* €€€€ Mpoumpoulínas 16, 10682. **Map 2 F2.** 210 380 5611. FAX 210 380 0507. The modern façade of this building hides a genteel interior. Situated opposite the National Archaeological Museum, it is frequented by academics. The rooms are clean and quiet. 🚌 P 🔥 🖥	58				■
ILISIA: *Hilton* W www.athens.hilton.com €€€€€ Leofóros Vasilíssis Sofías 46, 11528. **Map 4 D5.** 210 728 1000. FAX 210 728 1111. Athens' best-known modern hotel. All the rooms have large balconies, providing stunning views across the city. 🚌 P 🔥 🖥	517	●	■	●	■
ILISIA: *Holiday Inn* €€€€€ Michalakopoúlou 50, 11528. **Map 8 E1.** 210 727 8000. FAX 210 727 8600. This efficiently run hotel is popular with business travellers. It has large rooms, good restaurants and a rooftop swimming pool. 🚌 P 🔥 🖥	191	●	■	●	■
KAISARIANI: *Divani Caravel* €€€€€ Leofóros Vasiléos Alexándrou 2, 16121. **Map 8 D1.** 210 720 7000. FAX 210 723 6683. Popular for conferences, the Caravel has spacious rooms and several eating and drinking areas, including the Lord Byron piano bar. 🚌 P 🔥 🖥	470	●	■	●	■
KOLONAKI: *Athenian Inn* €€€€€ Cháritos 22, 10675. **Map 3 B5.** 210 723 9552. FAX 210 724 2268. This hotel offers clean, basic rooms and friendly management. Situated in the heart of Kolonáki, among a choice of shops, restaurants and cafés. 🚌 🖥	25				■
KOLONAKI: *St George Lycabettus* W www.sglycabettus.gr €€€€€ Kleoménous 2, 10675. **Map 3 B4.** 210 729 0711. FAX 210 729 0439. Situated beneath Lykavittós Hill, this small, luxury hotel offers large rooms with good views. The rooftop restaurant is excellent. 🚌 P 🔥 🖥	167	●		●	■
KOUKAKI: *Marble House* W www.marblehouse.gr €€€ Anastasíou Zínni 35, 11741. **Map 5 C4.** 210 923 4058. FAX 210 922 6461. At the end of a quiet cul-de-sac, this is a firm favourite among mid-range *pensions* for its cleanliness and helpful management. Most rooms are *en suite* and many have vine-covered balconies. Breakfast not included. 🚌	16	■			
KOUKAKI: *Tony's Hotel* €€€€ Zacharísta 26, 11741. **Map 5 C4.** 210 923 0561. FAX 210 923 6370. This hotel offers basic but clean studio accommodation with kitchenettes. The roof garden enjoys goods views of the city. 🚌	21		■		■

<table>
<tr><td>

Price categories are for a standard double room for one night in peak season, including tax, service charges and breakfast:
€ under 25 euros
€€ 25–35 euros
€€€ 35–45 euros
€€€€ 45–60 euros
€€€€€ over 60 euros.

</td><td>

RESTAURANT
Restaurant within the hotel sometimes reserved for residents only.
GARDEN OR TERRACE
Hotel with garden, courtyard or terrace, often providing tables for eating outside.
SWIMMING POOL
Hotel swimming pools are usually quite small and are outdoors unless otherwise stated.
AIR-CONDITIONING
Hotel with air-conditioning in all the rooms.

</td></tr>
</table>

	NUMBER OF ROOMS	RESTAURANT	GARDEN OR TERRACE	SWIMMING POOL	AIR-CONDITIONING
KOUKAKI: *Fíllipos* €€€€€ Mitsaíon 3, 11742. **Map** 6 D3. 210 922 3611. FAX 210 922 3615. Sister property to the Iródeion, this modern hotel offers basic but clean accommodation. Some rooms have balconies.	48				
MAKRYGIANNI: *Ira* €€€€€ Falírou 9, 11742. **Map** 6 D4. 210 923 5618. FAX 210 924 7334. The rooms and public areas in this modern hotel are spotless. The hotel also has a coffee shop and a rooftop terrace.	38		■		
MAKRYGIANNI: *Athens Gate* €€€€€ Leofóros A Syngroú 10, 11742. **Map** 6 E3. 210 923 8302. FAX 210 923 7493. This centrally located, modern hotel offers comfortable rooms and a rooftop garden with views of the Acropolis and Hadrian's Arch.	100	●	■		
MAKRIGIANNI: *Divani Palace Acropolis* €€€€€ Parthenónos 19–25, 11742. **Map** 6 D3. 210 928 0100. FAX 210 921 4993. Beautifully upgraded to deluxe standard, this hotel is just a short stroll from the Acropolis. An original section of the Themistoklean Long Walls is on view in the hotel lobby.	251	●	■	●	■
MAKRYGIANNI: *Iródeion* €€€€€ Rovértou Gkálli 4, 11742. **Map** 5 C3. 210 923 6832. FAX 210 921 1650. This hotel has large modern rooms, a patio shaded by pistachio trees and a roof terrace with views of the Acropolis.	90	●	■		
MAKRYGIANNI: *Royal Olympic* W www. royalolympic.com €€€€€ Athanasíou Diákou 28–34, 11743. **Map** 6 E3. 210 922 6411. FAX 210 923 3317. The Royal Olympic has wonderful large rooms, all with superb views of the Temple of Olympian Zeus. Good grill restaurant.	304	●	■	●	■
METAXOURGEIO: *Stanley* €€€€€ Odysséos 1, Plateía Karaïskáki, 10437. **Map** 1 B3. 210 524 1611. FAX 210 524 4611. The Stanley hotel has large fully equipped rooms with balconies, a rooftop garden and pool and a busy bar and restaurant.	384	●	■	●	■
MONASTIRAKI: *Hotel Témpi* W www.travelling.gr/tempihotel. €€€ Aiólou 29, 10551. **Map** 6 D1. 210 321 3175. FAX 210 325 4179. Rooms here are basic but the hotel enjoys an excellent central location on a pedestrian street overlooking Monastiráki flower market and the Acropolis. Communal kitchen and café.	24				■
MONASTIRAKI: *Attalos* €€€€€ Athinás 29, 19554. **Map** 2 D5. 210 321 2801. FAX 210 324 3124. Ideally situated for shopping, near Monastiráki and Athinás, the Attalos offers adequate rooms, some with balconies. The hotel also has a roof garden with good views of the Acropolis.	80		■		■
MONASTIRAKI: *Hotel Carolina* €€€€€ Kolokotróni 55, 10560. **Map** 2 E5. 210 324 3551. FAX 210 324 3550. This delightful, newly renovated hotel offers clean rooms, some with ensuite bathrooms. There are views of the Acropolis from the terrace.	34		■		■
NEOS KOSMOS: *Athenian Kallirhoe* €€€€€ Petmezá 15, 11743. **Map** 6 D4. 210 921 5353. FAX 210 921 5342. This is a small, luxurious hotel just a short walk from the Acropolis. The rooms are modern and comfortable.	68	●	■		
NEOS KOSMOS: *Athenaeum Inter-Continental* €€€€€ Leofóros Andrea Syngroú 89–93, 11745. **Map** 6 E4. 210 920 6000. FAX 210 920 6500. W www.interconti.com Decorated with modern Greek art, this luxurious hotel offers a choice of restaurants, bars and shops. Facilities include a gym.	520	●		●	■

For key to symbols see back flap

<table>
<tr><td colspan="2">

Price categories are for a standard double room for one night in peak season, including tax, service charges and breakfast:
€ under 25 euros
€€ 25–35 euros
€€€ 35–45 euros
€€€€ 45–60 euros
€€€€€ over 60 euros.

</td><td>

RESTAURANT
Restaurant within the hotel sometimes reserved for residents only.
GARDEN OR TERRACE
Hotel with garden, courtyard or terrace, often providing tables for eating outside.
SWIMMING POOL
Hotel swimming pools are usually quite small and are outdoors unless otherwise stated.
AIR-CONDITIONING
Hotel with air-conditioning in all the rooms.

</td></tr>
</table>

		NUMBER OF ROOMS	RESTAURANT	GARDEN OR TERRACE	SWIMMING POOL	AIR-CONDITIONING
NEOS KOSMOS: *Ledra Marriott* w www.marriott.com €€€€€ Leofóros Andrea Syngroú 115, 11745. **Map** 6 D4. **C** 210 930 0000. **FAX** 210 935 8603. As well as all the amenities expected from a luxury hotel, the Marriot's rooms are large and spacious and the hotel boasts superb restaurants, particularly the trendy Polynesian Kona Kai. ⊞ P & ⊜		259	●		●	▨
OMONOIA: *La Mirage* €€€ Maríkas Kotopoúli 3, 10431. **Map** 2 D3. **C** 210 523 4071. **FAX** 210 523 3992. A favourite for those who want to be close to the 24-hour hustle and bustle of Plateía Omonoías. All rooms are double glazed. ⊞ P & ⊜		208	●			▨
OMONOIA: *Zorba's Hotel* w www.zorbashotel.com €€€€ Gkilfórdou 10, 10434. **Map** 2 E1. **C** & **FAX** 210 823 4239. Basic accommodation but the hotel has a good central location just off Victoria Square. Rooms are small but clean and dorm beds are are also available. Large bathrooms and friendly staff. ⊞		18				▨
OMONOIA: *Dorian Inn* €€€€€ Peiraiós 17, 10552. **Map** 2 D3. **C** 210 523 9782. **FAX** 210 522 6196. Situated in the heart of the city centre, the roof garden of this smart hotel offers spectacular views over Athens and the Acropolis. ⊞ P & ⊜		146	●	▨	●	▨
OMONOIA: *Athens Acropolis* €€€€€ Peiraiós 1, 10552. **Map** 2 D3. **C** 210 523 1111. **FAX** 210 523 1361. This hotel has large and comfortable public lounge areas, including a restaurant and bar, where you can relax and enjoy the ambience. All the rooms are quiet. ⊞ P & ⊜		167	●	▨		▨
OMONOIA: *Titánia* €€€€€ Panepistimíou 52, 10678. **Map** 2 E4. **C** 210 330 0111. **FAX** 210 330 0700. The entrance to this well-appointed hotel is through a shopping arcade close to Plateía Omonoías. Rooms are well equipped and the rooftop terrace bar and ground-floor café are always busy. ⊞ P & ⊜		396	●	▨		▨
PLAKA: *Faídra* €€€€ Chairefóntos 16, 10558. **Map** 6 E2. **C** 210 323 8461. **FAX** 210 322 795. The hotel's location next to the Lysikrates monument more than makes up for the slightly tacky quality of its rooms and public areas.		21				
PLAKA: *John's Place* €€€€ Patróou 5, 10557. **Map** 6 E1. **C** 210 322 9719. One of the better bargain backpacking hotels. The rooms are small but very clean, and bathrooms are shared.		15				
PLAKA: *Koúros* €€€€ Kódrou 11, 10557. **Map** 6 E2. **C** 210 322 7431. Situated in the heart of Pláka, this cheap and cheerful small *pension* is housed in a converted Neo-Classical mansion house. Rooms are basic but clean and have balconies – some with a view of the Acropolis.		10				
PLAKA: *Acropolis House Pension* €€€€€ Kódrou 6–8, 10557. **Map** 6 E1. **C** 210 322 2344. **FAX** 210 324 4143. Housed in a converted 19th-century building, the rooms in this *pension* are large and airy. All rooms have private balconies. ⊞ ⊜		19				▨
PLAKA: *Neféli* €€€€€ Angelikís Chatzimicháli 2, 10558. **Map** 6 E1. **C** 210 322 8044. **FAX** 210 322 5800. A modern hotel, hidden away in a peaceful backwater in Pláka. The rooms are clean and of a good, basic standard. ⊞ & ⊜		18				▨

PLAKA: *Aphrodite* €€€€€ 84
Apóllonos 21, 10557. **Map 6** E1. **(** *210 323 4357*.
FAX *210 322 5244*.
This hotel is well located and offers clean, good-value rooms, some of
which enjoy wonderful views of the Acropolis. ☐ P & ◢

PLAKA: *Byron* €€€€€ 20
Výronos 19, 10558. **Map 6** E2. **(** *210 323 0327*. **FAX** *210 322 0276*.
Situated on the southern fringe of Pláka, this small and basic hotel
is close to the Acropolis. Some rooms have balconies. ☐

PLAKA: *Myrtó* €€€€€ 12
Níkis 40, 10558. **Map 6** F1. **(** *210 322 7237*. **FAX** *210 323 4560*.
Close to the central areas of Plateía Syntágmatos and Pláka, this small
hotel is ideal for short stays and is popular with young couples. ☐

PLAKA: *Omiros* €€€€€ 37
Apóllonos 15, 10557. **Map 6** E1. **(** *210 323 5486*. **FAX** *210 322 8059*.
A lovely roof garden distinguishes this otherwise basic hotel which is
located in a quiet area of Pláka. ☐ & ◢

PLAKA: *Adrian* €€€€€ 22
Adrianoú 74, 10556. **Map 6** E2. **(** *210 325 0461*. **FAX** *210 325 0461*.
Situated in central Pláka, this hotel has simple, comfortable rooms as well
as a quiet terrace to escape the bustle of the city. ☐ & ◢

PLAKA: *Pláka* €€€€€ 67
Mitropoleos & Kapnikareas 7, 10556. **Map 6** D1. **(** *210 322 2096*.
FAX *210 322 2412*.
Set in the heart of Pláka, with a superb view of the Acropolis, this is a
comfortable hotel with a friendly atmosphere. ☐ & ◢

PLAKA: *Ermís* €€€€€ 45
Apóllonos 19, 10557. **Map 6** E1. **(** *210 323 5514*. **FAX** *210 322 2412*.
The rooms of this newly-renovated hotel are large, some having
balconies overlooking a playground. ☐ & ◢

STATHMOS LARISSIS: *Oscar* €€€€€ 164
Filadelfeías 25, 10439. **Map 1** C1. **(** *210 883 4215*.
FAX *210 821 6368*.
Close to Laríssis railway station, this excellent modern hotel has large
rooms, a rooftop pool and a good restaurant. ☐ P ◢

STATHMOS LARISSIS: *Novotel Athens* €€€€€ 195
Michaíl Vóda 4–6, 10439. **Map 1** D1. **(** *210 820 0700*.
FAX *210 820 0777*.
Run by the French group, Novotel, this smart, centrally located
hotel has modern, well-equipped rooms and a stunning rooftop
garden and swimming pool. ☐ P & ◢

STREFI HILL: *Oríon* €€€€ 38
Anexartisías 5 & E Mpenáki 105, 11473. **Map 3** A2. **(** *210 382 7362*.
FAX *210 380 5193*.
Beside Stréfi Hill, just above the bustling Exárcheia area, this quiet hotel
is popular with students looking for short-term accommodation.

SYNTAGMA: *Metropolis* €€€€ 25
Mitropóleos 46, 10563. **Map 6** D1. **(** & **FAX** *210 321 7469*.
This five-storey hotel enjoys views over Athens' Mitrópoli (cathedral).
Rooms are large and clean and the staff friendly. No breakfasts
provided. ☐ & ◢

SYNTAGMA: *Amalía* €€€€€ 98
Leofóros Vasilíssis Amalías 10, 10557. **Map 6** F1. **(** *210 607 2135*.
FAX *210 322 3872*.
Although the rooms are fairly small, all the bathrooms are marble.
The hotel is centrally located and has good views of both the
Parliament building and the National Gardens. ☐ & ◢

SYNTAGMA: *Aretoúsa* €€€€€ 87
Mitropóleos 6–8 & Níkis 12, 10563. **Map 6** F1. **(** *210 322 9431*.
FAX *210 322 9439*.
Decent value characterizes this centrally located hotel. The rooms are
modern and there is a roof garden as well as a lively bar. ☐ & ◢

For key to symbols see back flap

<table>
<tr><td colspan="6">

Price categories are for a standard double room for one night in peak season, including tax, service charges and breakfast:
€ under 25 euros
€€ 25–35 euros
€€€ 35–45 euros
€€€€ 45–60 euros
€€€€€ over 60 euros.

RESTAURANT
Restaurant within the hotel sometimes reserved for residents only.
GARDEN OR TERRACE
Hotel with garden, courtyard or terrace, often providing tables for eating outside.
SWIMMING POOL
Hotel swimming pools are usually quite small and are outdoors unless otherwise stated.
AIR-CONDITIONING
Hotel with air-conditioning in all the rooms.

</td></tr>
</table>

	NUMBER OF ROOMS	RESTAURANT	GARDEN OR TERRACE	SWIMMING POOL	AIR-CONDITIONING
SYNTAGMA: *Astor* €€€€€ Karageórgi Servías 16, 10562. **Map** 6 F1. ℂ 210 335 1000. ℻ 210 325 5115. The popular all-year-round rooftop restaurant of this hotel boasts stunning views over Athens. The double rooms from the sixth floor upwards share this impressive view of the city. ▤ ♿ ✎	130	●	▦		▦
SYNTAGMA: *Athens Cypria* €€€€€ Diomeías 5, 10557. **Map** 6 E1. ℂ 210 323 8034. ℻ 210 324 8792. Located in a quiet street, a few minutes from Plateía Syntágmatos, this hotel offers good value for money. Acropolis views from top floor rooms. ▤ ✎	71				▦
SYNTAGMA: *Electra* €€€€€ Ermoú 5, 10557. **Map** 6 F1. ℂ 210 322 3223. ℻ 210 322 0310. This centrally located hotel is ideally situated for shopping expeditions to Monastiráki. All the rooms are clean and pleasant. ▤ ✎	110	●			▦
SYNTAGMA: *Esperia Palace* €€€€€ Stadíou 22, 10564. **Map** 2 E4. ℂ 210 323 8001. ℻ 210 323 8100. A smart city hotel with marble lobbies and tastefully decorated rooms. Its restaurant and bar are popular with Athenians. ▤ ♿ ✎	184	●			▦
SYNTAGMA: *Grande Bretagne* 🆆 www.hotelgrandebretagne-ath.gr €€€€€ Plateía Syntágmatos, 10563. **Map** 6 F1. ℂ 210 333 0000. ℻ 210 322 8034. This luxurious hotel was built in 1852 and is the landmark of Plateía Syntágmatos, the most desirable hotel location in Athens. The lobby and rooms are beautiful and the service is excellent. ▤ ♿ ✎	450	●			▦
SYNTAGMA: *Athens Plaza* €€€€€ Vasiléos Georgíou, 10564. **Map** 6 F1. ℂ 210 325 5301. ℻ 210 323 5856. This grand hotel offers luxurious blue and white rooms, all of which are soundproofed. There are good facilities and its Explorers' Lounge and Marco Polo restaurant are always busy. ▤ P ✎	177	●			▦
AROUND ATHENS					
ANAVYSOS: *Eden Beach Hotel Club* €€€€€ 3 km (2 miles) N of Anávysos, 19013. **Road map** D4. ℂ 22910 60031. ℻ 22910 60043. Boasting a prime, beachside location and set in beautiful gardens, this hotel offers good sports facilities including tennis courts, a seawater pool and watersports. ◗ Nov–Mar. ▤ P ♿ ✎	286	●	▦	●	▦
GLYFADA: *Hotel Ilion* €€€ Kondlyli 4, 16675. **Road map** D4. ℂ 210 894 6011. Situated in Glyfáda, 2 km (1 mile) north of Vouliágmeni, this is ideally located near the town's chic shops. Rooms are plainly decorated, but some have views of the sea. No breakfast supplied. ▤ P	34				
GLYFADA: *Oasis Hotel Apartments* 🆆 www.oasishotel.gr €€€€€ Poseidónos 27, 16675. **Road map** D4. ℂ 210 894 1662. ℻ 210 894 1724. This hotel offers deluxe apartments with kitchenettes, some with sea views. There is a courtyard with a pool and jacuzzi and the apartments are served by full hotel amenities including childcare. ▤ P ♿ ✎	70	●	▦	●	▦
KIFISIA: *Hotel Grand Chalet* €€€€€ Kokkinara 38, 14562. **Road map** D4. ℂ 210 623 3120. ℻ 210 808 5426. In an up-market northern suburb, this is a pleasant place to stay away from the bustle of the city centre. It has a restaurant serving international cuisine and an outdoor swimming pool in an attractive garden. ▤ ⛾ ✎	44	●	▦	●	▦

KIFISIA: *Kefalári Suites* w www.kefalarisuites.gr €€€€€ 13
Pentélis 1, 14562. **Road map** D4. 210 623 3333. FAX 210 623 3330.
Luxury suites each with a bedroom, sitting room and kitchenette. The
suites are individually themed. The Jaipur suite, for example, echoes
the Far East. There is a rooftop jacuzzi and sun deck. 🔲 🖂

KIFISIA: *Pentelikón* w www.hotelpentelikon.gr €€€€€ 44
Deligiánni 66, 14562. **Road map** D4. 210 623 0650-6. FAX 210 801 0314.
Set within landscaped gardens, this Neo-Classical deluxe hotel offers
beautiful, spacious rooms and discreet service. 🔲 🛇 🖂

KIFISIA: *Theoxenía Palace* w www.theoxeniapalace.gr €€€€€ 71
Filadélfeos 2, 14562. **Road map** D4. 210 623 3622. FAX 210 623 1675.
Set in a palatial building overlooking Kefalári Park, this luxurious hotel
offers clean, comfortable rooms and a good restaurant. 🔲 🅿 🖂

LAVRIO: *Grecotel Cape Sounio* w www.grecotel.gr €€€€€ 154
Lávrio–Soúnio road, 19500. **Road map** D4. 22920 39010. FAX 22920 39011.
This luxury complex of bungalows and villas is set in extensive
landscaped gardens and boasts spectacular views of the sea and
Temple of Poseidon. Luxury marble bathrooms and all mod cons
including DVD players. 🔲 🅿 🖂

MARATHONAS: *Golden Coast* €€€€€ 541
Marathónas beach, 19005. **Road map** D4. 22940 57100. FAX 22940 57300.
This luxury hotel is situated near the ancient site of Marathon. Amenities
include a night club, restaurants, four swimming pools (one for children)
and other sports facilities and shops. ⚫ *Oct–Mar.* 🔲 🅿 🛇 🖂

MOUNT PARNITHA: *Casino Mont Parnes* €€€€€ 108
4 km (2 miles) N of Acharnaí, 13571. **Road map** D4. 210 240 4221. FAX 210 246
0768. Overlooking the plain of Attica, this hotel is known primarily for its
casino. Whether you gamble or not, the fresh air and pine trees around
the hotel are a wonderful relief from the Athens summer heat. 🔲 🅿 🛇 🖂

PIRAEUS: *Cava D'Oro* €€€€€ 74
Vasiléos Pávlou 19, 18533. **Road map** D4. 210 412 2210. FAX 210 412 2210.
Overlooking Mikrolímano harbour, this smart hotel boasts a popular
disco and bar. The rooms are cool and airy. 🔲 🅿 🛇 🖂

PIRAEUS: *Kastélla* €€€€€ 32
Vasiléos Pávlou 75, 18533. **Road map** D4. 210 411 4735 FAX 210 417 5716.
Situated in the smart area of Kastélla, the modern rooms in this hotel
have views of the yacht marina below. 🔲 🅿 🛇 🖂

PIRAEUS: *Park* €€€€€ 80
Kolokotróni 103, 18535. **Road map** D4. 210 452 4611. FAX 210 452 4615.
The central location of the Park hotel makes it ideal for exploring
Piraeus. There is a breakfast terrace and the rooms are large. 🔲 🛇 🖂

SPATA: *Sofitel Athens Airport* w www.sofitel.com €€€€€ 345
Athens International Airport, 19004. **Road map** D4. 210 354 4000.
FAX 210 354 4444.
A five star hotel with excellent facilities including a well-equipped fitness
centre. Ideally situated for Athens' airport and Rafina. 🔲 🅿 🛇 🖂

VOULIAGMENI: *Aphrodite Astir Palace* w www.astir.gr €€€€€ 570
Apóllonos 40, 16671. **Road map** D4. 210 890 2000. FAX 210 896 2579.
A luxury hotel in a resort development, 23 km (14 miles)
south of Athens, by the sea. The plushest place to stay for
combining the sites of Athens with the pleasures of the beach.
⚫ *Oct–Apr.* 🔲 🅿 🛇

VOULIAGMENI: *Divani Apollon Palace* w www.divaniapollon.gr €€€€€ 286
10 Agios Nikólao & Ilíon, 16671. **Road map** D4. 210 891 1100. FAX 210 965 8010.
This superb hotel offers spacious rooms with marble bathrooms. Facilities
include out- and in-door pools, floodlit tennis courts and Spa and Thalasso
Centre. A shuttle bus serves Sýntagma. 🔲 🅿 🛇

VOULIAGMENI: *The Margi Hotel* w www.themargi.gr €€€€€ 17
Litoús 11, 16671. **Road map** D4. 210 896 2061. FAX 210 896 0229.
The rooms of this luxurious, boutique hotel boast 19th-century antiques
and marble bathrooms. Poolside sofas in the lounge bar. The hotel is a
few minutes walk from the beach. 🔲 🅿 🛇

WHERE TO EAT

TO EAT OUT IN GREECE is to experience the democratic tradition at work. Rich and poor, young and old, all enjoy their favourite local restaurant, taverna or café. Greeks consider the best places to be where the food is fresh, plentiful and well-cooked, not necessarily where the setting or the cuisine is the fanciest. Visitors too have come to appreciate the simplicity and health of the traditional Greek kitchen – olive oil, yoghurt, vegetables, a little meat and some wine, always shared with friends. The traditional three-hour lunch and siesta – still the daily rhythm of the countryside – is now only a fading memory for most city Greeks, who have adapted to a more Western European routine. But the combination of traditional cooking and outside influences has produced a vast range of eating places, with somewhere to suit almost everyone.

A local cheese from Métsovo

The Néon restaurant in the centre of Athens (see p102)

TYPES OF RESTAURANT

THE ESTIATORION or traditional Greek restaurant, is one of Europe's most enjoyable places to eat. Friendly, noisy and sometimes in lovely surroundings, estiatória are reliable purveyors of local recipes and wines, particularly if they have been owned by the same family for decades. Foreigners unfamiliar with Greek dishes may be invited into the kitchen to choose their fare. In Greece, the entire family dines together and takes plenty of time over the meal, especially at weekends.

Estiatória range from the very expensive in Athens' wealthy suburbs, to the incredibly inexpensive mageirió or koutoúki, popular with students and workers. Here there is little choice in either wines or dishes, all of which will be mageireftá (ready-cooked). The food, however, is home made and tasty and the barrel wine is at the very least drinkable, often good, and sometimes comes from the owner's home village.

Some restaurants may specialize in a particular type of cuisine. In the suburbs of Athens, where Asia Minor refugees settled after 1923, you may find food to be spicier than the Greek norm, with lots of red peppers and such dishes as giogurtlú (kebabs drenched in yoghurt and served on pitta bread) or lamb-brain salad.

The menu (see pp96–7) in a traditional restaurant tends to be short, comprising at most a dozen mezédes (starters or snacks), perhaps

Sign for a traditional Greek taverna

eight main dishes, four or five cooked vegetable dishes or salads, plus a dessert of fresh or cooked fruit, and a selection of local and national wines.

Many hotels have restaurants open to non-residents. Smaller hotels occasionally have excellent kitchens, and serve good local wines, so check on any that are close to where you are staying.

In the last few years a new breed of young Greek chefs has emerged in kultúra restaurants, developing a style of cooking that encompasses Greece's magnificent raw materials, flavours and colours. These dishes are served with the exciting new Greek wines.

Dining on the vine-covered veranda of a Greek restaurant

Waiter outside a restaurant in Pláka, Athens

TAVERNAS

ONE OF THE GREAT pleasures for the visitor to Greece is the tradition of the taverna, a place to eat and drink, even if you simply snack on *mezédes* (Greeks rarely drink without eating). Traditional tavernas are open from mid-evening and stay open late; occasionally they are open for lunch as well. Menus are short and seasonal – perhaps six or eight *mezédes* and four main courses comprising casseroles and dishes cooked *tis óras* (to order), along with the usual accompaniments of vegetables, salads, fruit and wine.

Like traditional restaurants, some tavernas specialize in the foods and wines of the owner's home region, some in a particular cooking style and others in certain foods.

A *psarotavérna* is the place to find good fish dishes but, because fish is expensive, these tavernas often resemble restaurants and are patronized mainly by wealthy Greeks and tourists. In smaller fishing villages along the coast it is quite different and you may find the rickety tables of a *psarotavérna* literally on the beach.

For delicious grills try a *psistariá*, a taverna that specializes in spit-roasts and char-grilling *(sta kárvouna)*. Lamb, kid, pork, chicken, game, offal, lambs' heads and even testicles are char-grilled, and whole lamb is roasted on the spit.

At the harbourside, fish and shellfish are grilled and served with fresh lemon juice and olive oil. Family-run tavernas and cafés will invariably provide simple meals, such as omelettes and salads throughout the day, but many of these places close quite early in the evening. After your meal in the taverna, follow the Greeks and enjoy a visit to the local *zacharoplasteío* *(see p94)* for sweets and pastries.

CAFÉS AND BARS

CAFES, KNOWN AS *kafeneía*, are the pulse of Greek life, and even the tiniest hamlet has a place to drink coffee or wine. Equally important is the function it performs as the centre of communication – mail is collected here, telephone calls made, and newspapers read, dissected and discussed. *Kafeneía* serve Greek coffee, sometimes *frappé* (instant coffee served cold, in a tall glass), soft drinks, beer, ouzo and wine. Most also serve some kind of snack to order. All open early and remain open until late at night.

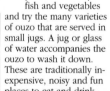

Bottle of ouzo

As the social hub of their communities, country *kafeneía*, as well as many in the city, open seven days a week.

A *galaktopoleío*, or "milk shop", has a seating area where you can enjoy fine yoghurt and honey; those around Plateía Omonoías in Athens remain open for most of the night.

A *kapileío* (wine shop with a café-bar attached) is the place to try local wines from the cask, and you may find a few bottled wines as well. The owner is invariably from a wine village or family and will often cook some simple regional specialities to accompany the wine.

In a *mezedopoleío*, or *mezés* shop, the owner will not only serve the local wine and the *mezédes* that go with it, but also ouzo and the infamous spirit, raki, both distilled from the remnants of the grape harvest. Their accompanying *mezédes* are less salty than those served with wine.

No holiday in Greece is complete without a visit to an *ouzerí*. Some of the best of these are to be found in Athens' central arcades. You can order a dozen or more little plates of savoury meats, fish and vegetables and try the many varieties of ouzo that are served in small jugs. A jug or glass of water accompanies the ouzo to wash it down. These are traditionally inexpensive, noisy and fun places to eat and drink.

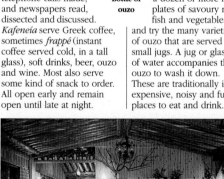

O Vláchos taverna *(see p104)* at Mount Párnitha, north of Athens

Waitress at To Geráni restaurant in Pláka, Athens (see p102)

FAST FOOD AND SNACKS

V ISITORS can be forgiven for thinking Greeks never stop eating, for there seem to be snack bars on every street and vendors selling sweets, nuts, rolls, and seasonal corn and chestnuts at every turn.

Although American-style fast-food outlets dominate city streets, it is easy to avoid them by trying the traditional Greek eateries. The extremely cheap *souvlatzídiko* offers chunks of meat, fish or vegetables roasted on a skewer and served with bread, while an *ovelistírio* serves *gýros* – meat from a revolving spit in a pitta bread pocket. The food is sold *sto chéri* (in the hand).

Many bakeries serve savoury pies and a variety of tasty bread rolls, and in busy city neighbourhoods you can always find a *kafeneío* serving substantial snacks and salads. Street vendors sell *koulou-rákia* (rolls), small pies, corn on the cob, roast chestnuts, nut brittle and candies. Other snacks include tiny open pizza-like pies, pies of wild greens or cheese, and small flavourful sausages.

If you have a sweet tooth you will love the *zacharo-plasteío* (literally, "shop of the sugar sculptor"). The baker there makes traditional sweet pastries *(see p98)*, and a whole variety of fragrant honey cakes.

BREAKFAST

F OR GREEKS, this is the least important meal of the day. In traditional homes and cafés a small cup of Greek coffee accompanies *paximádia* (slices of rusk-like bread) or *koulourákia* (firm, sesame-covered or slightly sweet rolls in rings or s-shapes) or pound cakes with home-made jam. Elsewhere, and in many city *kafeneía*, this has been replaced by a large cup of brewed coffee and French-style croissants or delicious brioche-style rolls, also called *koulourákia*. In the summer, some *kafeneía* will still serve fresh figs, thick yoghurt, pungent honey and slightly sweet currant bread.

RESERVATIONS

T HE MORE expensive the restaurant, the more advisable it is to make a reservation, and it is always worth doing so at the week-end. In the suburbs, it is the practice to visit the restaurant or taverna earlier in the day, or the day before, and check on the dishes to be served. The proprietor will take your order and reserve any special dish that you request.

Serving gýros on an Athens street

WINE

R ESTAURATEURS IN Greece are only now learning to look after bottled wines. If the wine list contains the better bottles, such as Ktíma

Merkoúri, Seméli or Strofiliá, the proprietor probably knows how to look after the wine and it will be safe to order a more expensive bottle. For a good-value bottle there are the nationally known Cambás or Boutári wines.

Traditional restaurants and tavernas may only stock carafe wine, which is served straight from the barrel and is always inexpensive. Carafe wines are often of the region and, among Greek wines, the rosé in par-ticular is noted for having an unusual but pleasing flavour.

HOW TO PAY

G REECE IS STILL largely a cash society. If you need to pay by credit card, check first that the restaurant takes credit cards, and if so, that they take the card you intend to use – many proprietors accept some but not others. *Kafeneía* almost never take credit cards, and café-bars rarely, but many will be happy to take travellers' cheques. Country tavernas, restaurants and *kafeneía* will only accept cash. The listings in this guide indicate whether or not credit cards are accepted at each establishment.

SERVICE AND TIPPING

G REEKS TAKE PLENTY of time when they eat out and expect a high level of attention. This means a great deal of running around on the part of

Patrons outside Thanásis kebab restaurant, Athens (see p101)

Sign for a typical Athenian ouzerí

the waiter, but in return they receive generous tips – as much as 20 per cent if the service is good, though more often a tip is 10–15 per cent. Prices in traditional establishments do include service, but the waiters still expect a tip so always have coins ready to hand.

Western-style restaurants and tourist tavernas sometimes add a service charge to the bill; their prices can be much higher because of trimmings, such as telephones and air-conditioning.

Bread ring seller, Athens

DRESS CODE

THE GREEKS dress quite formally when dining out. Visitors should wear whatever is comfortable, but skimpy tops and shorts and active sportswear are not acceptable, except near the beach, although it is unlikely that tourist establishments would turn custom away. Some of the most expensive city restaurants, especially those attached to hotels, request formal dress.

In summer, if you intend dining outside, take a jacket or sweater for the evening.

CHILDREN

GREEK CHILDREN become restaurant and taverna habitués at a very early age – it is an essential part of their education. Consequently, children are welcome everywhere in Greece except in

the bars. In formal restaurants children are expected to be well behaved, but in summer, when Greeks enjoy eating outside, it is perfectly acceptable for children to play and enjoy themselves too. Facilities such as highchairs are unknown except in the most considerate hotel dining rooms, but more casual restaurants and tavernas are fine for dining with children of any age.

SMOKING

SMOKING is commonplace in Greece and until recently establishments maintaining a no-smoking policy have been difficult to find. However, new EU regulations make it obligatory for all restaurants to have no-smoking areas. In practice, of course, change is slow but for at least half the year you can always dine outdoors.

Enjoying food, drink and live music at a traditional taverna in Pláka, Athens

WHEELCHAIR ACCESS

IN CITY RESTAURANTS wheelchair access is often restricted. The streets themselves have uneven pavements and many restaurants have narrow doorways and possibly steps. Restaurants that do have wheelchair access are indicated in the listings pages of this guide. Also, the organizations that are listed on page 117 provide information for disabled travellers in Greece.

VEGETARIAN FOOD

GREEK CUISINE provides plenty of choice for vegetarians. Greeks enjoy such a variety of dishes for each course that it is easy to order just vegetable dishes for first and main courses in traditional restaurants, tavernas or *kafeneía*. Vegetable dishes are substantial, inexpensive, imaginatively prepared and satisfying.

Vegans may have more of a problem, for there are few places in Greece catering for special diets. However, as Greek cooking relies little on dairy products, it is possible to follow a vegan diet almost anywhere in Greece.

PICNICS

THE BEST TIME to picnic in Greece is in spring, when the countryside is at its most beautiful and the weather is not too hot. The traditional seasonal foods, such as Lenten olive oil bread, sweet Easter bread, pies filled with wild greens, fresh cheese and new retsina wine, all make perfect fare for picnics. The best foods for summer snacks are peaches and figs, yoghurt and cheese, and tomatoes, various breads and olives. Mount Párnitha *(see p75)* is a popular picnic area for Athenians wishing to escape the noise and bustle of the city.

The Classic Greek Menu

THE TRADITIONAL FIRST COURSE is a selection of *mezédes*, or snacks; these can also be eaten in *ouzerís*, or bars, throughout the day. Meat or fish dishes follow next, usually served with a salad. The wine list tends to be simple, and coffee and cakes are generally consumed after the meal in a nearby pastry shop. In rural areas traditional dishes can be chosen straight from the kitchen.

Mezédes are both a first course and a snack with wine or other drinks.

Taramosaláta *is a purée of salted mullet roe and breadcrumbs or potato. Traditionally a dish for Lent, it is now on every taverna menu.*

Souvlákia *are tiny chunks of pork, flavoured with lemon, herbs and olive oil, grilled on skewers. Here they are served with* **tzatzíki**, *a refreshing mixture of creamy yoghurt, cucumber, garlic and mint.*

Olives

Melitzanosaláta and revithosaláta *are both purées. Melitzanosaláta, left, is grilled aubergines and herbs; and revithosaláta, right, is chickpeas, coriander and garlic.*

Fish are at their best around the coast and on the islands.

Melitzánes imám baïldí *are aubergines filled with a ragoût of onions, tomatoes and herbs.* **Ntolmádes** *(bottom) are parcels of vine leaves tightly stuffed with currants, pine nuts and rice.*

Fried squid

ΜΕΖΕΣ
Mezés

Ελιές
Eliés

Ταραμοσαλάτα
Taramosaláta

Τζατζίκι
Tzatzíki

Σουβλάκια
Souvlákia

Ρεβυθοσαλάτα
Revythosaláta

Μελιτζανοσαλάτα
Melitzanosaláta

Ντολμάδες
Ntolmádes

Μελιτζάνες ιμάμ μπαϊλντί
Melitzánes imám baïldí

Χωριάτικη σαλάτα
Choriátiki saláta

ΨΑΡΙΑ
Psária

Πλακί
Plakí

Σχάρας
Scháras

Τηγανιτά καλαμάρια
Tiganitá kalamária

Choriátiki saláta, *Greek salad, combines tomatoes, cucumber, onions, herbs, capers and feta cheese.*

Scháras *means "from the grill". This summer dish of grilled swordfish is served with a salad of bitter greens.*

Psária plakí *is a whole fish baked in an open dish with carrots, leeks and potatoes in a tomato, fennel and olive oil sauce.*

BREAD IN GREECE

Bread is considered by Greeks to be the staff of life and is served at every meal. Village bakers vary the bread each day with flavourings of currants, herbs, wild greens or cheese. The many Orthodox festivals are celebrated with special breads.

Olive rolls with herbs

Pitta bread, unleavened

Paximádia (twice-baked bread)

Koulourákia (sweet or plain rolls)

Tsouréki (festival bread loaf)

ΚΡΕΑΣ
Kréas

Μουσακάς
Mousakás

Κεφτέδες
Keftédes

Χοιρινό σουβλάκι
Choirinó souvláki

Κλέφτικο
Kléftiko

ΛΑΧΑΝΙΚΑ ΚΑΙ ΣΑΛΑΤΙΚΑ
Lachaniká kai salatiká

Μελιτζάνες και κολοκυθάκια τηγανιτά
Melitzánes kai kolokythákia tiganitá

Αγκινάρες α λα πολίτα
Agkináres a la políta

Σπαράγγια σαλάτα
Sparángia saláta

ΓΛΥΚΑ
Glyká

Φρέσκα φρούτα
Fréska froúta

Σύκα στο φούρνο με μαυροδάφνη
Sýka sto foúrno me mavrodáfni

Γιαούρτι και μέλι
Giaoúrti kai méli

Meat is more readily available on the mainland than the islands.

Kebabs of grilled pork

Vegetables and salads often use wild produce.

Fried aubergines and courgettes

Artichokes with potatoes, dill, lemon and oil

Asparagus in olive oil and lemon

Desserts are simple affairs of pastry, fruit or yoghurt.

Fresh fruit varies according to what is in season.

Mousakás *is made of layers of fried aubergine and potato slices, spicy minced meat and savoury béchamel sauce, topped with cheese.*

Keftédes *are pork mince with egg and breadcrumbs, flavoured with herbs, mint and cumin and fried in olive oil. They are served here with saffron rice.*

Sýka sto foúrno me Mavrodáfni *are fresh figs baked in Mavrodaphne wine sauce, served as a dessert or sweet treat. The sauce, of wine, spices and honey, is flavoured with orangeflower water.*

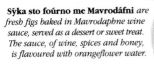

Giaoúrti kai méli *(yoghurt with honey) is the most wonderful snack in Greece, served in speciality "milk shops", to be eaten there or taken home.*

Kléftiko *is usually goat meat wrapped in parchment paper and cooked so that the juices and flavours are sealed in.*

What to Eat in Athens

Fresh fruit and vegetable market

Slices of melon

ANCIENT GREECE regarded cooking as both a science and an art. In Athens, and through Attica, you still find the ingredients that inspired the chefs of antiquity and, later, the cuisine of the Ottoman Empire with its highly flavoured meat dishes. The simplicity of Greek cooking and its reliance on fresh raw materials are what make it distinctive.

Athens is a city of immigrants from the countryside, the islands and the shores of the eastern Mediterranean. Its diversity is reflected in the markets and the cuisine.

Sparángia kai agináres *is lightly boiled wild asparagus and artichoke hearts in an olive oil and lemon juice sauce, a typical early spring mezés.*

Avgotáracho *is the smoked and salted roe of the grey mullet. It is a rare and expensive treat.*

Souvlákia *are chunks of pork or lamb, marinated in lemon juice and herbs, then grilled on a skewer. Here they are served with saffron pilaf.*

Kotópoulo riganáto *is chicken slowly roasted on a spit or grill, glistening with olive oil and pungent with oregano, accompanied here by okra.*

Mprizóles *is a thin beef or pork steak basted with olive oil and lemon juice. Here it is served with a chopped salad.*

Ravaní

Pistachios in filo pastry

Sweet pastries *filled with nuts and honey, syrup-drenched cakes, pies, doughnuts and glyká (candied fruits) are mainly eaten in cafés.*

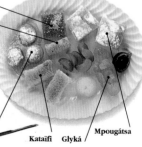

Loukoumádes

Mpougátsa

Kataïfi   Glyká

Sweets *such as nougat,* pastéli *(honey-sesame candy),* loukoúmia *(yeast doughnuts in syrup) and* chalvás *(halva, or sweetmeats) have been a part of Athens street life since the days of Aristotle. They are sold in small shops or stalls.*

Coffee *in Greece is traditionally made from very finely ground beans boiled up with water in a long handled* mpríki *(coffee pot) and drunk from a tiny cup. It is served in cafés rather than tavernas.*

Ingredients here are as varied as the terrain: fish from the sea and, from the mountains, sheep, goat and game. From the hills come several varieties of cheese, olives and honey.

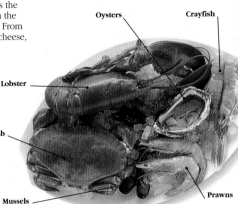

Oysters

Crayfish

Lobster

Crab

Mussels

Prawns

Fakés *is a warm or cold vegetable side dish of green lentils, black olives, lemon juice, fresh herbs and olive oil. It is also served as a mezés, or as a main course with cheese and bread.*

Shellfish and crustaceans, *especially lobster and crab, are the prize catch of the Mediterranean. Delicious straight from the sea, they are traditionally char-grilled or pan-fried, sprinkled with fresh herbs, sea salt, olive oil and lemon juice.*

OLIVES AND OLIVE OIL IN GREEK COOKING

Greece produces the largest variety of olives in the world and is also a major exporter. Greek olives can be brine-cured, dry-cured in rock salt, oil-cured or water-cured, methods that have been used for thousands of years. Olives are also pressed to extract rich olive oil. The best quality olive oil, extra-virgin, is made by pressing just-ripe olives only.

Throúmpes

Ionian green

Nafplíou

Kalamátas

Cracked green

Amfíssas

Extra-virgin oil from the Máni

Tin of blended olive oil for everyday use

Arní me vótana *is a country casserole of lamb on the bone, herbs and early summer vegetables: beans, carrots, tomatoes and potatoes.*

Choriátiko choirinó *is a pork chop marinated in olive oil, lemon juice, sea salt and oregano, then grilled. It is often served with a salad of* chórta *(wild greens).*

Sýka Mavrodáfni *is a dessert of dried figs, which are simmered in Mavrodaphne wine and spices, and served with slices of mature kefalotýri cheese.*

Kaïmáki *is a very thick cream. It is served with sweet pastries and occasionally rice puddings or, as here, with walnuts drenched in honey.*

Choosing a Restaurant

THE RESTAURANTS in this guide have been selected across a wide range of price categories for their good value, traditional food and interesting location. This chart lists the restaurants by area, starting with Athens. Use the colour-coded thumb tabs, which indicate the areas covered on each page, to guide you to the relevant section of the chart.

	AIR-CONDITIONING	OUTDOOR TABLES	LIVE ENTERTAINMENT	LOCAL WINES

ATHENS

ACROPOLIS: *Strofí*   €€
Rovértou Gkálli 25, 11742. **Map** 5 C3. 210 921 4130.
The rooftop views of the Acropolis attract a constant stream of diners.
The menu features all the mainstays of a Greek taverna. ● *lunch; Sun.*

ACROPOLIS: *Sympósio*   €€€€€
Erechtheíou 46, 11742. **Map** 6 D3. 210 922 5321.
Housed in a Neo-Classical building overlooking the Acropolis, Sympósio offers
cuisine from the Epirus region. Wild boar and venison feature. Specialities
include river crayfish with wild mushrooms. ● *lunch; Sun evening.*

EXARCHEIA: *Mpármpa Giánnis*   €
Emmanouíl Mpenáki 94, 10681. **Map** 2 F3. 210 382 4138.
This popular taverna offers such dishes as octopus and macaroni, baked cod
and tomatoes, and seasonal cooked vegetables. ● *Sun evening; Aug.*

EXARCHEIA: *Yiántes*   €
Valtetsíou 44, 10681. **Map** 2 F3. 210 330 1369.
Set in a beautiful garden, this taverna offers wonderful dishes, such as
chicken stuffed with grapes, all made with organic produce.

EXARCHEIA: *Rosalia*   €
Valtetsiou 58, 10681. **Map** 2 F2. 210 330 2933.
This busy taverna is especially popular in summer, when eating takes place
outside. The food is simple, but good.

EXARCHEIA: *Ama Lachei*   €€
Kallidromíon 69, 10681. **Map** 3 A2. 210 384 5978.
The well known *mezedopoleío* is about as authentic as they get. It is situated
in the heart of Exárcheia, well off the usual tourist track. ● *lunch; Sun.*

EXARCHEIA: *La Crêperie*   €€
Ippokratous 148, 10681. **Map** 2 F4. 210 646 8493.
Generously filled sweet and savoury crêpes, washed down with a very good
house wine, make this a pancake-lover's dream.

KOLONAKI: *The Food Company*   €
Corner of Anagnostopoúlou & Dimokrítou, 10673. **Map** 3 A4. 210 363 0373.
Anyone in need of wholesome, tasty food offered at excellent prices should
go to this café, which is run by two American women. On offer are unusal
salads, great pasta and delicious cakes. ● *1–15 Aug.*

KOLONAKI: *Filíppos*   €€
Xenokrátous 19, 10675. **Map** 3 C5. 210 721 6390.
This Kolonáki favourite offers all the standard taverna fare. Roast chicken with
lemon potatoes and *ntolmádes* are particularly good. ● *Sat evenings, Sun; Aug 15.*

KOLONAKI: *Lykóvrysi*   €€
Plateía Kolonakíou, 10673. **Map** 3 B5. 210 361 6712.
A popular meeting place, the Lykóvrysi serves a few Greek dishes such
as *fasouláda* (bean soup) alongside traditional international dishes.

KOLONAKI: *Dimókritos*   €€€
Dimokrítou 23, 10673. **Map** 3 A5. 210 361 3588.
The excellent food in this stylish taverna includes cuttlefish cooked in red
wine, tongue with lemon sauce, and a wide range of starters. ● *Sun; Aug.*

KOLONAKI: *To Kafeneío*   €€€
Loukianoú 26, 10675. **Map** 3 B5. 210 722 9056.
Excellent *mezédes* are served at this up-market Kolonáki *mezedopoleío*. Also
featured are some of the better new-generation Greek wines. ● *Sun; Aug.*

Average prices for a three-course meal for one, including a half-bottle of house wine, tax and service:
€ up to 12 euros
€€ 12–18 euros
€€€ 18–24 euros
€€€€ 24–32 euros
€€€€€ over 32 euros

AIR-CONDITIONING
Restaurant with air-conditioning.

OUTDOOR TABLES
Tables for eating outdoors, often with a good view.

LIVE ENTERTAINMENT
Dancing or live music performances on various days of the week.

LOCAL WINES
A specialized selection of local Greek wines.

	AIR-CONDITIONING	OUTDOOR TABLES	LIVE ENTERTAINMENT	LOCAL WINES
KOLONAKI: *Vivliothíki* €€€ Plateía Kolonakiou 18, 10673. **Map** 3 A5. 210 363 7897. The meals at this smart, French-style brasserie include smoked salmon, steak tartare, pasta and salads.	●	■		■
KOLONAKI: *Academy of Food and Wine* €€€€ Akadamias 24, 10673. **Map** 2 F5. 210 364 1434. Good quality food and wines, presented with great flair and attention to detail, are served here. ● *lunch; Sun.*	●			■
KOLONAKI: *Dekaoktó* €€€€ Souidías 51, 10676. **Map** 3 C5. 210 723 5561. A dozen candlelit tables, seductive *mezédes*, perfectly grilled fish and a good wine list make for a romantic place to dine.	●			■
KOLONAKI: *Kíku* €€€€€ Dimokrítou 12, 10673. **Map** 3 A5. 210 364 7033. The city's finest Japanese restaurant has all the ingredients you would expect: understated decor, perfect *sushi* and *sashimi*. ● *lunch; Sun; mid-Jul–mid-Aug.*	●			■
KOLONAKI: *Sale e Pepe* €€€€€ Aristíppou 34, 10673. **Map** 3 B4. 210 723 4102. A chic Italian restaurant with a sophisticated menu. Specialities include ravioli with white truffles and foie gras in pancetta and leek sauce. ● *Sat lunch, Sun.*	●			■
KOUKAKI: *Edódi* €€€€€ Veíkou 80, 11741. **Map** 5 B5. 210 921 3013. This small, intimate establishment serves classic international dishes as well as more unusual combinations. Examples include lamb with lobster and coffee sauce, venison with chocolate and fig-stuffed pheasant. ● *lunch, Sun evening.*	●			■
MONASTIRAKI: *Ipeiros* € Agiou Filíppou 16, 10555. **Map** 5 C1. 210 324 5572. Well located near the flea market and the Ancient Agora, this good-value lunchtime taverna serves large portions of local food. ● *evenings; Easter Sun; mid-Aug.*		■		■
MONASTIRAKI: *Thanásis* € Mitropóleos 69, 10555. **Map** 6 D1. 210 324 4705. This is a favourite pit stop for some of the best and cheapest grilled food in the city. Try the kebabs of spiced meat, onions or tomato and parsley wrapped in grilled pitta bread. ● *1 Jan, Easter Sun, 25 Dec.*	●			
MONASTIRAKI: *O Plátanos* €€ Diogénous 4, 10556. **Map** 6 D1. 210 322 0666. In business since 1932, this restaurant offers traditional Greek cuisine. Dishes include lamb with okra and barbecued squid. Good value. ● *Sun evening.*		■		■
MONASTIRAKI: *Cafe Avissynía* €€€€ Plateía Avissynías, 10555. **Map** 5 C1. 210 321 7047. Tables are always packed for the accordionist and singer who perform every weekend. During the week, when the café is quieter, is a better time to sample the unusual Macedonian dishes. ● *evenings; Aug.*	●	■	●	■
MONASTIRAKI: *Multi Culti* €€€€ Ag. Théklas 8, 10554. **Map** 2 D5. 210 324 4643. This restaurant offers a combination of Italian- and Middle Eastern-style cuisine against a backdrop of ethnic music. ● *May–Oct.*	●			■
LYKAVITTOS: *Orízontes* €€€€€ Lykavittós Hill, 10676. **Map** 3 C3. 210 722 7065. This upmarket restaurant situated at the top of Lykavittós Hill offers Mediterranean and fusion cuisine. Specialities include unusual fish dishes such as fillet of *synagrída* in sweet pepper butter, leeks and mushrooms. Superb views over Athens.	●	■	●	■

For key to symbols see back flap

<table>
<tr><td>

Average prices for a three-course meal for one, including a half-bottle of house wine, tax and service:
€ up to 12 euros
€€ 12–18 euros
€€€ 18–24 euros
€€€€ 24–32 euros
€€€€€ over 32 euros

</td><td>

AIR-CONDITIONING
Restaurant with air-conditioning.

OUTDOOR TABLES
Tables for eating outdoors, often with a good view.

LIVE ENTERTAINMENT
Dancing or live music performances on various days of the week.

LOCAL WINES
A specialized selection of local Greek wines.

</td></tr>
</table>

	AIR-CONDITIONING	OUTDOOR TABLES	LIVE ENTERTAINMENT	LOCAL WINES
OMONOIA: *Andréas* €€ Themistokléous 18, 10678. **Map** 2 E3. ☎ 210 382 1522. Set in a small alley off Themistokléous, this *ouzerí* specializes in seafood such as octopus, shellfish, anchovies and fried squid. ● *Sun; 1–20 Aug.*		■		■
OMONOIA: *Athinaikón* €€ Themistokléous 2, 10678. **Map** 2 E3. ☎ 210 383 8485. This old establishment serves a wide range of well-executed and delicious fish and meat *mezédes*. Meals are accompanied by carafes of ouzo and wine. ● *Sun; Aug.*	●			■
OMONOIA: *Ideal* €€€ Panepistimíou 46, 10678. **Map** 2 E3. ☎ 210 330 3000. Since 1922, this much-loved institution has been serving excellent Greek and international cuisine. Specials include milk-fed veal with aubergine, stuffed courgettes and *agkináres a la políta* (artichokes in lemon juice). ● *Sun.* 🗨	●			
OMONOIA: *Néon* €€ Omónoia Square 1, 10431. **Map** 2 E3. ☎ 210 523 6409. All-day eating at this self-service chain restaurant includes a salad bar, fresh pasta, grills and typical oven-baked Greek dishes.	●			
PANGRATI: *O Vyrinis* € Archimidous 11, 11636. **Map** 7 B3. ☎ 210 701 2153. Always busy, especially in summer, this taverna serves simple but tasty food at very reasonable prices. ● *lunchtime; Sun.*		■		■
PANGRATI: *Friday's* €€€ Ymittou 110, Millenium Shopping Mall, 11636. **Map** 7 B2. ☎ 210 756 0544. Part of the TGI Fridays chain, this restaurant serves steaks, burgers and other classic American dishes. Excellent desserts and cocktails. 🗨	●			
PANGRATI: *Kallimármaron* €€€ Effioríonos 13, 11636. **Map** 7 B2. ☎ 210 701 9727. Situated behind the Kallimármaro stadium, this relaxed restaurant provides hearty Greek cooking. Try the unusual *kókoras* (cockerel) with macaroni or wild boar with garlic sauce. ● *Mon; mid–31 Aug.* 🗨		■		■
PANGRATI: *The Sushi Bar* €€€€ Plateía Varnáva, 11636. **Map** 7 B4. ☎ 210 752 4354. Choose between several Japanese snacks or have a more substantial meal at this tiny but popular sushi bar. ● *lunch.*		■		
PANGRATI: *Spondí* €€€€€ Pýrronos 5, 11636. **Map** 7 B4. ☎ 210 752 0658. This award-winning restaurant in a Neo-Classical house serves food with Greek and Pacific influences. Dishes include steamed grouper. ● *lunch; Aug.* 🗨	●	■		
PLAKA: *O Damígos* € Kydathinaíon 41, 10558. **Map** 6 E2. ☎ 210 322 5084. This basement taverna specializes in salt cod and garlic sauce, chunky chips and salad. The chilled retsina is excellent. ● *Jul & Aug.*				■
PLAKA: *To Geráni ("Scholarcheio")* € Tripódon 14, 10557. **Map** 6 E2. ☎ 210 324 7605. A popular restaurant set in a Neo-Classical house with balcony seating and walls crowded with Greek ephemera. Try the sausages flambéed in ouzo and *saganáki* (fried cheese).	●	■		
PLAKA: *Byzantinó* €€ Kydathinaíon 18, 10558. **Map** 6 E2. ☎ 210 322 7368. Excellent daily specials such as the *chtapódi krasáto* (octopus in wine) and baked vegetable dishes entice the locals to this old-fashioned taverna. 🗨	●	■		

PLAKA: *Eden* €€
Lysíou 12, off Mnisikléous,10556. **Map** 6 E1. 210 324 8858.
Housed in a Neo-Classical building with modern interior, this is Athens' oldest vegetarian restaurant. Food is made with organically grown produce. ● *Tue.*

PLAKA: *Symposion* €€
Mnisikléous 24, 10556. **Map** 6 D1. 210 325 4940.
This lively *ouzerí* serves traditional Greek food such as *ntolmádes*. Retsina is served from the barrel and live *rempétika* music is played every day.

PLAKA: *Xynoú* €€
Aggelou Géronta 4, 10558. **Map** 6 E2. 210 322 1065.
Favoured by the old Athenian aristocracy, who enjoy the simple setting and food. Unsophisticated murals and a strolling trio of guitarists add to the charm of this simple taverna. ● *lunch; Sat, Sun; Jul.*

PLAKA: *Dáfni* €€€€
Lysikrátous 4, 10557. **Map** 6 E2. 210 322 7971.
Garish frescoes adorn the walls of this converted Neo-Classical mansion. Stick to the simple dishes, such as swordfish or *keftédes* (pork or beef meatballs). ● *lunch; Nov–Apr: Sun.*

PSYRRI: *Evripos* €€€
Navárchou Apostóli 3, 10554. **Map** 1 C5. 210 323 1351.
Housed in former royal stables, the Evripos serves *mezedopoleío* and unusual dishes such as ostrich with damsons and *penne* in vodka sauce. ● *Mon.*

PSYRRI: *Tavérna tou Psyrrí* €
Aischýlou 12, 10554. **Map** 2 D5. 210 321 4923.
With an owner from the Cycladic island of Náxos, the food in this taverna relies heavily on the island's delicious vegetables, meat and fish. End the meal with a slice of Náxos *graviéra* cheese. ● *Sun evenings; 15–20 Aug.*

PSYRRI: *To Díporto* €
Sokrátous 9, 10552. **Map** 2 D4. 210 321 1463.
This archetypal taverna, hidden beneath an olive shop, serves a few delicious dishes each day such as *revíthia* (chickpeas), *fasouláda* (bean soup), grilled sardines, and always a meat stew. Open to 8pm only. ● *Sun; Easter Day; 25 Dec.*

PSYRRI: *Plateía Iróon* €€
Plateía Iróon 1, 10554. **Map** 1 C5. 210 321 1915.
Good food and drink along with *rempétika* music contribute to the noisy, amiable atmosphere of this small café.

PSYRRI: *Stoá tou Vagéli* €€
Evripídou 63, 10554. **Map** 2 D4. 210 325 1513.
Tucked away in an alley, this old taverna has been serving warming beef stews, grills and soups for many years. Birds in a large cage and faded Aegean photographs amuse the clientele. ● *lunch; Aug.*

PSYRRI: *Faós* €€€
Lepeniótou 26 (first floor), 10554. **Map** 1 C5. 210 324 7833.
This stylish bar and restaurant offers modern food accompanied by live music on Friday nights and Saturday afternoons. Pricey wines are more than compensated by the tasty and imaginative cuisine served here. ● *Mon, Sun dinner.*

PSYRRI: *Kouzina* €€€€
Sarri 44, 10554. **Map** 1 C5. 210 321 5534.
Grilled lamb with noodles and orange chicken with basmati rice are two unusual dishes served at this cosy taverna. Roof garden.
● *lunch except Sun.*

SYNTAGMA: *Delfoí* €€
Nikis 13, 10557. **Map** 6 F1. 210 323 4869.
This discreet restaurant offers a large selection of fine grills, slow-baked stews and a variety of salads. ● *Sun.*

SYNTAGMA: *Kentrikón* €€
Kolokotróni 3, 10562. **Map** 2 E5. 210 323 2482.
This quiet, understated restaurant offers a wide spectrum of Greek dishes, such as lamb in lemon sauce, pilaffs and grilled liver.
● *evenings; Sun.*

For key to symbols see back flap

Average prices for a three-course meal for one, including a half-bottle of house wine, tax and service:

€ up to 12 euros
€€ 12–18 euros
€€€ 18–24 euros
€€€€ 24–32 euros
€€€€€ over 32 euros

AIR-CONDITIONING
Restaurant with air-conditioning.

OUTDOOR TABLES
Tables for eating outdoors, often with a good view.

LIVE ENTERTAINMENT
Dancing or live music performances on various days of the week.

LOCAL WINES
A specialized selection of local Greek wines.

	AIR-CONDITIONING	OUTDOOR TABLES	LIVE ENTERTAINMENT	LOCAL WINES

SYNTAGMA: *Diros*   €€€
Xenofontos 10–12, 10557. **Map** 6 F1. 📞 *210 323 2392.*
This charming restaurant specializes in good, home-cooked Greek dishes such as *lamb jardinière* and *avgolémono* (rice and egg soup). 🌑 *Easter Day.* 🍴

| | ● | ▪ | | ▪ |

SYNTAGMA: *Palia Vouli*   €€€€
Plateía Karytsi 7, 10561. **Map** 2 E5. 📞 *210 323 4803.*
This piano bar/restaurant offers a wide range of wines by the glass as well as food, including a few interesting *mezédes*. 🌑 *Sun lunch; Jun–mid-Sep.*

| | ● | ▪ | | ▪ |

SYNTAGMA: *Aigli Bistrot*   €€€€€
Záppeion Gardens, 10563. **Map** 7 A2. 📞 *210 336 9363.*
Set in a beautiful building in the middle of Záppeion Gardens, this atmospheric restaurant offers good quality food and service. Classic dishes are served alongside more unusual combinations such as pork in honey and soya sauce. 🍴

| | ● | ▪ | | ▪ |

SYNTAGMA: *GB Corner*   €€€€€
Hotel Grande Bretagne, Plateía Syntágmatos, 10563. **Map** 6 F1. 📞 *210 333 0000.*
This is a long-established restaurant serving high-class Greek and international food. The service is impeccable. 🍴

| | ● | ▪ | | ▪ |

THISEIO: *Kírki*   €€
Apostólou Pavlou 31, 11851. **Map** 5 B1. 📞 *210 346 6960*
Forty different *mezé* are offered at this *mezedopoleío*, which is a great place to sit and watch the world go by or enjoy the views of the Acropolis.

| | ● | | | |

THISEIO: *Pil Poul*   €€€€€
Corner of Apostólou Pávlou & Poulopoúlou, 11851. **Map** 5 B1. 📞 *210 342 3665.*
Fashionable Mediterranean cooking and views of the Acropolis draw the crowds to this busy and expensive restaurant. 🌑 *lunch; Sun.* 🍴

| | ● | ▪ | ● | ▪ |

AROUND ATHENS

ANAVYSOS: *O Vláchos*   €
Leofóros Anavýsou, 19013. **Road map** D4. 📞 *22910 54669.*
Meat grills, dips such as *tzatzíki* (yoghurt and cucumber) and other standard Greek fare can be enjoyed at this traditional taverna with a wooden interior. The vine-covered patio is a pleasant place to dine during the summer.

| | | ▪ | | ▪ |

GLYFADA: *O Tzórtzis*   €€
Konstantinoupóleos 4, 16675. **Road map** D4. 📞 *210 894 6020.*
Situated in Glyfáda, 2 km (1 mile) north of Vouliagméni, this classic taverna survives amidst Glyfáda's blaring fast-food joints. *Biftéki* (hamburgers), chicken and fried courgettes are some of the specialities.

| | ● | ▪ | | |

KALLITHEA: *Valentína*   €€
Lykoúrgou 235, 17675. **Road map** D4. 📞 *210 943 1871.*
In the area of Kallithéa, 2 km (1 mile) southwest of the Acropolis, this tiny taverna with its ethnic Pontian cuisine and chilled vodka is popular with Russian diners. Food includes pickles, breads and stuffed cabbage leaves.

| | | ▪ | | ▪ |

KIFISIA: *Beau Brummel Grille*   €€€€€
Agíou Dimitriou 9 & Agíon Theodóron, 14561. **Road map** D4. 📞 *210 623 6780.*
One of the most celebrated restaurants in Athens, Beau Brummel boasts a luxurious setting and offers excellent, organically-grown food with a French twist. 🌑 *Sun evening.* 🍴

| | ● | ▪ | | ▪ |

KOROPI: *To Alsos*   €€
Leofóros Lavríou 21, 19400. **Road map** D4. 📞 *210 664 2714.*
Situated in Koropí, 6 km (4 miles) south of Paianía, this grill-house offers perfectly roasted lamb and pork, served with large helpings of salads and vegetables, in a quiet garden setting.

| | | ▪ | | |

MAROUSI: *Altamíra*
Perikléous 28, 15122. **Road map** D4. 210 612 8841.
Mexican, Arabic and Asian cuisines meet in a mad culinary mix at this popular
restaurant in Maroúsi, 15 km (9 miles) north of Athens. *lunch; Sun; 1–15 Aug.*
€€€€

MOUNT PARNITHA: *O Vláchos*
Leofóros Párnithos, Párnitha, 13671. **Road map** D4. 210 246 3762.
Situated in the foothills of Mount Párnitha, this atmospheric taverna
offers traditional Greek cuisine. Specializes in meat grills.
€

PIRAEUS: *Allí Skála*
Serífou 57, Kamínia, 18541. **Road map** D4. 210 482 7722.
Real home cooking and a courtyard filled with banana trees distinguish
this elegant restaurant. The food is outstanding and includes cuttlefish,
offal dishes and stuffed peppers with caper leaves. *lunch; Sun.*
€€

PIRAEUS: *Mágaro*
Chatzikyriákou 126, 18538. **Road map** D4. 210 451 4226.
Small but popular taverna serving grilled fish dishes and salads at
reasonable prices. No bookings taken so arrive early. *Sun evening; Aug.*
€€

PIRAEUS: *Archéon Géfsis*
Epidaúrou 10, Kastélla, 18533. **Road map** D4. 210 413 8617.
This restaurant recreates the world of Ancient Greece. Staff are dressed in
robes and the menu offers dishes such as suckling pig stuffed with liver, apple
and chestnuts, and pork served with plums.
€€€

PIRAEUS: *Kóllias*
Stratigoú Plastíra 3, Taboúria, 18756. **Road map** D4. 210 462 9620.
In typically Aegean surroundings, superb fish and starters such as *garidósoupa*
(prawn and tomato soup) are on offer. *Mon–Sat lunch; Sun evening; 1–15 Aug.*
€€€

PIRAEUS: *Vasílenas*
Aitolikoú 72, 18545. **Road map** D4. 210 461 2457.
This restaurant offers a perfect introduction to Greek cuisine, with 16
dishes brought to the table in succession. *lunch; Sun; 1–20 Aug.*
€€€

PIRAEUS: *Dourámbeis*
Aktí Protopsálti 27, 18533. **Road map** D4. 210 412 2092.
Opened in 1932, this is arguably the best fish restaurant in Piraeus. All the fish
comes from the islands of Ios, Náxos and Páros. Good salads. *lunch; Aug.*
€€€€€

PIRAEUS: *Island, Várkiza*
Leofóros Athinón–Souníon, Várkiza, 16672. **Road map** D4. 210 965 3563/4.
Mediterranean fusion food and sushi are on offer at this hip restaurant, an
hour's drive from Athens. Overlooks the sea and has late-night dancing.
€€€€€

PIRAEUS: *Jimmy and the Fish*
Aktí Koumoundoúrou 46, Mikrolímano, 18533. **Road map** D4. 210 412 4417.
This classic fish restaurant enjoys a harbourside setting. Grilled fresh fish and
unusual dishes such as spaghetti with crayfish are served on the terrace.
€€€€€

PIRAEUS: *Varoúlko*
Deligiórgi 14, 18533. **Road map** D4. 210 411 2043.
Reservations are necessary at this backstreet restaurant. The innovative
chef, Leftéris Lázarou, prepares such dishes as prawns and artichokes,
seafood *ntolmádes*, and mussel and lentil salad. *Sun lunch; Aug.*
€€€€€

VARI: *Ta Vláchika*
Leofóros Váris 35, 16672. **Road map** D4. 210 895 6141.
One of the best of the many meat restaurants in Vári, 2 km (1 mile) north of
Vouliagméni, Ta Vláchika specializes in spit-roast kid, lamb and suckling pig.
Try the oven-roasted goat and *kokorétsi* (piquant heart and liver sausage).
€€

VARKIZA: *Esplanade*
Leofóros Poseidónos 16, 16672. **Road map** D4. 210 897 1760.
An old-fashioned waterfront café that offers Greek and international
dishes, as well as a patisserie, ice creams and drinks.
€€€

VOULIAGMENI: *Lámpros*
Leofóros Poseidónos 20, 16671. **Road map** D4. 210 896 0144.
Located at the water's edge since 1889, this famed restaurant has a
variety of seafood, salads and meat dishes. A good wine list
complements the freshly grilled mullet and sea bream.
€€€€€

For key to symbols see back flap

SHOPPING IN ATHENS

SHOPPING IN ATHENS offers many delights. There are open-air street markets, quiet arcades, traditional arts and crafts shops, and designer fashion boutiques to rival Paris and New York. Most Athenians go to the triangle which is formed by Omónoia, Sýntagma and Monastiráki squares to buy everyday household items, clothes and shoes. For leather goods, bargain hunters should head for Mitropóleos, Ermoú, Aiólou and nearby streets. Along the smarter Stadíou and Panepistimíou, there are world-class jewellers and large clothing stores. The maze of arcades in the

centre also houses smart leather-goods shops, booksellers, cafés and *ouzerís*. The most stylish shopping is to be found in Kolonáki where some of the city's most expensive art galleries and antique shops are clustered among the foreign and Greek designer outlets selling the latest fashions. Around Athinás, Monastiráki and Pláka there is an eclectic mix of aromatic herb and spice stores, religious retailers selling icons and church candlesticks, second-hand bookshops with rare posters and prints, and catering stores packed with household goods such as pots and pans.

Colourful shadow puppet

OPENING HOURS

SHOPS GENERALLY open from 8am–2pm or 9am–3pm, Monday to Saturday. On Tuesdays, Thursdays and Fridays there is late shopping from 5:30–8:30pm. The exceptions are department stores, tourist shops, supermarkets, florists and *zacharoplasteía* (cake shops) which often open for longer. Many shops also close every year throughout August, the time when many Greeks take their holidays.

DEPARTMENT STORES AND SUPERMARKETS

THE MAIN STORES are **Fokás** and **Lambrópoulos**. They stock a wide range of beauty

Lambrópoulous, one of the largest department stores in Athens

products, clothes, gifts, and electrical and household goods. Fokás is not as big as Lambrópoulos but it is more exclusive, with departments for clothes, cosmetics and gifts. **Carrefour** is a supermarket chain as are **AB Vassilópoulos** and **Marinópoulos**, both of which are in the city centre.

MARKETS

ATHENS IS FAMOUS FOR its flea markets. **Monastiráki** market starts early in the morning every Sunday, when dealers set out their wares along Adrianoú and neighbouring streets. Hawkers of *salépi* (a drink made from sesame seeds) and gypsy clarinet players weave through the crowds.

The commercial tourist and antique shops of Pandrósou and Ifaístou, which collec-

Shoppers in Adrianoú at the centre of Monastiráki flea market

tively refer to themselves as "Monastiráki Flea Market", are open every day. Friday, Saturday and Sunday mornings are the best times to visit Plateía Avissynías, when dealers arrive with piles of bric-a-brac.

For food, the **Central Market** is excellent, as are the popular *laïkés agorés* (street markets) selling fruit and vegetables, which occur daily in different areas. Centrally located *laïkés agorés* include one on **Xenokrátous** in Kolonáki which takes place each Friday.

Greeks buy in bulk and stallholders will find it strange if you try to buy very small quantities of things. It is not really acceptable to buy less than half a kilo (1lb) of a fruit or vegetable. In most cases, you will be given a bag to serve yourself – do not be afraid to touch, smell and even taste.

ART AND ANTIQUES

AS AUTHENTIC GREEK antiques become increasingly hard to find, many shops are forced to import furniture, glassware and porcelain from around the globe. Fortunately, however, there are still reasonable buys in old Greek jewellery, brass and copperware, carpets and embroidery, engravings and prints. Some can be found at **Antiqua**, just off Plateía Syntágmatos. Kolonáki is a prime area for small, exclusive stores around Sólonos, Skoufá and their side streets. Try **Patrick François** for early Greek advertising posters and **Serafetinídis** for excellent antique kilims and carpets. They are both on Cháritos. Kolonáki is also the art centre with well-established galleries selling paintings and prints. The **Zoumpouláki Galleries** specialize in art and antiques.

Monastiráki also has many antique shops. Look out for **Giórgos Goútis** – these are two stores selling 19th-century jewellery and costumes. Try **Iákovos Serapian** for popular art and glassware and **Vergína** for copperware, particularly nautical items. **Martínos** has some beautiful, ornate icons and silverware.

Antique jewellery and ornaments in Giórgos Goútis

TRADITIONAL FOLK ART AND CRAFTS

Affordable popular folk art, crafts and souvenirs are plentiful in Monastiráki and Pláka. There are innumerable stores filled with ecclesiastical ephemera and cramped icon painters' studios. In addition, there are more unusual shops offering a unique service. **Stávros Melissinós**, a self-styled poet sandal-maker, makes a wide

The famous shoemaker and poet Stávros Melissinós

variety of sturdy sandals and leather goods and is famous for handing out translations of his work as a parting gift. Many shops stock elegant wood carvings, rustic painted wooden trays and richly coloured *flokáti* rugs *(see p209)*. **Amorgós** is packed with fine wood carvings and puppets as seen in the Karagkiózis theatre in Maroúsi *(see p151)*.

The **National Welfare Organization** offers an excellent selection of different goods including tapestries, rugs and needlepoint cushions. Beautiful carved shepherds' crooks from Epirus as well as a large variety of finely crafted ceramics can be found at the fascinating **Centre of Hellenic Tradition**.

JEWELLERY

Athens is justly famed for its jewellery stores. There is no shortage in Monastiráki and Pláka, which is full of small shops selling gold and silver. But the best known are to be found in Voukourestíou, which is packed with such exclusive jewellers as **Anagnostópoulos** and **Vourákis**. Window displays also dazzle at the designer of world class fame, **Zolótas**, whose own pieces copy museum treasures. Another famous name is that of the designer Ilías Lalaoúnis, whose collections, inspired by Classical and other

archaeological sources, such as the gold of Mycenae, are eagerly sought by the rich and famous. At the **Ilías Lalaoúnis Jewellery Museum** over 3,000 of his designs are exhibited, and there is also a workshop where you can watch the craftsmen demonstrate the skills of the goldsmith and buy some of the jewellery.

MUSEUM COPIES

Museum shops provide some of the better buys in the city. Well-crafted, mostly tasteful copies draw on the wide range of ancient and Byzantine Greek art. They come in all shapes and sizes, from a life-size Classical statue to a simple Cycladic marble bowl. Many fine reproductions of the exhibits in the **Benáki Museum** *(see pp78–9)* can be bought from a collection of silverware, ceramics, embroidery and jewellery in the museum shop.

The **Museum of Cycladic Art** *(see pp74–5)* has some fine Tanagran and Cycladic figurines, bowls and vases for sale. There is a large selection of reproduction statues and pottery at the **National Archaeological Museum** *(see pp68–71)* souvenir shop. Apart from the museums, the Monastiráki shop **Orféas** offers good quality marble and pottery copies of Classical Greek works as well as glittering Byzantine icons.

Display of red- and black-figure reproduction vases for sale

Períptero in Kolonáki selling English and Greek newspapers

BOOKS, NEWSPAPERS AND MAGAZINES

ALL THE PERIPTERA (kiosks) in the city centre sell foreign newspapers and magazines. English publications include the weekly *Athens News* and the monthly magazine *Odyssey*. Athens' wealth of bookshops includes many selling foreign language publications. **Raÿmóndos**, situated on Voukourestíou, offers the widest selection of foreign magazines, but for foreign books, go to the huge branch of **Eleftheroudákis** on Panepistimíou, with seven floors of English and Greek books, and a café. Try **Andromēda Books** for Classical and archaeological subjects and **Ekdotikí Athinón** for history and guide books.

One of the many designer stores to be found in Kolonáki

CLOTHES

ALTHOUGH THERE are some famous Greek designers, such as **Aslánis** who produces colourful party dresses, and **Parthénis** whose hallmark is black and white minimalism, most fashion stores concentrate on imported clothes. However, there are plenty of high-quality clothes: every designer label can be found in the city's main fashion centre, Kolonáki. There are branches of such internationally famous names as **Ralph Lauren** and **Max Mara**. Such upmarket stores as **Sótiris** and **Mohnblumchen** typify the area's urban chic. For good-quality high-street fashion there is **Marks & Spencer**.

KITCHENWARE

CAVERNOUS CATERING stores in the side streets around the Central Market specialize in classic Greek kitchen- and tableware. There are tiny white cups and copper saucepans used to make Greek coffee, long rolling pins for making filo pastry, and metal olive oil pourers. **Kotsóvolos** in 3 Septemvriou has a huge range of cheap and cheerful equipment, including traditional *kantária* (wine-measuring jugs), used to serve retsina in restaurants, round *tapsiá* (metal roasting dishes), and *saganákia* (two-handled pans) used for frying cheese. More stylish products can be found at **Méli Interiors** in Kolonáki. A good selection of tinware is on display, as well as traditional Greek pottery and miniature taverna chairs.

FOOD AND DRINK

THERE ARE MYRIAD gourmet treats in Athens, including unusual *avgotáracho* (smoked cod roe preserved in beeswax), herbs and spices, cheeses and wines. The bakeries and *zacharoplasteía* (patisseries) are irresistible, brimming with delicious breads and biscuits, home-made ice cream and yoghurt. **Aristokratikón**, off Plateía Syntágmatos, sells luxurious chocolates and marzipan. One of Athens' best patisseries, **Asimakópoulos**, is crammed with decadent *mpaklavás* and crystallized fruits.

The Central Market on Athinás is one of the most enticing places for food shopping. It is surrounded by stores packed with cheeses, pistachio nuts, dried fruits and pulses such as *fáva* (yellow split peas) and *gígantes* (butter beans). You will find over 20 different types of olive and pickle at **Papalexandrís**, and a range of herbs and spices at **Bahar**, in particular dried savory and sage, lemon verbena and saffron. A new delight is **Green Farm**, part of a chain of organic supermarkets.

Two enterprising *cáves* (wine merchants), **Oino-Pnévmata** in Irakleítou and **Cellier** in Kriezótou, offer a broad range of wines and spirits from the new generation of small Greek wineries. **Vrettós** in Pláka has an attractive and varied display of own-label spirits and liqueurs.

A crammed Athenian kitchenware store

DIRECTORY

DEPARTMENT STORES AND SUPERMARKETS

AB Vassilópoulos
Stadíou 19, Sýntagma.
Map 2 F5.
℡ 210 322 2405.
One of several branches.

Carrefour
Palaistínis 1, Alimos.
℡ 210 989 3100.

Fokás
Ermou 11 & Voulis,
Sýntagma. **Map** 6 E1.
℡ 210 285 5524.

Lambrópoulos
Aiólou 99 and Lykoúrgou
26, Omónoia. **Map** 2 E4.
℡ 210 324 5811.

Marinópoulos
Kanári 9, Kolonáki.
Map 3 A5.
℡ 210 362 4907.
One of several branches.

MARKETS

Central Market
Athinás, Omónoia.
Map 2 D4.

Monastiráki
Adrianoú & Pandrósou,
Pláka.
Map 6 E1.

Xenokrátous
Xenokrátous, Kolonáki.
Map 3 C5.

ART AND ANTIQUES

Antiquities
Pandrósou 58,
Monastiráki. **Map** 6 D1.
℡ 210 325 0539.

Antiqua
Amaliás 2,
Sýntagma.
Map 4 F2.
℡ 210 323 2220.

Giórgos Goútis
Dimokrítou 10,
Kolonáki. **Map** 3 A5.
℡ 210 361 3557.

Iákovos Serapian
Ifaístou 6, Monastiráki.
Map 5 C1.
℡ 210 321 0169.

Katerina Avdelopoulou-Vonta
Lykavittoú 8, Kolonáki.
Map 3 A5.
℡ 210 361 6386.

Martínos
Pandrósou 50, Pláka.
Map 6 D1.
℡ 210 321 3110.

Patrick François
Cháritos 27, Kolonáki.
Map 3 B5.
℡ 210 725 7716.

Serafetinídis
Pat. Ioakim 21, Kolonáki.
Map 3 B5.
℡ 210 721 4186.

Vergína
Adrianoú 37, Pláka.
Map 6 E1.
℡ 210 321 7065.

Zoumpouláki Galleries
Kriezótou 7, Kolonáki.
Map 2 F5.
℡ 210 363 4454.
One of three branches.

TRADITIONAL FOLK ART AND CRAFTS

Amorgós
Kódrou 3, Plaka.
Map 6 E1.
℡ 210 324 3836.

Centre of Hellenic Tradition
Mitropóleos 59 (Arcade) –
Pandrósou 36,
Monastiráki. **Map** 6 D1.
℡ 210 321 3023.

National Welfare Organization
Ypatías 6 and Apóllonos,
Monastiráki. **Map** 6 E1.
℡ 210 321 8272.

Stávros Melissinós
Pandrósou 89,
Monastiráki. **Map** 6 D1.
℡ 210 321 9247.

JEWELLERY

Anagnostópoulos
Voukourestíou 21,
Kolonáki. **Map** 2 F5.
℡ 210 360 4426.

Ilías Lalaoúnis Jewellery Museum
Karyatidon & P. Kallisperi
12, Pláka. **Map** 6 D3.
℡ 210 922 1044.

Vourákis
Voukourestíou 8,
Kolonáki. **Map** 2 F5.
℡ 210 331 1089.

Zolótas
Stadiou 9 & Kolokotroni,
Kolonáki. **Map** 2 F5.
℡ 210 322 1222.

MUSEUM COPIES

Orféas
Pandrósou 28B, Pláka.
Map 6 D1.
℡ 210 324 5034.

BOOKS, NEWSPAPERS AND MAGAZINES

Androméda Books
Mavromicháli 46,
Exárcheia. **Map** 2 F3.
℡ 210 360 0825.

Ekdotikí Athinón
Akadímias 34, Kolonáki.
Map 2 F5.
℡ 210 360 8911.

Eleftheroudákis
Panepistimíou 17,
Kolonáki. **Map** 2 F5.
℡ 210 331 4180.

Raÿmóndos
Voukourestíou 18,
Kolonáki. **Map** 2 F5.
℡ 210 364 8189.

CLOTHES

Aslánis
Anagnostopoúlou 16,
Kolonáki. **Map** 3 A4.
℡ 210 360 0049.

Nike
Tsakálof & Dimokrítou 34,
Kolonáki. **Map** 3 A5.
℡ 210 363 6188.

Marks & Spencer
Ermou 33–35, Sýntagma.
Map 6 E1.

Max Mara
Akadímias 14, Kolonáki.
Map 3 A5.
℡ 210 360 2142.

Mohnblumchen
Plateía Dexamenís 7,
Dexaméni.
Map 3 B5.
℡ 210 723 6960.

Parthénis
Dimokrítou 20, Kolonáki.
Map 3 A5.
℡ 210 363 3158.

Ralph Lauren
Kassavéti 19, Kifisiá.
℡ 210 808 5550.
One of two branches.

Sótiris
Anagnostopoúlou 30,
Kolonáki. **Map** 3 A4.
℡ 210 363 9281.
One of two branches.

KITCHENWARE

Kotsóvolos
3 Septemvriou 10,
Omónoia.
Map 2 D4.
℡ 210 289 1000.

Méli Interiors
Voukourestiou 41,
Kolonáki. **Map** 3 A5.
℡ 210 360 9324.

FOOD AND DRINK

Aristokratikón
Karagiórgi Servías 9,
Sýntagma. **Map** 2 E5.
℡ 210 322 0546.

Asimakópoulos
Chariláou Trikoúpi 82,
Exárcheia. **Map** 3 A3.
℡ 210 361 0092.

Bahar
Evripídou 31, Omónoia.
Map 2 D4.
℡ 210 321 7225.

Cellier
Kriezótou 1, Kolonáki.
Map 3 A5.
℡ 210 361 0040.

Green Farm
Dimokrítou 13, Kolonáki.
Map 3 A5.
℡ 210 361 4001.

Oino-Pnévmata
Irakleítou 9A, Kolonáki.
Map 3 A5.
℡ 210 360 2932.

Papalexandrís
Sokrátous 9, Omónoia.
Map 2 D4.
℡ 210 321 1461.

Vrettós
Kydathinaíon 41, Pláka.
Map 6 E2.
℡ 210 323 2110.

ENTERTAINMENT IN ATHENS

ATHENS EXCELS in the sheer variety of its open-air summer entertainment. Visitors can go to outdoor showings of the latest film releases, spend lazy evenings in garden bars with the heady aroma of jasmine, or try a concert in the atmospheric setting of the Herodes Atticus Theatre, which sits beneath the Acropolis.

Two Athens listings magazines

The Mousikís Mégaron Concert Hall has given the city a first-class classical concert venue and draws some of the best names in the music world. For most Athenians, however, entertainment means late-night dining in tavernas, followed by bar- and club-hopping until the early hours. There is also an enormous number of large discotheques, music halls and intimate *rempétika* clubs, playing traditional Greek music, throughout Athens. Whatever your musical taste, there is something for everyone in this lively city. Sports and outdoor facilities are also widely available, in particular watersports, which are within easy reach of Athens along the Attic coast.

LISTINGS MAGAZINES

THE MOST comprehensive Greek weekly listings magazines are *Athinorama* and *Time Out*, both published on Thursdays. Both list events and concerts, and the latest bars and clubs. The English language publications such as the weekly *Athens News*, the weekly (Thursday) *Hellenic Star* and the bimonthly *Odyssey* also have listings sections. All are generally available at kiosks.

BOOKING TICKETS

ALTHOUGH IT IS NECESSARY to book tickets in advance for the summer Athens Festival (mid-Jun–mid Sep) and for concerts at the Mégaron Concert Hall, most theatres and music clubs sell tickets at the door on the day of the performance. However, there is also a central ticket office, open daily from 10am to 4pm, located near Plateía Syntágmatos, where tickets can be purchased for concerts at both the Mégaron Concert Hall and for the various events of the summer Athens Festival.

THEATRE AND DANCE

THERE ARE MANY FINE theatres scattered around the city centre, often hidden in converted Neo-Classical mansion houses or arcades. Numerous popular revues that combine an entertaining mixture of contemporary political satire and comedy are regularly performed in theatres such as the **Lampéti**.

Some excellent productions of 19th-century Greek and European plays are staged at

Ibsen at the Evros Theatre, Psyrrí

the **National Theatre**. Playhouses such as the Evros, **Athinón**, **Alfa** and **Vrettánia** also mount Greek-language productions of works by well-known 19th- and 20th-century playwrights such as Ibsen.

The major classical venues, including the National Theatre, put on contemporary dance and ballet as well as plays and operas. The **Dóra Strátou Dance Theatre** on Filopáppos Hill performs traditional regional Greek dancing nightly between May and September.

The Dóra Strátou Dance Theatre performing traditional Greek dancing outdoors

The doorway to the outdoor Refresh Dexamení cinema

CINEMA

ATHENIANS LOVE GOING to the
cinema, especially from
late May to September when
the warm weather means that
local open-air cinemas are
open. All foreign-language
films are subtitled, with the
exception of children's films
which are usually dubbed. The
last showing is always at 11pm,
which makes it possible to
dine before seeing a movie.

The city centre has several
excellent, large-screen cinemas
showing the latest international
releases. **Ideál**, **Elly** and
Astor Nescafé are large,
comfortable, indoor cinemas
equipped with with Dolby
Stereo sound systems. The
Alphaville-Bar-Cinema
and **Aavóra** tend to show a
comprehensive range of art-
house and cult movies.

Athenians like to hang out
at the bars and tavernas next
to open-air cinemas, such as
Refresh Dexamení
in Kolonáki or the
Riviéra in Exarcheía,
before catching the
last performance.
The acoustics are
not always perfect
but the relaxed at-
mosphere, in the
evening warmth,
with street noises,
typically cats and
cars, permeating
the soundtrack,
is an unforgettable
experience. These
cinemas seem
more like clubs,
with tables beside
the seats for
drinks and snacks.
The outdoor

Thiseíon cinema comes with
the added attraction of a stunning view of the Acropolis.

CLASSICAL MUSIC

THE ANNUAL Athens Festival,
held throughout the
summer, attracts the major
international ballet and opera
companies, orchestras and
theatrical troupes to the open-
air **Herodes Atticus Theatre**,
which seats 5,000 people, and
to other venues around
the city. This has always
been the premier event
of the classical music
calendar. In 1991, the
**Mousikís Mégaron
Concert Hall** was
inaugurated, providing a
year-round venue for
opera, ballet and classical
music performances.
This majestic marble building
contains two recital halls with
superlative acoustics, an
exhibition space, a shop and

a restaurant. The Olympia
Theatre is home to the **Lyrikí
Skiní** (National Opera), and
stages excellent ballet productions as well as opera.

Details of concerts held at
cultural centres such as the
French Institute can be
found in listings magazines
and newspapers.

TRADITIONAL
GREEK MUSIC

THE LIVELY GREEK music
scene thrives in a variety
of venues throughout central
Athens. The large music halls
of Syngróu advertise on omni-
present billboards around the
city. **Diogénis Studio**, **Fever**
and **Rex** attract the top stars
and their loyal fans. The
more old-fashioned venues
in Pláka, such as **Zoom** and
Mnisikléous, offer more
intimate surroundings for the
haunting sounds of *rempétika*
music, which draws its
inspiration and defiant
stance from the lives of
the urban poor.

Rempétiki Istoría and
Taksími are two of
the places at which
you can hear genuine
bouzouki (Greek man-
dolin) music. Both
bars have well-known
bouzouki players, and
reasonable prices.

Mpoémissa attracts a
much younger crowd, more
concerned with dancing the
night away than with the
authenticity of the music.

Accordionist
in Plateía
Kolonakíou

A classical concert at the Herodes Atticus Theatre

ROCK AND JAZZ MUSIC

INTERNATIONAL ACTS usually perform at large stadiums or the open-air **Lykavittós Theatre** as part of the annual Athens Festival. The **Ródon**, a successfully converted cinema, also attracts the very cream of foreign and Greek rock bands. Greek bands can be enjoyed at the **An Club**, and at the **Decadence** club, which offers patrons the intriguing prospect of Greek rock-and-roll dinner dancing.

The city's premier jazz venue is the **Half Note Jazz Club**. Housed in a former stonemason's workshop, opposite the First Cemetery, this cosy club presents the best of foreign contemporary jazz. For blues, check out the aptly named **Blues** in Ambelopiki.

Alternatively, to hear Afro-Latin music, head for **Café Asante** or the **Cubanita Havana Club** which feature Cuban bands whose performances are often as lively as their music.

Live music in the Ródon, one of the city's popular rock clubs

NIGHTCLUBS

ATHENS IS A HIVE of bars and nightclubs that come and go at an alarming rate. Most offer special DJ nights that attract the paparazzi and the dedicated followers of fashion. Many large dance clubs, such as **Horostásio**, **+Soda** and the **Camel Club**, offer a hedonistic atmosphere and dancing until the early hours. Also worth trying are the designer-sleek **Kalúa**, **Wild Rose** and **Exodus**, all with a sophisticated crowd.

Marathon runner in Athens retracing the path of his ancestors

SPORT

MOST TAXI DRIVERS will reel off their favourite football team to passengers before they have had a chance to mention their destination. Such is the Athenian passion for football that the two main rival teams, Panathenaïkós and Olympiakós, are always the subject of fervent debate. Each team is backed by a consortium of private companies, each of which also owns a basketball team of the same name. Football matches are played every Wednesday and Sunday during the September to May season. The basketball teams play weekly, in what is the latest popular national sport.

Lack of adequate parkland within the city means that joggers are a rare sight, despite the annual **Athens Open Marathon** every October. The athletes run from Marathon to the Kallimármaro Stadium in the centre of Athens *(see p63)*. The **Olympiakó Stadium** in Maroúsi seats 80,000 spectators and was built in 1982. The Panathenaïkós football team are based here. It has excellent facilities for all sports and includes an indoor sports hall and tennis courts in its 100 ha (250 acres) of grounds. The **Karaïskáki Stadium** in Piraeus is the home of the Olympiakós football team. There are also facilities there for many other sports including volleyball and basketball.

Another famous event is the **Acropolis Rally**, a celebration of vintage cars, held around the Acropolis every spring. It attracts between 50 and 100 cars.

Outside the city centre, there are more facilities on offer, including bowling at the **Bowling Centre of Piraeus** and golf at the fine 18-hole **Glyfáda Golf Course**, which is located close to the airport. Tennis courts are available for players to hire at various places, including the **Pefki Tennis Club**.

Proximity to the Attic coast means that a large variety of watersports is on offer. Windsurfing and water-skiing are widely available on most beaches. Contact the **Hellenic Water-Ski Federation** for details of water-skiing schools offering tuition. There are several scuba-diving clubs, such as the **Piraeus Karteliás School,** which offers diving lessons to beginners as well as more advanced divers.

Basketball, an increasingly popular national sport among the Greeks

DIRECTORY

THEATRE AND DANCE

Alfa
Patisíon 37 & Stournári,
Exárcheia. **Map** 2 E2.
210 523 8742.

Athinón
Voukourestíou 10,
Kolonáki. **Map** 2 E5.
210 331 2343.

**Dóra Strátou
Dance Theatre**
Filopáppou Hill,
Filopáppou. **Map** 5 B4.
210 921 4650.

Lampéti
Leof Alexándras 106,
Avérof. **Map** 4 D2.
210 646 3685.

National Theatre
Agíou Konstantínou 22,
Omónoia. **Map** 1 D3.
210 522 3242.

Vrettánia
Panepistimíou 7,
Sýntagma. **Map** 2 E4.
210 322 1579.

CINEMA

Aavóra-Nescafé
Ippokrátous 180,
Neápolis. **Map** 2 E4.
210 646 2253.

**Alphaville-
Bar-Cinema**
Mavromicháli 168,
Neápolis. **Map** 2 F4.
210 646 0521.

Astor Nescafé
Stadiou 28,
Kolonáki. **Map** 2 E5.
210 323 1297.

Attikon Renault
Stadiou 19, Kolonáki.
Map 2 E5.
210 322 8821.

Elly
Akadimias 64,
Omónia. **Map** 2 E3.
210 363 2789.

Ideál-Lux
Panepistimíou 1,
Omónoia. **Map** 2 E4.
210 382 6720.

Refresh Dexamení
Plateía Dexamenís,
Dexamení. **Map** 3 B5.
210 362 3942.

Riviéra
Valtetsioú 46,
Exárcheia. **Map** 2 F3.
210 384 4827.

Thiseíon
Apostólou Pávlou 7,
Thiseío. **Map** 5 B2.
210 347 0980.

CLASSICAL MUSIC

French Institute
Sína 29–31, Kolonáki.
Map 3 A4.
210 339 8601.

**Herodes Atticus
Theatre**
Dionysíou Areopagítou,
Acropolis. **Map** 6 C2.
210 323 9132.

**Lyrikí Skiní,
Olympia Theatre**
Akadimías 59,
Omónoia. **Map** 2 F4.
210 361 2461.

**Mousikís Mégaron
Concert Hall**
V Sofías & Kókkali,
Stégi Patrídos. **Map** 4 E4.
210 728 2333.

TRADITIONAL GREEK MUSIC

**Diogénis
Studio**
Leof A Syngroú 259,
N. Smyrni.
210 942 5754.

Fever
Leof. A Syngrou &
Lagousitsi 25, Kallithéa.
210 921 7333.

Mnisikléous
Mnisikleous 22,
Pláka. **Map** 6 D1.
210 322 5558.

Mpoémissa
Solomoú 19,
Exárcheia. **Map** 2 D2.
210 384 3836.

Rempétiki Istoría
Ippokrátous 181,
Neápoli. **Map** 3 C2.
210 642 4937.

Rex
Panepistimíou 48,
Sýntagma. **Map** 2 E4.
210 381 4591.

Taksími
C Trikoúpi & Isávron 29,
Neápoli. **Map** 3 A2.
210 363 9919.

Zoom
Kydathinaíon 39,
Pláka. **Map** 6 E2.
210 322 5920.

ROCK, JAZZ AND ETHNIC MUSIC

An Club
Solomoú 13–15,
Exárcheia. **Map** 2 E2.
210 330 5056.

Blues
Panórmou 20,
Ambelokipi. **Map** 4 F2.
210 643 3372.

Café Asante
Damaréos 78,
Pangrati. **Map** 8 E3.
210 756 0102.

**Cubanita
Havana Club**
Karaiskáki 28, Psyrri.
Map 1 C5.
210 331 4605.

Decadence
Voulgaroktónou 69 &
Poulcherias 2, Strefi Hill.
Map 3 A2.
210 882 3544.

**Half Note
Jazz Club**
Trivonianoú 17,
Stádio.
Map 6 F4.
210 921 3310.

Lykavittós Theatre
Lykavittós Hill.
Map 3 B4.
210 722 7209.

Ródon
Márni 24,
Váthis.
Map 1 C3.
210 524 7427.

NIGHTCLUBS

Camel Club
Irakleidón 74, Thiselo.
Map 5 B1.
210 347 6847.

Exodus
Ermou 116, Psyrrí.
Map 1 B5.
210 331 6766.

Horostásio
Skouleníou 2, Plateía
Klathmónos. **Map** 2 E5.
210 331 4330.

Kalúa
Amerikís 6,
Sýntagma. **Map** 2 F5.
210 360 8304.

+Soda
Ermoú 161,
Thiselo. **Map** 1 A5.
210 345 6187.

Wild Rose
Panepistimíou 10,
Sýntagma. **Map** 2 E4.
210 364 2160.

SPORT

**Bowling Centre
of Piraeus**
Profítis Ilías,
Kastélla.
210 412 7077.

Glyfáda Golf Course
Glyfáda.
210 894 2338.

**Hellenic Water-Ski
Federation**
Leof Possidónos,
16777 Athens.
210 894 7413.

Karaïskáki Stadium
Néo Fáliro.
210 481 2902.

Olympiakó Stadium
Leof Kifisías 37, Maroúsi.
210 683 4000.

Pefki Tennis Club
Peloponnissou 3,
Ano Pefki
210 806 6162.

**Piraeus Karteliás
School**
Mikrás Asías 3,
Néo Fáliro
210 482 5887.

SURVIVAL
GUIDE

PRACTICAL INFORMATION

ROM WARM SEAS TO Classical temples and magnificent Byzantine architecture, Greece has much to offer the visitor. Its capital city is a major cultural centre, best visited in late spring or early autumn when the weather is mild and the atmosphere relaxed. Knowing the nuts and bolts of Greek life – when to visit, what to bring, how to get around and what to do if things

Soldier in ceremonial dress

go wrong – will help avoid unnecessary frustrations. Public transport, vehicle hire, eating out and hotel accommodation in Greece are still relatively inexpensive compared with most other European countries. Tourist information is available through the many EOT offices *(see p118)*, which offer plenty of advice on the practical aspects of your stay in Athens and beyond.

WHEN TO VISIT

HIGH SEASON in Greece – late June to early September – is the hottest and most expensive time to visit, as well as being very crowded. December to March are the coldest and wettest months everywhere, with reduced public transport, and many hotels and restaurants closed for the winter.

Spring (late April–May) is one of the loveliest times to visit – the weather is sunny but not yet debilitatingly hot, there are relatively few tourists about, and the countryside is ablaze with brightly coloured wild flowers and fresh, brilliant greenery.

WHAT TO BRING

MOST OF LIFE'S comforts are available in Greece, although it is advisable to take a good map of the area in which you intend to stay *(see p133)*, an AC adaptor for your electrical gadgetry *(see p119)*, sun-

glasses and a sun hat, mosquito repellent, any medical supplies you might need and a high factor (15 and up) suntan lotion.

Apart from swimwear, light clothing is all you need for most of the year, though a sweater or light jacket for the evening is also recommended, and is essential in May and October. During winter and spring, rainwear should be taken, as well as warm clothes. Many religious buildings have dress codes that should always be adhered to *(see p119)*.

| ΕΛΕΓΧΟΣ ΔΙΑΒΑΤΗΡΙΩΝ |
| PASSPORT CONTROL |

Greek airport passport control sign

VISA REQUIREMENTS

VISITORS FROM EU countries, the US, Canada, Australia and New Zealand need only a valid passport for entry to Greece (no visa is required), and can stay for a period of up to 90 days. For longer stays a resident's permit must be

obtained from the **Aliens' Bureau** in Athens, or the local police in remoter areas.

Any non-EU citizen planning to work or study in Greece should contact their local Greek consulate a few months in advance about visa requirements and work permits.

CUSTOMS

VISITORS ENTERING Greece from within the EU are no longer subject to any customs controls or other formalities. Limits for duty-paid goods have been similarly relaxed in recent years, though anything valuable should be recorded in your passport upon entry if it is to be re-exported. Visitors coming from non-EU countries may be subject to the occasional spot check on arrival in Greece.

However, visitors should be aware that the unauthorized export of antiquities and archaeological artifacts from Greece is treated as a serious offence, with penalties ranging from hefty fines to prison sentences.

Any prescription drugs that are brought into the country should be accompanied by a copy of the prescription for the purposes of the customs authorities *(see pp120–21)*.

On 30 June 1999, the intra-EU Duty and Tax Free Allowances, better known as Duty Free and mainly affecting such luxury items as alcohol, perfumes and tobacco, were abolished. EU residents can now import greater amounts of these goods, as long as they are for personal use.

Visitors on the beach in high summer

◁ **One of the many attractive harbours of Greece's fishing villages**

A family arriving at Athens airport

TRAVELLING WITH CHILDREN

CHILDREN ARE much loved by the Greeks and welcomed just about everywhere. Baby-sitting facilities are provided by most hotels on request, though you should check this before you book in.

Concessions of up to 50 per cent are offered on most forms of public transport for children aged 10 and under, but in some cases it is 8 and under.

Swimming in the sea is generally safe for kids, but keep a close eye on them as lifeguards are rare in Greece. Also be aware of the hazards of overexposure to the sun and dehydration.

WOMEN TRAVELLERS

GREECE IS A VERY SAFE country and local communities are generally welcoming. Foreign women travelling alone are usually treated with respect, especially if dressed modestly *(see p119)*. However, like elsewhere, hitchhiking alone in Greece carries potential risks and is not advisable.

STUDENT AND YOUTH TRAVELLERS

WITHIN Greece itself, no concessions are offered on ferry, bus or train travel, except to students actually studying in Greece. However, there are plenty of deals to be had getting to Greece, especially during low season. There are scores of agencies for student and youth travel, including **STA Travel**, which has 120 offices worldwide. IYHF (International Youth Hostel Federation) membership cards are rarely asked for in Greek hostels, but to be on the safe side it is worth joining before setting off. Most state-run museums and archaeological sites are free to EU students with a valid International Student Identity Card (ISIC); non-EU students with an ISIC card are usually entitled to a 50 per cent reduction. There are no youth concessions available for these entrance fees, but occasional discounts are possible with a "Go 25" card, which can be obtained from any STA office by travellers who are under 26.

International student identity card

FACILITIES FOR THE DISABLED

THERE ARE FEW facilities in Greece for assisting the disabled, so careful planning is essential – sights that have wheelchair access are indicated at the beginning of each entry in this guide. Organizations such as **Holiday Care Service**, **RADAR** and **Tripscope** are worth contacting for advice. Agencies such as **Accessible Travel and Leisure** and **OPUS 23** organize holidays specifically for disabled travellers.

A sign directing access for wheelchairs at a Greek airport

DIRECTORY

GREEK TOURIST OFFICES (EOT)

Greek National Tourist Board Internet Site
W www.gnto.gr

Athens
Amerikis 2, 10564 Athens.
(210 331 0692 or 331 0561.
FAX 210 325 2895

Australia
51–57 Pitt St, Sydney, NSW 2000.
((2) 9241 1663.

Canada
2nd Floor, 91 Scollard Street, Toronto, Ontario M5R 1G4.
((416) 968-2220.

United Kingdom and Republic of Ireland
4 Conduit St, London W1S 2DJ.
(020-7495 9330.

USA
Olympic Tower, 645 Fifth Ave, New York, NY 10022.
((212) 421-5777.

USEFUL ADDRESSES

Accessible Travel and Leisure
Avionics House, Naas Lane, Quedegeley Enterprise Centre, Quedegely, Gloucester GL2 4SN.
(0870 241 6127.

Aliens' Bureau
Leofóros Alexándras 173, Athens.
(210 647 6000.

Holiday Care Service
2nd Floor, Imperial Buildings, Victoria Rd, Horley RH6 7PZ.
(0845 124 9971.

Pacific Travel
Nikis 26, 10557 Athens.
(210 324 1007.

OPUS 23
Sourdock Hill, Barkisland, Halifax, West Yorkshire HX4 0AG.
(01422 310 330.

RADAR
12 City Forum, 250 City Road, London EC1V 8AF.
(020-7250 3222.

STA Travel
86 Old Brompton Rd, London SW7 3LQ.
(0870 1600 599.

Tripscope
The Courtyard, Evelyn Rd, London W4 5JL. (08457 585641.
W www.tripscope.org.uk

Holiday Essentials

The EOT's Greek tourism emblem

FOR A CAREFREE holiday in Greece, it is best to adopt the philosophy *sigá, sigá* (slowly, slowly). Within this principle is the ritual of the afternoon siesta, a practice that should be taken seriously, particularly during the hottest months when it is almost a physiological necessity. Almost everything closes for a few hours after lunch, reopening later in the day when the air cools and Greece comes to life again. The shops reopen their doors, the restaurants start filling up and practically everyone partakes in the *vólta*, or evening stroll – a delightful Greek institution.

TOURIST INFORMATION

TOURIST INFORMATION is available in many towns and villages in Greece, either in the form of government-run **EOT** offices (Ellinikós Organismós Tourismoú, or National Tourist Organization of Greece), municipally run tourist offices, the local tourist police *(see p120)*, or privately owned travel agencies. The EOT publishes an array of tourist literature, including maps, brochures and leaflets on transport and accommodation – be aware though that not all of their information is up-to-date and reliable. The addresses and phone numbers of the EOT and municipal tourist offices, as well as the tourist police, are listed throughout this guide.

GREEK TIME

GREECE IS ALWAYS 2 hours ahead of Britain (GMT), 1 hour ahead of European countries on Central European Time (such as France), 7 hours ahead of New York, 10 hours ahead of Los Angeles and 8 hours behind Sydney.

As Greece is now part of the EU, it follows the rule that all EU countries must put their clocks forward to summertime, and back again to wintertime on the same days, in order to avoid any confusion when travelling between countries. This should lessen the chance of missing a ferry or flight due to confusion over the time!

Entry ticket to an archaeological site

OPENING HOURS

OPENING HOURS tend to be vague in Greece, varying from day to day, season to season and place to place. It is therefore advisable to use the times given in this book as rough guidelines only and to check with local information centres for accurate times.

State-run museums and archaeological sites generally open from around 8:30am to 2:45pm (the major ones stay open as late as 8 or 9pm in the summer months).

Mondays and main public holidays *(see box on opposite page)* are the usual closing days for most tourist attractions. Locally run and private museums may be closed on additional

A *períptero*, or kiosk, with a wide array of papers and periodicals

public holidays and also on local festival days. Monasteries and convents are open during daylight hours, but will close for a few hours in the afternoon.

Opening times for shops are covered on page 106, pharmacies on page 121, banks on page 122, post offices on page 125 and OTE (telephone) offices on page 124.

Most shops and offices are closed on public holidays and local festival days, with the exception of some shops within tourist resorts.

ADMISSION CHARGES

MOST STATE-RUN museums and archaeological sites charge an entrance fee of between 1.5 and 6 euros. Reductions are available, however, ranging from around 25 per cent for EU citizens aged 60 years and over (use your passport as proof of age) to 50 per cent for non-EU students armed with an international student identity card (ISIC) *(see p117)*.

Though most museums and sites are closed on public holidays, the ones that do remain open are free of charge.

EVENTS

THE ENGLISH-LANGUAGE paper *Athens News* has a What's On column, gazetting events all over the city and also those of special interest to children. The tourist office in Amerikis Street has a free monthly English-language magazine, *Now in Athens*, which details cultural events and entertainment in Athens, as does the weekly Greek-language *Athinorama* *(see pp110–13)*.

For information on Greek festivals it is worth enquiring at your nearest tourist office or logging onto the EOT website *(see p117)* for information. Other forms of entertainment include the outdoor cinema in summer, which is very popular with the Greeks; most films are in English with Greek subtitles.

MAIN PUBLIC HOLIDAYS

Museums and public sites are closed on the following dates:

Agios Vasíleios
1 Jan

Independence Day
25 Mar

Protomagiá
1 May

Megáli Paraskeví
Good Friday

Páscha
Easter Sunday

Christoúgenna
25 Dec

Sýnaxis tis Theotókou
26 Dec

There are also bars, discos and nightclubs in abundance as well as tavernas and *kafeneía* (coffee shops). In small villages these coffee shops are often the centre of social life.

RELIGION

Greece is almost entirely Greek Orthodox. The symbols and rituals of the religion are deeply rooted in Greek culture and are visible everywhere. Saints' days are celebrated throughout Greece, sometimes on a local scale and sometimes across the entire country.

The largest religious minority are the Muslims of Thrace, though they constitute less than 2 per cent of the country's total population. Places of worship for other religions are mostly situated within Athens and its environs.

ETIQUETTE

Like anywhere else, common courtesy and respect is appreciated in Greece, so try speaking a few words of the language, even if your vocabulary only extends as far as the basics *(see pp164–8)*.

Though formal attire is rarely needed, modest clothing (trousers for men and skirts for women) is *de rigueur* for visits to churches and monasteries.

Topless sunbathing is generally tolerated, but nude bathing is officially restricted to a few designated beaches.

In restaurants, the service charge is always included in the bill, but tips are still appreciated – the custom is to leave between 10 and 15 per cent. Public toilet attendants should also be tipped. Taxi drivers do not expect a tip, but they are not averse to them either; likewise hotel porters and chambermaids.

PHOTOGRAPHY

Photographic film is readily available in Greece, though it is often quite expensive in tourist areas and close to the major sights.

Taking photographs inside churches and monasteries is officially forbidden; within museums photography is usually permitted, but flashes and tripods are often not. In most cases where a stills camera is allowed, a video camera will also be fine, but you may have to pay an extra fee. At sites, museums or religious buildings it is best to gain permission before using a camera, as rules do vary.

A Greek priest

ELECTRICAL APPLIANCES

Two-pin adaptor, for use with all British appliances when in Greece

Greece, like other European countries, runs on 220 volts/50 Hz AC. Plugs have two round pins, or three round pins for appliances that need to be earthed. The adaptors required for British electrical appliances are difficult to find in Greece so bring one with you. Similarly, transformers are needed for North American equipment.

CONVERSION CHART

Greece uses the metric system, with two small exceptions: sea distances are expressed in nautical miles and land is measured in *strémmata*, the equivalent of about 0.1 ha (0.25 acre).

Imperial to Metric
1 inch = 2.54 centimetres
1 foot = 30 centimetres
1 mile = 1.6 kilometres
1 ounce = 28 grams
1 pound = 454 grams
1 pint = 0.6 litres
1 gallon = 4.6 litres

Metric to Imperial
1 millimetre = 0.04 inches
1 centimetre = 0.4 inches
1 metre = 3 feet 3 inches
1 kilometre = 0.64 miles
1 gram = 0.04 ounces
1 kilogram = 2.2 pounds
1 litre = 1.8 pints

Personal Health and Security

Gᴿᴇᴇᴄᴇ ɪꜱ ᴏɴᴇ of the safest European countries to visit, with a time-honoured tradition of honesty that still survives despite the onslaught of mass tourism. But, like travelling anywhere else, it is still advisable to take out a comprehensive travel insurance policy. One place where danger is ever present, however, is on the road. Driving is a volatile matter in Greece, and it now has the highest accident rate in Europe. Considerable caution is recommended, for drivers and pedestrians.

Fire service emblem

PERSONAL SECURITY

Tʜᴇ ᴄʀɪᴍᴇ ʀᴀᴛᴇ in Greece is very low compared with other European countries. Nevertheless, a few precautions are worth taking, like keeping cars and hotel rooms locked, watching your handbag in public, and not keeping all your documents together in one place. If you do have anything stolen, contact the police or tourist police.

POLICE

Gʀᴇᴇᴄᴇ'ꜱ ᴘᴏʟɪᴄᴇ are split into three forces: the regular police, the port police and the tourist police. The tourist police are the most useful for holiday-makers, combining normal police duties with tourist advice. Should you suffer a theft, lose your passport or have cause to complain about shops, restaurants, tour guides or taxi drivers, your case should first be made to them. As every tourist police office claims to have at least one English speaker, they can act as interpreters if the case needs to involve the local police. Their offices also offer maps, brochures, and advice on finding accommodation.

LEGAL ASSISTANCE FOR TOURISTS

Eᴜʀᴏᴘᴇᴀɴ ᴄᴏɴꜱᴜᴍᴇʀꜱ' associations together with the European Commission have created a programme, known as **EKPIZO**, to inform tourists of their rights. Its aim is specifically to help holiday-makers who experience problems with hotels, travel agencies

A policeman giving directions to holiday-makers

and so forth. They will furnish tourists with the relevant information and, if necessary, arrange legal advice from lawyers in English, French or German. The main Athens branch has local telephone numbers.

MEDICAL TREATMENT AND INSURANCE

Bʀɪᴛɪꜱʜ and other EU citizens are entitled to free medical care in Greece on presentation of an E111 form (available from most UK post offices), and emergency treatment in public hospitals is free to all foreign nationals. Be aware, however, that public health facilities are limited in Greece and private clinics are expensive. Visitors are strongly advised to take out comprehensive travel insurance – available from travel agents, banks and insurance brokers – covering both private medical treatment and loss or theft of personal possessions. Be sure, too, to read the small print: not all policies, for instance,

will cover you for activities of a "dangerous" nature, such as motorcycling and trekking; not all policies will pay for doctors' or hospital fees direct, and only some will cover you for ambulances and emergency flights home. Paying for your flight with a credit card such as Visa or American Express will also provide limited travel insurance, including reimbursement of your air fare if the agent happens to go bankrupt.

HEALTH PRECAUTIONS

Iᴛ ᴄᴏꜱᴛꜱ ʟɪᴛᴛʟᴇ or nothing to take a few sensible precautions when travelling abroad, and certain measures are essential if holidaying in the extreme heat of high summer. The most obvious thing to avoid is overexposure to the sun, particularly for the fair skinned: wear a hat and good-quality sunglasses, as well as a high-factor suntan lotion. If you do burn, calamine lotion is soothing. Heat stroke is a real hazard for which medical attention should be sought immediately, while heat exhaustion and dehydration (made worse by alcohol consumption) are also serious.

Be sure to drink plenty of water, even if you don't feel thirsty, and if in any doubt invest in a packet of electrolyte tablets (a mixture of potassium salts and glucose) available at any Greek pharmacy, to avoid dehydration and replace lost minerals.

Port policeman's uniform　　**City policeman uniform**

An ambulance with the emergency number emblazoned on its side

Fire engine

Police car

Always go prepared with an adequate supply of any medication you may need while away, as well as a copy of the prescription with the generic name of the drug – this is useful not only in case you run out, but also for the purposes of customs when you enter the country. Also be aware that codeine, a painkiller commonly found in headache tablets, is illegal in Greece.

Tap water in Greece is generally safe to drink, but in remote communities it is a good precaution to check with the locals. Bottled spring water is for sale throughout the country, and often has the advantage of being chilled.

However tempting the sea may look, swimming after a meal is not recommended for at least two hours, since stomach cramps out at sea can be fatal. Underwater hazards to be aware of are weaver fish, jellyfish and sea urchins. The latter are not uncommon and are extremely unpleasant if trodden on. If you do tread on one, the spine will need to be extracted using olive oil and a sterilized needle. Jellyfish stings can be relieved by vinegar, baking soda, or by various remedies sold at Greek pharmacies. Though a rare occurrence, the sand-dwelling weaver fish has a powerful sting, its poison causing extreme pain. The immediate treatment is to immerse the affected area in very hot water to dilute the venom's strength.

No inoculations are required for visitors to Greece, though tetanus and typhoid boosters may be recommended by your doctor.

PHARMACIES

GREEK PHARMACISTS are highly qualified and can not only advise on minor ailments, but also dispense medication not usually available over the counter back home. Their premises, *farmakeía*, are identified by a red or green cross on a white background. Pharmacies are open from 8:30am to 2pm, but are usually closed in the afternoon and on Saturday mornings. However, in larger towns there is usually a rota system to maintain a service from 7:30am to 2pm and from 5:30 to 10pm. Details are posted in pharmacy windows, in both Greek and English.

Pharmacy sign

EMERGENCY SERVICES

IN CASE OF EMERGENCIES the appropriate services to call are listed in the directory below. For accidents or other medical emergencies, a 24-hour ambulance service operates within Athens. Outside Athens, in more rural towns it is unlikely that ambulances will be on 24-hour call. If necessary, patients can be transferred from local ESY (Greek National Health Service) hospitals or surgeries to a main ESY hospital in Athens by ambulance or helicopter.

A complete list of ESY hospitals, private hospitals and clinics is available from the tourist police.

DIRECTORY

NATIONWIDE EMERGENCY NUMBERS

Police
(*100*.

Ambulance
(*166*.

Fire
(*199*.

Road assistance
(*104*.

Coastguard patrol
(*108*.

ATHENS EMERGENCY NUMBERS

Tourist police
(*171*.

Doctors
(*1016 (2pm–7am)*.

Pharmacies
For information on 24-hour pharmacies:
(*107 (central Athens)*.
(*102 (suburbs)*.

Poison treatment centre
(*210 779 3777*.

EKPIZO BUREAU

Athens branch
Valtetsiou 43–45,
10681 Athens.
(*210 330 4444*.

Banking and Local Currency

Eurocheque logo

GREECE HAS NOW CONVERTED to the common European currency, the euro, which replaces the former drachma. Changing money from other currencies into euros is straightforward and can be done at banks or post offices. Even in small towns and resorts you can expect to find a car-hire firm or travel agency that will change travellers' cheques and cash, albeit with a sizeable commission. Larger towns and tourist centres all have the usual banking facilities, including a growing number of cash machines (ATMs).

Visitors changing money at a foreign exchange bureau

BANKING HOURS

ALL BANKS ARE OPEN from 8am to 2pm Monday to Thursday, and from 8am to 1:30pm on Friday. In the larger cities and tourist resorts there is usually at least one bank that reopens its exchange desk for a few hours in the evening and on Saturday mornings during the summer season.

Cash machines, though seldom found outside the major towns and resorts, are in operation 24 hours a day. All banks are closed on public holidays (see p119) and may also be closed on any local festival days.

BANKS AND EXCHANGE FACILITIES

THERE ARE BANKS in all major towns and resorts, as well as exchange facilities at post offices (which tend to charge lower commissions and are found in the more remote areas of Greece), travel agents, hotels, tourist offices and car-hire agencies. Always take your passport with you when cashing travellers' cheques, and check exchange rates and commission charges beforehand, as they vary greatly. In major towns and tourist areas you may find a foreign exchange machine

Foreign exchange machine

for changing money at any time of day or night. These operate in several languages, as do the ATMs.

CARDS, CHEQUES AND EUROCHEQUES

VISA, MASTERCARD (Access), American Express and Diners Club are the most widely accepted credit cards in Greece. They are the most convenient way to pay for air tickets, international ferry journeys, car hire, some hotels and larger purchases. Cheaper tavernas, shops and hotels as a rule do not accept credit cards.

You can get a cash advance on a foreign credit card at some banks, though the minimum amount is 44 euros, and you will need to take your passport with you as proof of identity. A credit card can be used for drawing local currency at cash machines. At a bank or ATM, a 1.5 per cent processing charge is usually levied for Visa, but none for other cards.

Cirrus and Plus debit card systems operate in Greece. Cash can be obtained using the Cirrus system at National Bank of Greece ATMs and the Plus system at Commercial Bank ATMs.

Travellers' cheques are the safest way to carry large sums of money. They are refundable if lost or stolen, though the process can be time-consuming. American Express and Travelex are the best-known brands of travellers' cheques in Greece. They usually incur two sets of commissions: one when you buy them (1–1.5 per cent) and another when you cash them. Rates for the latter vary considerably, so shop around

before changing your money. Travellers' cheques can be cashed at large post offices (see p125) – an important consideration if you are travelling to a rural area or remote island.

Eurocheques, available only to holders of a European bank account in the form of a chequebook, are honoured at banks and post offices throughout Greece, as well as many hotels, shops and travel agencies. There is no commission charged when cashing Eurocheques, though there is an annual fee of about £8 for holding a European account and a fee of about 2 per cent for each cheque used. All fees are debited directly from the account.

DIRECTORY

To report a lost or stolen credit card call the following numbers collect from Greece:

American Express
 00 44 1273 696933.

Diners Club
 00 44 1252 513500.

MasterCard
 00 800 11887 0303.

Visa
 00 800 11638 0304.

To report lost or stolen travellers' cheques call the following free-phone numbers from Greece:

American Express
 00 800 44 127569.

Travelex
 00 800 44 131409.

Visa
 00 800 44 128366.

THE EURO

INTRODUCTION OF the single European currency, the euro, is taking place in 12 of the 15 member states of the EU. Austria, Belgium, Finland, France, Germany, Greece, Ireland, Italy, Luxembourg, the Netherlands, Portugal and Spain chose to join the new currency; the UK, Denmark and Sweden stayed out, with an option to review their decision. The euro was introduced in most countries, but only for banking purposes, on 1 January, 1999. Greece adopted it on 1 January 2001. In all countries, a transition period saw euros and local currency used simultaneously.

In Greece, euro notes and coins came into circulation on 1 January 2002 and became the sole legal tender at the beginning of March 2002.

Bank Notes

Euro bank notes have seven denominations. The 5-euro note (grey in colour) is the smallest, followed by the 10-euro note (pink), 20-euro note (blue), 50-euro note (orange), 100-euro note (green), 200-euro note (yellow) and 500-euro note (purple). All notes show the stars of the European Union.

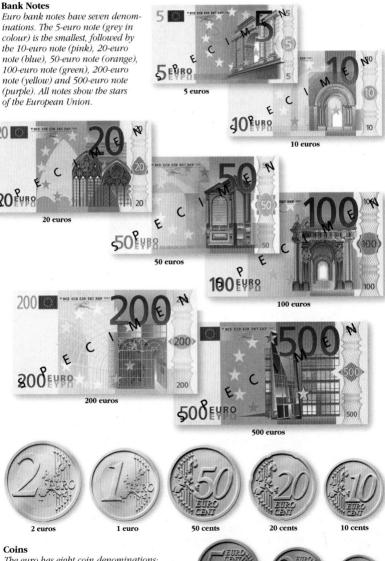

5 euros

10 euros

20 euros

50 euros

100 euros

200 euros

500 euros

2 euros

1 euro

50 cents

20 cents

10 cents

Coins

The euro has eight coin denominations: 2 euros and 1 euro (both silver-and-gold); 50 cents, 20 cents, 10 cents (all gold); 5 cents, 2 cents and 1 cent (all bronze). The reverse of each coin is the same in all Eurozone countries; the obverse is different in each country.

5 cents

2 cents

1 cent

Communications

Post office logo

THE GREEK NATIONAL telephone company is the OTE (Organismós Tilepikoinonión Elládos). Telecommunications have improved dramatically in recent years, and now there are direct lines to all major countries. These are often better than local lines, but the rates are among the highest in Europe. Greek post is reasonably reliable and efficient, especially from the larger towns and resorts; faxes are also easy to send and receive. The Greeks are avid newspaper readers, and in addition to a vast array of Greek publications, there are also a few good English-language papers and magazines.

TELEPHONES AND FAXES

PUBLIC TELEPHONES can be found in many locales – hotel foyers, telephone booths, street kiosks, or the local OTE office. Long-distance calls are best made in a telephone booth using a phonecard – available at any kiosk in a variety of different values. Alternatively, they can be made at a metered phone in an OTE office, where you can also make reverse-charge calls. OTE offices are open daily from 7am to 10pm or midnight in the larger towns, or until around 3pm in smaller communities. Call charges are variable, but in general local calls are cheap, out-of-town domestic calls are surprisingly expensive, and long-distance calls are extortionate. You can ring the operator first to find out specific rates, as well as for information about peak and cheap times, which vary depending on the country you are phoning.

Ship-to-shore and shore-to-ship calls can be made through INMARSAT; for information on this service call the marine operator from Greece on 158.

Faxes can be sent from OTE offices, a few city post offices, and some car-hire and travel agencies, though expect to pay a heavy surcharge wherever you go. The easiest way to receive a fax is to become friendly with your nearest car-hire or travel agency – both will usually oblige and keep faxes aside for you – otherwise the OTE office is the place to go.

RADIO AND TV

WITH THREE state-owned radio channels and a plethora of local stations, the airwaves are positively jammed in Greece, and reception is not always dependable. There are many Greek music stations to listen to, as well as classical music stations such as ER-3, one of the three state-run channels, which can be heard on 95.6 FM. Daily news summaries are broadcast in English, French and German, and with a shortwave radio you will be able to pick up the BBC World Service in most parts of Greece. Its frequency varies, but in the Greater Athens area it can be heard on 107.1 FM. There is another 24-hour English-language station, Galaxy, which is on 92 FM.

Greek TV is broadcast by two state-run, and several privately run, channels, plus a host of cable and satellite stations from across Europe. Most Greek stations cater to popular taste, with a mix of dubbed foreign soap operas, game shows, sport and films. Fortunately for visitors, foreign language films tend to be subtitled rather than dubbed.

Satellite stations CNN and Euronews televise international news in English as it breaks around the clock. Guides that give details of the coming week's television programmes are published in all the English-language papers.

A public phone

USING A PHONECARD TELEPHONE IN GREECE

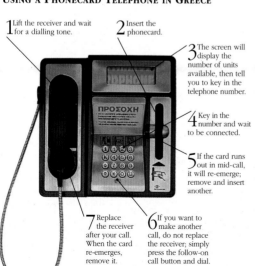

1 Lift the receiver and wait for a dialling tone.

2 Insert the phonecard.

3 The screen will display the number of units available, then tell you to key in the telephone number.

4 Key in the number and wait to be connected.

5 If the card runs out in mid-call, it will re-emerge; remove and insert another.

6 If you want to make another call, do not replace the receiver; simply press the follow-on call button and dial.

7 Replace the receiver after your call. When the card re-emerges, remove it.

A pictorial telephone card

Red post box / **Yellow post box**
for express mail / **for all other post**

NEWSPAPERS AND MAGAZINES

THE TRUSTY corner *períptera* (kiosks), bookshops in larger towns and tourist shops in the resorts often sell day-old foreign newspapers and magazines, though the mark-up is substantial. Much cheaper, and also widely available, is the English-language paper published in Athens, *Athens News*, which is printed every day except Monday. The *Odyssey*, a bi-monthly, glossy magazine, is available in most resorts as well as the capital. These two publications are excellent sources of information on local entertainment, festivals and cultural goings-on, while also providing coverage of domestic and international news. The most popular Greek language newspapers are

Stamp machine

Eleftherotypía, Eléftheros Týpos and *Kathemeriní*.

POST

GREEK POST offices *(tachydromeía)* are generally open from 7:30am to 2pm Monday to Friday, with some main branches staying open as late as 8pm (main branches occasionally open for a few hours at weekends). All post offices are closed on public holidays *(see p119)*. Those with an "Exchange" sign will change money in addition to the usual services.

Post boxes are usually bright yellow; those with two slots are marked *esoterikó*, meaning domestic, and *exoterikó*, meaning overseas. Bright red post boxes are reserved for express mail, both domestic and overseas. Express is a little more expensive, but cuts delivery time by a few days.

Stamps *(grammatósima)* can be bought over the counter at post offices and also at *períptera*, the latter usually charging a 10 per cent commission.

Airmail letters to most European countries take three to six days, and anywhere from five days to a week or more to North America, Australia and New Zealand. If you are sending postcards allow additional time for reaching any destination.

The poste restante system – whereby mail can be sent to, and picked up from, a post office – is widely used in Greece. Mail should be clearly marked "Poste Restante", with the recipient's surname underlined so that it gets filed in the right place. A passport, or some other proof of identity, is needed when collecting the post, which is kept for a maximum of 30 days before being returned to the sender.

If you are sending a parcel from Greece to a non-EU country, do not seal it before going to the post office. The contents will need to be inspected by security before it is sent, and if the package is sealed they will unwrap it.

The main post offices in the centre of Athens are indicated on the Street Finder map, at Plateía Omonoías, Plateía Syntágmatos and on Aiólou.

Athenians reading newspapers on a clothes line at a street kiosk

TRAVEL INFORMATION

RELIABLY HOT, SUNNY WEATHER makes Greece a popular destination for holiday-makers, particularly from the colder parts of northern Europe. During high season (May to October) countless flights bring visitors to Athens, many of whom pass through the city on their way to the islands. For those with more time, it is also possible to reach Greece by car, rail and coach. Travelling on the Greek mainland is easy enough. There is an extensive bus network and frequent services covering all major routes. Greece's rail network is skeletal by comparison and, aside from the intercity expresses, service is much slower. Travelling around by car offers the most flexibility, allowing the visitor to dictate the pace, and to reach places that are not accessible by public transport. However, road conditions in remoter parts can often be poor. Some of the larger centres and popular tourist destinations can also be visited by plane from Athens and Thessaloníki.

Olympic Airways passenger aeroplane

GETTING TO GREECE BY AIR

THE MAIN AIRLINES operating direct scheduled flights from London to Athens and Thessaloníki are **Olympic Airways** (the Greek national airline) and **British Airways**. Athens now has a new airport, Elefthérios Venizélos, which handles all international and domestic flights. The old airport (Hellinikon) is no longer used.

From Europe, there are around 20 international airports in Greece that can be reached directly. On the mainland, only Athens and Thessaloníki handle scheduled flights. The other mainland international airports – Préveza, Kalamáta and Kavála – can be reached directly only by charter flights. From outside Europe, all scheduled flights to Greece arrive in Athens, although only a few airlines offer direct flights – most will require changing planes, and often airlines, at a connecting European city.

There are direct flights daily from New York operated by Olympic and **Delta**.

From Australia, Olympic Airways operates flights out of Sydney, Brisbane and Melbourne. These generally necessitate a stop-off in Southeast Asia or Europe, but there are two direct flights a week from Australia, which leave from Melbourne and Sydney. Flights from New Zealand are also via Melbourne or Sydney. Other carriers with services from Australasian cities to Athens include **Singapore Airlines** and **KLM**.

Travellers with airport shopping

Check-in desks at Athens' new Elefthérios Venizélos Airport

CHARTERS AND PACKAGE DEALS

CHARTER FLIGHTS to Greece are nearly all from within Europe, and mostly operate between May and October. Tickets are sold by travel agencies either as part of an all-inclusive package holiday or as a flight-only deal.

Although they tend to be the cheapest flights available, charters do carry certain restrictions: departure dates cannot be changed once booked and there are usually minimum and maximum limits to one's stay (typically between three days and a month). And if you plan to visit Turkey from Greece, bear in mind that charter passengers can only do so for a day trip; staying any longer will forfeit the return ticket for your flight home from Greece.

Athens' new international airport nearing completion in 2001

Booking agency in Athens

FLIGHT TIMES

FLYING TO ATHENS from London or Amsterdam takes about 3.5 hours; the journey time from Paris and Berlin is around 3 hours – the trip from Berlin being a little quicker. From Madrid it takes just over 4 hours and from Rome a little under 2 hours. There are direct flights to Athens from New York, which take 10 hours, although a non-direct flight can take more than 12. From Los Angeles the flight's duration is from 17 to 19 hours, depending on the European connection. From Sydney, via Bangkok, it is a 19-hour flight.

AIR FARES

FARES TO GREECE are generally at their highest from June to September, but how much you pay will depend more on the type of ticket you decide to purchase. Charters are usually the cheapest option during peak season, though discounted scheduled flights are also common and worth considering for longer visits or during the low season, when there are few charters available. Reasonable savings can also be made by booking an APEX (Advance Purchase Excursion) ticket well in advance but, like charters, these are subject to minimum and maximum limits to one's stay and other

Departure gate symbol

restrictions. Budget travellers can often pick up bargains through agents advertising in the national press, and cheap last-minute deals are also advertised on Teletext and Ceefax in the UK. Whoever you book through, be sure that the company is a fully bonded and licensed member of ABTA (the Association of British Travel Agents) or an equivalent authority – this will ensure that you can get home should the company go bankrupt during your stay; it also should ensure that you receive compensation. Note that domestic flights in Greece are subject to an airport tax (see p128).

ATHENS' NEW AIRPORT

GREECE'S LARGEST and most prestigious infrastructure development project for the new millennium opened to air traffic in 2001. Located at Spata, 27 km (17 miles) north-east of the city centre, Athens' brand new airport now handles all the city's passenger and cargo flights. It has two runways, designed for simultaneous, round-the-clock operation, and a Main Terminal Building for all arrivals and departures. Arrivals are located on the ground floor (level 1) and departures on the first floor (level 2). The smaller Satellite Building is accessed along an underground corridor with moving walkways. The airport has been designed to allow for a 45-minute connection time between two scheduled flights.

The airport's modern business and service facilities include a shopping mall, restaurants and cafés in the Main Terminal Building and a four-star hotel in the airport complex. Car-rental firms, banks, bureaux de change and travel agencies are in the arrivals area.

TRANSPORT FROM ATHENS AIRPORT

A NEW SIX-LANE highway is being built to link the airport to the Athens City Ring Road, while metro and

Light, space and accessibility are features of Athens' airport

rail networks that extend to the airport are planned for the future. From the airport, the E95 bus runs to and from Plateía Syntágmatos in the city centre every 15 minutes with a journey time of about one hour. Bus E96 runs to and from Piraeus every 20 minutes, taking about 100 minutes. Tickets for both journeys cost around 3 euros. These tickets are in effect one-day travel cards and can also be used to travel around the city (see p139). A taxi-ride into town costs 12–15 euros.

One of the smaller planes in Olympic's fleet, for short-haul flights

Athens' new airport, designed in the blue and white national colours

FLIGHT CONNECTIONS IN GREECE

As well as having the largest number of international flights in Greece, Athens also has the most connecting air services to other parts of the country. Both international and domestic flights now arrive at and depart from the main terminal at the city's Elefthérios Venizélos airport. Thessaloníki also handles scheduled flights, but only from within Europe. Greece's other international airports are served by charters only, mostly from the UK, Germany, the Netherlands and Scandinavia.

DOMESTIC FLIGHTS

Greece's domestic airline network is extensive. **Olympic Airways** and its affiliate, **Olympic Aviation**, operate most internal flights, though there are also a number of private companies, such as **Aegean Airlines**, providing services between Athens and the major island destinations. Fares for domestic flights are at least double the equivalent bus journey or deck-class ferry trip. Tickets and timetables for Olympic flights are available from any Olympic Airways office in Greece or abroad, as well as from most major travel agencies. Reservations are essential in peak season.

Olympic Airways operates direct flights from Athens to eight mainland towns, including Thessaloníki, Ioánnina and Alexandroúpoli, and to over two dozen islands. A number of inter-island services operate during the summer, and about a dozen of these fly year round *(see p127)*.

A small airport departure tax is charged on domestic flights of between 62 and 466 air miles. For "international" flights (that is, those over 466 air miles) the tax is doubled.

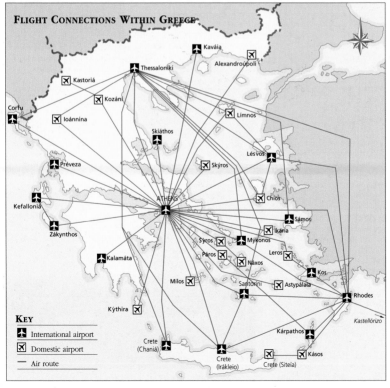

FLIGHT CONNECTIONS WITHIN GREECE

KEY

✈ International airport

✕ Domestic airport

— Air route

Island	Distance	Flying Time	Island	Distance	Flying Time
Corfu	381 km (237 miles)	40 minutes	Crete (Chaniá)	318 km (198 miles)	45 minutes
Rhodes	426 km (265 miles)	45 minutes	Santoríni	228 km (142 miles)	40 minutes
Skýros	128 km (80 miles)	40 minutes	Kos	324 km (201 miles)	45 minutes
Skiáthos	135 km (84 miles)	30 minutes	Mýkonos	153 km (95 miles)	30 minutes
Límnos	252 km (157 miles)	45 minutes	Páros	157 km (98 miles)	35 minutes

DIRECTORY

ATHENS AIRPORT

Elefthérios Venizélos – Athens International Airport
5th km Spata-Loutsa Ave.,
10904 Spata.
☎ 210 353 0000.
FAX 210 369 8883.
W www.aia.gr

OLYMPIC AIRWAYS

Arrivals and Departures
☎ 210 353 0000.
☎ 1440.

Athens Office
Syngroú 96,
11741 Athens.
☎ 210 926 7251.

Thessaloníki Office
Kountouriótou 3,
Thessaloníki.
☎ 2310 368 311.
W www.olympic-airways.gr

OTHER AIRLINES

Aegean Airlines
Leof. Vouliagménis 572,
16451 Athens.
☎ 801 112 0000.
W www.airgreece.com
W www.aegeanair.com

Air Canada
Ziridi 10,
15124 Athens.

☎ 210 617 5321.
W www.aircanada.ca

Air France
Leof. Vouliagménis 18,
16674 Athens.
☎ 210 960 1100.
W www.airfrance.com

British Airways
Vouliagménis &
Themistokleous 1,
16674 Athens.
☎ 210 890 6666.
(Phone for details of Qantas Airline services).
Thessaloníki:
☎ 2310 220 227.
W www.british-airways.com

Delta Airlines
Othonos 4,
10557 Athens.
☎ 210 331 1668.
W www.delta.com

Easyjet
☎ 210 967 0000.
W www.easyjet.com

KLM
Vouliagménis 41,
16675 Athens.
☎ 210 911 0000.
W www.klm.com

Singapore Airlines
Xenofóntos 9,
10557 Athens.
☎ 210 372 8000.
W www.singapore air.com

United Airlines
Syngroú 5,
11743 Athens.

☎ 210 924 2645.
W www.ual.com
(reservations).

PRIVATE AIRLINES (FOR DOMESTIC TRAVEL)

Greek Air Ltd
Efxenia Pontou 45,
Ano Glyfada.
☎ 210 992 8108.

Interjet
Leof. Vouliagménis 6,
16674 Athens.
☎ 210 940 2151.

Olympic Aviation
Syngrou 96,
11741 Athens.
☎ 210 356 8600.
(reservations),
(or via Olympic Airways).

TRAVEL AGENCIES IN ATHENS

American Express Travel Services
Ermoú 2,
10225 Athens.
☎ 210 324 4975.

Blue Star Ferries
Attica Premium,
Attica Posidonos.
☎ 210 891 9935.

Ginis Vacances
3rd floor,
Ermoú 23–25,
10563 Athens.
☎ 210 325 0401.

Pacific Travel
Níkis 26,
10557 Athens.
☎ 210 324 1007.
@ isyts@travelling.gr

Oxygen Travel
Eslin 4,
Athens.
☎ 210 641 0881.
@ angeki@eexi.gr

OLYMPIC AIRWAYS OFFICES ABROAD

Australia
37–49 Pitt Street,
Suite 303,
Level 3,
Underwood House,
Royal Exchange,
Sydney,
NSW 2001.
☎ (02) 9251 1047.

Canada
80 Bloor Street,
Suite 502,
Toronto,
Ontario
M5S F2V1.
☎ (416) 964 7137.

UK
11 Conduit Street,
London
W1R OLP.
☎ (020) 7399 1500.
☎ 0870 606 0460
(reservations).

USA
Satellite Airlines Terminal,
125 Park Avenue, New
York, NY 10017.
☎ (718) 269-2200.

Travelling by Train

G REECE'S RAIL NETWORK is limited to the mainland, and the system is fairly skeletal by European standards. With the exception of intercity express trains, service tends to be slow. In compensation, non-express tickets are very inexpensive (much less than coaches in fact) and some lines are pleasurable in themselves, travelling as they do through rugged and beautiful countryside. Fast and efficient intercity trains operate on some of the major lines, though tickets for these trains are more expensive. An overnight sleeper service is also available on the Athens–Thessaloníki and Thessaloníki–Alexandroúpoli routes.

Greek railway's OSE logo

via Belgrade; the line via Alexandroúpoli splits, going to Sofia and Istanbul; and the line to Flórina continues to Skopje. Intercity express trains run from Athens to Thessaloníki, Alexandroúpoli, Vólos and Kozáni; and from Pireaus to Pátra, Kyparissía and Thessaloníki. From Thessaloníki express trains run to Kozáni, Alexandroúpoli and Vólos.

First- and second-class carriages of a non-express train

TRAVELLING TO GREECE BY TRAIN

T RAVELLING TO GREECE by train is expensive, but may be useful if you wish to make stopovers en route. From London to Athens, the main route takes around three and a half days. The journey is through France, Switzerland and Italy, then by ferry from the Adriatic ports of Bari or Brindisi, via the Greek island of Corfu, to the port of Pátra, and finally on to Athens.

The other route is through the region of the former Yugoslavia, and does not necessitate a ferry crossing. The train travels overland via Budapest in Hungary, on to Belgrade and Skopje to arrive in Greece at Thessaloníki.

TRAVELLING AROUND GREECE BY TRAIN

G REECE'S RAIL NETWORK is run by the state-owned **OSE** (Organismós Sidirodrómon Elládos), and Athens forms the hub of the system. A north-bound line from Laríssis station links Athens and Thessaloníki, with branch lines to Chalkída (Evvoia);

Vólos; Kardítsa, Tríkala and Kalampáka; and Edessa and Kozáni. The southern narrow-gauge railway runs from Athens' Peloponnísou station to towns in the Peloponnese, linking Athens to Kalamáta via Pátra and Pýrgos, or via Argos and Trípoli. Some routes are extremely picturesque, two of the best being the rack-and-pinion line between Diakoftó and Kalávryta in the Peloponnese, and the elevated section of line between Leivadiá and Lamía in central Greece.

From Thessaloníki there are three lines. The Polýkastro line continues to Budapest,

TRAIN TICKETS

T RAIN TICKETS can be bought at any OSE office or railway station, plus some authorized travel agencies. It is worth getting your ticket – and reserving a seat at no extra charge – several days in advance, especially in summer when there are often more passengers than seats. A 50 per cent surcharge is levied for tickets issued on the train.

There are three basic types of ticket: first class, second class and intercity express. The first two are at least half the price of the equivalent coach journey, though service tends to be slower; tickets for intercity express trains are more costly but worth it for the time they save. A 20 per cent reduction is offered on all return journeys, and a 30 per cent discount for groups of six or more. In addition, a Greek Rail Pass is available which allows the user 10, 20 or 30 days of unlimited rail travel on first and second class trains, anywhere in Greece. The only exclusion

Athens' Laríssis station, for trains to northern Greece

Peloponnísou station ticket window

with this pass is travel on the intercity express trains, which is not included in the fixed price. InterRail and Eurail passes are both honoured in Greece, though supplements are payable on some lines.

TRAIN STATIONS IN ATHENS

ATHENS HAS two train stations, virtually next door to each other, about a 15-minute walk northwest of Plateía Omonoías. Lárissis station, on Deligiánni, serves northern Greece (Thessaloníki, Vólos and Lárisa), the Balkans, Turkey and western Europe. Additionally, tickets for OSE coaches abroad are sold here, and there are baggage storage facilities. Peloponnísou station is a five-minute walk to the south over a metal bridge that crosses the railway tracks. This serves trains for the Peloponnese, including Pátra which is the main port for ferries to Italy. Lárissis station is served by the metro, and by trolleybus No. 1 from Plateía Syntágmatos. Alternatively, taxis are abundant in Athens and fares are inexpensive compared with most other European cities.

The distinctive front end of an intercity express train

GREEK RAIL NETWORK

Sofía
Kastaniés
Istanbul
Sofía
Belgrade
Skopje
Sidirókastro
Sérres   Xánthi
Polýkastro   Kilkís   Dráma   Komotiní
Edessa   Féres
Flórina   Thessaloníki   Alexandroúpoli
Amýntaio
Véroia
Kozáni   Kateríni
Litóchoro
Kalampáka
Lárisa
Tríkala
Kardítsa   Vólos
Stilída
Lamía
Leivadiá   Chalkída
Pátra Aígio
Diakoftó   Thebes
Xylókastro
Kyllíni Kalávryta   ATHENS
Corinth   Piraeus   Spáta
Pýrgos Olympía Argos
Tripoli   Náfplio
Kyparissía
Megalópoli
Messíni
Kalamáta

KEY

— Principal rail routes

0 kilometres   200

0 miles   100

DIRECTORY

OSE OFFICES

Athens
Sína 6.
📞 210 362 4402.
Karólou 1 (information).
📞 210 529 7777.

Thessaloníki
Aristotélous 18.
📞 2310 598112 or 598115.

Lárisa
Papakyriazi 137.
📞 2410 590239.

Vólos
Iásonos 42.
📞 24210 28555.

OSE website
🖥 www.ose.gr

RECORDED INFORMATION

📞 1440

RAILWAY STATIONS

Athens
Laríssis station.
📞 210 823 1514.
Peloponnísou station.
📞 210 513 1601.

Thessaloníki
📞 2310 517517.

Pátra
📞 2610 639108 or 639109.

Lárisa
📞 2410 236250.

Vólos
📞 24210 24056.

RAIL TRAVEL FROM THE UK

Rail Europe (InterRail)
French Rail House,
10 Leake Street,
London SE1 7NN.
📞 08705-848 848.
🖥 www.raileurope.co.uk

Campus Travel (Eurotrain)
52 Grosvenor Gardens,
London SW1W OAG.
📞 020-7938 2948.

Travelling by Road

Road sign to port

TRAVELLING AROUND GREECE by car gives you the flexibility to explore at your own pace. There are express highways between Athens, Thessaloníki, Vólos and Pátra, which are very fast, though tolls are charged for their use. The maps in this guide categorize the roads into four groups, from the express routes in blue to non-asphalt roads in yellow. The road system is continually being upgraded, and most routes are now surfaced.

An express recovery vehicle

You have priority

You have right of way

Do not use car horn

Wild animals crossing

Hairpin bend ahead

Roundabout ahead

TRAVELLING TO GREECE BY CAR

OWING TO POLITICAL upheaval in the former Yugoslavia, the most direct overland routes to Greece are currently not recommended. The **AA** and **RAC** can supply up-to-date information on the advisability of routes and, for a small fee, will compile individual itineraries. It is worth asking their advice on insurance needs and on any special driving regulations for those countries en route.

In order to drive in Greece, you will need to take a full, valid national driving licence, and have insurance cover (at least third party is compulsory). **ELPA** (the Automobile and Touring Club of Greece) also offer useful information on driving in Greece.

RULES OF THE ROAD

DRIVING IS ON the right in Greece and road signs conform to European norms. There may be exceptions on small rural back roads, where the names of villages are often signposted in Greek only.

The speed limit on national highways is 120 km/h (75 mph) for cars; on country roads is 90 km/h (55 mph) and in towns 50 km/h (30 mph). The speed limit on national highways for motorbikes up to 100 cc is 70 km/h (45 mph), and 90 km/h (55 mph) for larger motorbikes.

Although usually ignored, the use of seatbelts in cars is required by law, and children under the age of ten are not allowed to sit in the front seat. Parking and speeding tickets must be paid at the local police station or your car-hire agency.

Sign for car hire

CAR HIRE

THERE ARE SCORES of car-hire agencies in every tourist resort and major town, offering a full range of cars and four-wheel-drive vehicles.

A line of mopeds for hire

International companies such as **Budget**, **Avis**, **Hertz** and **Advantage** tend to be more expensive than their local counterparts, though the latter are generally as reliable.

The car-hire agency should have an agreement with an emergency recovery company, such as **Express**, **Hellas** or the **InterAmerican Towing Company** in the event of a vehicle breakdown. Also, be sure to check the insurance policy cover: third party is required by law, but personal accident insurance is strongly recommended. A valid national driving licence that has been held for at least one year is needed, and there is a minimum age requirement, ranging from 21 to 25 years.

MOTORBIKE, MOPED AND BICYCLE HIRE

MOTORBIKES AND MOPEDS are readily available for hire in Greece. Mopeds are ideal for short distances on fairly flat terrain, but for travel in more remote or mountainous areas a motorbike is essential.

Whatever you decide to hire, make sure that the vehicle is in good condition before you set out, and that you have adequate insurance cover; also check whether your own travel insurance covers you for motorbike accidents (many do not).

Speeding in Greece is penalized by fines, drink-driving laws are strict and helmets are compulsory.

Though less widely available, bicycles can be hired in some tourist resorts.

Rack of bicycles for hire at a coastal resort

The hot weather and tough terrain make cycling extremely hard work but, on the positive side, bikes can be transported free on most Greek ferries and buses, and for a small fee on trains.

PETROL STATIONS

PETROL STATIONS are plentiful in towns, though in rural areas they are few and far between – always set out with a full tank to be on the safe side. Fuel is sold by the litre, and the price is comparable to most other European countries. There are usually either three or four grades available: super (95 octane), unleaded, super unleaded and diesel, which is confusingly called *petrélaio* in Greece.

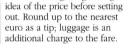

Unleaded and super petrol

Filling stations set their own working hours in Greece. Generally they are open seven days a week, from around 7am or 8am to between 7pm and 9pm. Some stations in the larger towns remain open 24 hours a day.

TAXIS

TAXIS PROVIDE a reasonably priced way of making short trips around Greece. All taxis are metered, but for longer journeys a price can usually be negotiated per diem, or per trip. Also, drivers are generally amenable to

Dual-language road sign, found on most routes

dropping you off somewhere and returning to pick you up a few hours later.

In Athens taxis are plentiful and can simply be hailed. In smaller towns it is best to find one at a taxi rank, which is likely to be either in the centre or by the bus or train station. Most rural villages have at least one taxi, and the best place to arrange for one is at the local *kafeneío* (café). In Greece taxis are often shared with other passengers; each pays for their part of the journey. Although taxis are metered, it is worth getting a rough idea of the price before setting out. Round up to the nearest euro as a tip; luggage is an additional charge to the fare.

HITCHHIKING

GREECE IS A RELATIVELY safe place for hitchhiking but, like anywhere else, there are potential risks. Women especially are advised against hitching alone.

If you do hitchhike, finding a lift is usually easier in the less populated, rural areas, than on busy roads heading out from major towns and cities.

MAPS

NOT TOO MUCH reliance should be given to maps issued by local travel agents and car-hire agencies. Visitors intending to do much motoring are advised to bring with them the GeoCenter regional road maps (1:300,000 range), the single-sheet Freytag & Berndt maps (1:650,000), or to buy regional Road Editions maps when in Greece.

Travelling by Coach and Bus

GREECE'S BUS SYSTEM is operated by KTEL (Koinó Tameío Eispráxeon Leoforeíon), a syndicate of privately run companies. The network is comprehensive in that it provides every community with services of some sort. In rural villages this may be once a day or, in remoter places, once or twice a week. Services between the larger centres are frequent and efficient. Time permitting, bus travel is a good way of experiencing the country.

International coaches also connect Greece with the rest of Europe, though fares do not compare well with charter bargains during the summer holiday season.

EUROPEAN COACH SERVICES TO GREECE

COACH JOURNEYS from London to Athens take many days and are not as cheap as a bargain air fare. However, if you are not in a hurry, it is cheaper than taking the train.

Eurolines is a very reliable company, with a huge network of European destinations. Its coaches have reclining seats, toilets and washing facilities, and there are frequent short stops en route. Tickets can be booked in person, or by telephone using a credit card. Eurolines coaches stop at Thessaloníki, with express coach services going from there to Athens. Alternatively, you could take the bus as far as Naples or Brindisi in Italy and then take the ferry across to Greece.

Top Deck is an adventure tour operator used mainly by young travellers. Tours to Greece take about 20 days, with many stops on the way.

UK COACH OFFICES

Eurolines
52 Grosvenor Gardens, Victoria, London SW1.
☎ 020-7730 8235.

Top Deck
125 Earls Court Road, London SW5 9RH.
☎ 020-7244 8000.
W www.topdecktravel.co.uk

TRAVELLING IN GREECE BY COACH AND BUS

THE GREEK coach and bus system is extensive, with services to even the remotest destinations and frequent

Domestic coach, run by KTEL

express coaches on all the major routes. Large centres, such as Athens, usually have more than one terminal, and each serves a different set of destinations.

Ticket sales are computerized for all major routes, with reserved seating on modern, air-conditioned coaches. It pays to buy your ticket at least 20 minutes before the coach is scheduled to depart, as seats often get sold out on popular routes, and Greek coaches have a habit of leaving a few minutes early.

In the villages of the countryside, the local *kafeneío* (café) often serves as the bus and coach station. You can usually buy your ticket from the proprietor of the *kafeneío*, who may also have a timetable. Otherwise it is possible to buy a ticket when you board.

KTEL logo

COACH TOURS

IN THE RESORT AREAS, travel agents offer a wide range of excursions on air-conditioned coaches accompanied by qualified guides. These include trips to major archaeological and historical sites, other towns and seaside resorts, popular beaches and specially organized events. Depending on the destination, some coach tours leave very early in the morning, so they are best booked a day in advance.

COACH SERVICES FROM ATHENS

FROM ATHENS there are frequent coach services to all the larger mainland towns, apart from those in Thrace, which are served by coaches from Thessaloníki. Athens' Terminal A is situated 4 km (2 miles) northeast of the city centre at Kifisoú 10 *(see p139)*. The terminal serves Epirus, Macedonia, the Peloponnese and the Ionian islands of Corfu, Kefalloniá, Lefkáda and Zákynthos (ferry crossings are included in the price of the ticket). It takes 7.5 hours to Thessaloníki, and 7 hours to the port of Párga.

Terminal B is at Liosíon 260, north of Agios Nikólaos metro station, but most easily reached by taxi. It serves most destinations in central Greece, including Delphi, which takes 3 hours, and Vólos, which takes 6.

Coaches to destinations around Attica, including Soúnio, Lávrio, Rafína and Marathónas, leave from the Mavrommataío coach terminal in Athens, a short walk north from the National Archaeological Museum on the corner of Leofóros Alexándras and 28 Oktovríou (Patisíon).

Eurolines international coach

Travelling by Sea

Greek catamaran

GREECE HAS ALWAYS been a nation of seafarers and, with its hundreds of islands and thousands of miles of coastline, the sea plays an important part in the life and history of the country. Today, it is a major source of revenue for Greece, with millions of tourists descending each year for seaside holidays in the Mediterranean and Aegean. The Greek mainland and islands are linked by a vast network of ferries, hydrofoils and catamarans.

TRAVELLING TO GREECE BY SEA

THERE ARE REGULAR year-round ferry crossings from the Italian ports of Ancona, Bari and Brindisi to the Greek ports of Igoumenítsa in Epirus and Pátra in the Peloponnese, plus summer sailings from Venice and Trieste. Journey times and fares vary greatly, depending on time of year, point of embarkation, ferry company, type of ticket and reductions (for young people, students or rail-card holders). Dozens of shipping lines cover the Italy–Greece routes, so it is best to shop around. In summer, reservations are advisable, especially if you have a car or want a cabin.

GREEK FERRY SERVICE

THE GOVERNMENT is implementing stricter checks on ferries, which should result in higher safety standards. However, ferry service schedules and departure times are notoriously flexible. From the smaller ports, your only concern will be getting a ferry that leaves on the day and for the destination that you want. Check the timetable on arrival for frequency and times of services, as schedules are changed each week.

Matters get more complicated from Piraeus, Greece's busiest port. Each of the many competing companies have agents at the quayside. Tickets and bookings (essential in high season) should be made through them, or at a travel agency.

Greece also has a network of hydrofoils and catamarans. They are twice as fast as ferries, though twice as expensive. As well as serving the islands, many stop at ports along the mainland coast. Most depart from Rafína, but those going to the Peloponnese coast leave from Piraeus, nearly all from Zéa port. Advanced booking is usually essential.

The Greek tourist office's weekly schedules can serve as a useful guideline for all departures, and some of the English-language papers also print summer sailings.

If you are travelling out of season, expect all services to be significantly reduced and some routes to be suspended.

Dane Sea Lines funnel

Passengers on the walkways of a car ferry leaving dock

PIRAEUS PORT MAP

This shows where you are likely to find ferries to various destinations.

Piraeus Port Authority:
01 422 6000.
Coastal Services Timetables: 1440.

KEY TO DEPARTURE POINTS

- Argo-Saronic islands
- Northeast Aegean islands
- Dodecanese
- Cyclades
- Crete
- International ferries
- Hydrofoils and catamarans

For key to symbols see back flap

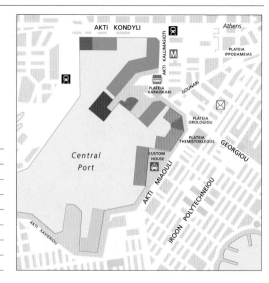

AKTI KONDYLI   Athens

PLATEIA IPPODAMEIAS

PLATEIA KARAISKAKI

PLATEIA OROLOGIOU

PLATEIA THEMISTOKLEOUS

Central Port

CUSTOM HOUSE

AKTI MIAOULI

AKTI KALIMASIOTI

GOUNARI

GEORGIOU

IROON POLYTECHNEIOU

AKTI XAVERIOU

Getting Around Athens

Trolleybus stop sign

THE SIGHTS OF ATHENS' city centre are closely packed, and almost everything of interest can be reached on foot. Given the appalling traffic congestion which makes city transport slow, this is the best way of sightseeing. The expansion of the metro system already provides a good alternative to the roads. However, the bus and trolleybus network still provides the majority of public transport in the capital for Athenians and visitors alike. Taxis are a useful alternative and, with the lowest tariffs of any EU capital, are worth considering even for longer journeys. During the Olympics, holders of event tickets can use public transport for free on the day of the event.

Orange and white regional bus for the Attica area

One of the large fleet of blue and white buses

BUS SERVICES IN ATHENS

ATHENS IS SERVED by an extensive bus network. Bus journeys are inexpensive, but can be slow and uncomfortably crowded, particularly in the city centre and during rush hours; the worst times are from 7am to 8:30am, 2pm to 3:30pm and 7:30pm to 9pm.

Tickets can be bought individually or in a book of ten, but either way, they must be purchased in advance from a *períptero* (street kiosk), a transport booth, or certain other designated places. The brown, red and white logo, with the words *eisitíria edó*, indicates where you can buy bus tickets. The same ticket can be used on any bus or trolleybus, and must be stamped in a special ticket machine to cancel it when you board. There is a penalty fine for not stamping your ticket. Tickets are valid for one ride only, regardless of the distance and, within the central area, are not transferable from one vehicle to another.

Athens bus ticket booth

USEFUL ROUTES IN ATHENS

Work continues on the Metro extension to Kerameikós. The metro station for the site will be Botanikós and it is due to be in operation by 2006.

Ⓜ **Botanikós (open 2006)**

National Historical Museum

Plateía Omonoías Ⓜ

National Archaeological Museum

KEY

— Bus A5

— Bus 230

— Trolleybus 1

— Trolleybus 3

— Trolleybus 7

— Trolleybus 8

— Trolleybus 9

— Minibus 60

— Minibus 100

Ⓜ Metro

Ancient Agora Ⓜ

Acropolis Ⓜ

Plateía Syntágmatos Ⓜ

National Gallery of Art

Lykavittós Hill

Benáki Museum

Museum of Cycladic Art

Pláka

ΜΟΝΑΣΤΗΡΙΟΝ
Monastirion

Monastiráki metro sign

ATHENS BUS NETWORKS

THERE ARE FOUR principal bus networks serving greater Athens and the Attica region. They are colour coded blue and white; red; orange and white; and green. Blue and white buses cover an extensive network of over 300 routes in greater Athens, connecting districts to each other and to central Athens. A small network of minibuses with red stop signs operates in the city centre only.

Orange and white buses serve the Attica area (*see pp66–7*) – on these you pay the conductor. The two terminals for orange and white buses are both situated on Mavrommataíon, by Pedío tou Areos (Areos Park). Though you can board at any designated orange stop, usually you cannot get off until you are outside the city area. These buses are less frequent than the blue and white service, and on some routes stop running in the early evening.

Green express buses, the fourth category, travel between central Athens and Piraeus. Numbers 040 and 049 are very frequent – about every 6 minutes – running from Athinas, by Plateía Omonoías, to various stops in Piraeus, including Plateía Karaïskáki, at the main harbour.

TROLLEYBUSES IN ATHENS

ATHENS HAS a good network of trolleybuses, which are orange-yellow or purple and yellow in colour. There are about 19 routes that criss-cross the city. They provide a good way of getting around the central sights. All routes pass the Pláka area. Route 3 is useful for visiting the National Archaeological Museum from Plateía Syntágmatos, and route 1 links Lárissis railway station with Plateía Omonoías and Plateía Syntágmatos.

A new line now links central Athens to the coast at Palaió Fáliro. Here it connects to a second line running between Néo Fáliro to the north and Glyfáda to the south. The lines

Front view of an Athens trolleybus

allow easy access to the Olympic venues on the coast, and central Athens terminals are located at Záppeion and Fix.

ATHENS' METRO

THE METRO is a fast and reliable means of transport in Athens. Line 1, the original line, runs from Kifissiá in the north to Piraeus in the south, with central stations at Thiseío, Monastiráki, Omónoia and Victoria. The majority of the line is overland and only runs underground between Attikí and Monastiráki stations through the city centre. The line is used mainly by commuters, but offers visitors a useful alternative means of reaching Piraeus (*see p139*).

Lines 2 and 3 form part of a huge expansion of the system, most of which has been completed in time for the Olympic Games. The new lines have been built 20 m (66 ft) underground in order to avoid material of archaeological interest.

Line 2 now runs from Agios Antónios in northwest Athens to Aléxandros Panagóulis in the southeast. Line 3 runs from Sýntagma to Doukíssis Plakentías in the northeast where the line meets the suburban railway to Eleftheríos Venizélos airport. Line 3 also now runs between Sýntagma and Monastiráki.

One ticket allows travel on any of the three lines and is valid for 90 minutes in one direction. This means you can exit a station, go back to continue your journey within the time limit. A cheaper ticket is sold for single journeys on Line 1. Tickets can be bought at any metro station and must be validated before entering the train – use the machines at the entrances to all platforms. Trains run every five minutes from 5am to 12:30am on Line 1, and from 5:30am to midnight on Lines 2 and 3.

Archaeological remains on display at Sýntagma metro station

DRIVING IN ATHENS

DRIVING IN ATHENS can be a nerve-racking experience, especially if you are not accustomed to Greek road habits. Many streets in the centre are pedestrianized and there are also plenty of one-way streets, so you need to plan routes carefully. Finding a parking space can also be very difficult. Despite appearances to the contrary, parking in front of a no-parking sign or on a single yellow line is illegal. There are pay-and-display machines for legal on-street parking, as well as underground car parks, though these usually fill up quickly.

In an attempt to reduce dangerously high air pollution levels, there is an "odd-even" driving system in force. Cars that have an odd number at the end of their licence plates can enter the central grid, also called the *daktýlios*, only on dates with an odd number, and cars with an even number at the end of their plates are allowed into it only on dates with an even number. To avoid this, some people have two cars – with an odd and even plate. The rule does not apply to foreign cars but, if possible, avoid taking your car into the city centre.

No parking on odd-numbered days of the month

No parking on even-numbered days of the month

Yellow Athens Taxi

ATHENIAN TAXIS

SWARMS OF YELLOW taxis can be seen cruising around Athens at most times of the day or night. However, trying to persuade one to stop for you can be difficult, especially between 2pm and 3pm when taxi drivers usually change shifts. Then, they will only pick you up if you happen to be going in a direction that is convenient for them.

To hail a taxi, stand on the edge of the pavement and shout out your destination to any cab that slows down. If a cab's "TAXI" sign is lit up, then it is definitely for hire (but often a taxi is also for hire when the sign is not lit). It is also common practice for drivers to pick up extra passengers along the way, so do not ignore the occupied cabs. If you are not the first passenger, take note of the meter reading immediately: there is no fare-sharing, so you should be charged for your portion of the journey only, (or the minimum fare of 1.5 euros, whichever is greater).

Athenian taxis are extremely cheap by European standards – depending on traffic, you should not have to pay more than 2.5 euros to go anywhere in the downtown area, and between 4.5 and 7.5 euros from the centre to Piraeus. Double tariffs come into effect between midnight and 5am, and for journeys that exceed certain distances from the city centre. Fares to the airport, which is out of town at Spata, are between 12 and 15 euros. There are also small surcharges for extra pieces of luggage weighing over 10 kg (22 lbs), and for journeys from the ferry or railway terminals. Taxi fares are increased during holiday periods, such as Christmas and Easter.

For an extra charge, (1–2.5 euros), you can make a phone call to a radio taxi company and arrange for a car to pick you up at an appointed place and time. Radio taxis are plentiful in the Athens area. Listed below are the telephone numbers of a few companies:

Express
℄ 210 993 4812.
Kosmos
℄ 1300.
Hellas
℄ 210 645 7000.

WALKING

THE CENTRE OF ATHENS is very compact, and almost all major sights and museums are to be found within a 20- or 25-minute walk of Plateía Syntágmatos, which is generally regarded as the city's centre. This is worth bearing in mind, particularly when traffic

Sign for a pedestrianized area

is congested, all buses are full, and no taxi will stop. Athens is still one of the safest European cities in which to walk around, though, as in any sizable metropolis, it pays to be vigilant, especially at night.

Visitors to Athens, walking up Areopagos hill

ATHENS TRANSPORT LINKS

THE HUB OF ATHENS' city transport is the area around Plateía Syntágmatos and Plateía Omonoías. From this central area trolleybuses or buses can be taken to the airport, the sea port at Piraeus, Athens' two train stations, and its domestic and international coach terminals.

Bus E95 runs between the airport and Syntágmatos and bus E96 between the airport and Piraeus *(see p127)*.

Buses 040 and 049 link Piraeus harbour with Syntágmatos and Omonoías in the city centre. The metro also

extends to Piraeus harbour and the journey from the city centre to the harbour takes about half an hour.

Trolleybus route 1 goes past Lárissis metro station, as well as Lárissis train station, with the Peloponnísou station *(see p130)* a short walk away from them. Bus 024 goes to coach terminal B, on Liosíon, and bus 051 to coach terminal A, on Kifisoú *(see p134)*.

Though more expensive than public transport, the most convenient way of getting to and from any of these destinations is by taxi. The journey times vary greatly but, if traffic is free-flowing, from the city centre to the airport takes

about 40 minutes; the journey from the city centre to the port of Piraeus takes around 40 minutes; and the journey from Piraeus to the airport takes about 90 minutes.

Bus from the port of Piraeus to Athens' city centre

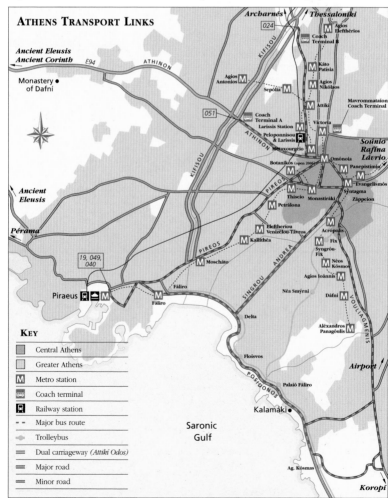

ATHENS TRANSPORT LINKS

Archarnés

Thessaloniki

024

Agios Elefthérios

Coach Terminal B

Ancient Eleusis
Ancient Corinth

E94

ATHINON

Káto Patisia

Monastery of Dafní

Agios Antonios Ⓜ

Agios Nikólaos

Sepólia Ⓜ

Attikí

Mavrommataío Coach Terminal

051

Coach Terminal A
Larissis Station

Victoria

KIFISOU

Peloponnísou & Larissis

Ⓜ

Souuío
Rafina
Lávrio

ATHINON

Metaxourgeío

Botanikós (open 2006)

Omónoia Ⓜ

Panepistimio

Ancient Eleusis

KIFISOU

Thiseío Ⓜ

Monastiráki Ⓜ

Syntagma
Záppeion

Evangelismós

Ⓜ Petrálona

Pérama

Eleftheriou Venizélou-Távros Ⓜ

Acrópolis Ⓜ

19, 049, 040

Kallithéa Ⓜ

Fix Ⓜ

Syngróu-Fix

PIREOS

Ⓜ Moscháto

Néos Kósmos Ⓜ

Agios Ioánnis Ⓜ

Fáliro

Néa Smýrni

Dáfni Ⓜ

Piraeus 🚉 ⛴ Ⓜ

Ⓜ Fáliro

Delta

Aléxandros Panagoúlis

SINGROU

ANDREA

VOULIAGMENIS

KEY

▪	Central Athens
▫	Greater Athens
Ⓜ	Metro station
🚏	Coach terminal
🚉	Railway station
--	Major bus route
⬥	Trolleybus
═	Dual carriageway *(Attikí Odos)*
═	Major road
═	Minor road

Floísvos

POSIDONOS

Palaió Fáliro

Airport

Kalamáki ●

Saronic Gulf

Ag. Kósmas

Koropí

ATHENS STREET FINDER

M AP REFERENCES given for sights in Athens refer to the maps on the following pages. References are also given for Athens hotels *(see pp86–90)*, Athens restaurants *(see pp100–4)* and for useful addresses in the *Survival Guide* section *(see pp114–139)*. The first figure in the reference tells you which Street Finder map to turn to, and the letter and number refer to the grid reference. The map below shows the area of Athens covered by the eight Street Finder maps (the map numbers are shown in black). The symbols used for sights and features are listed in the key below.

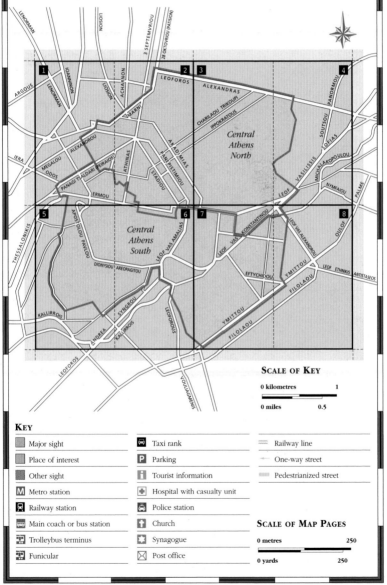

SCALE OF KEY

0 kilometres   1

0 miles   0.5

KEY

▢ Major sight	🚕 Taxi rank	▭▭ Railway line
▢ Place of interest	🅿 Parking	← One-way street
▢ Other sight	ℹ Tourist information	▭▭ Pedestrianized street
Ⓜ Metro station	✚ Hospital with casualty unit	
🚉 Railway station	🛡 Police station	
🚌 Main coach or bus station	✝ Church	
🚎 Trolleybus terminus	✡ Synagogue	**SCALE OF MAP PAGES**
🚟 Funicular	⊠ Post office	0 metres 250
		0 yards 250

Street Finder Index

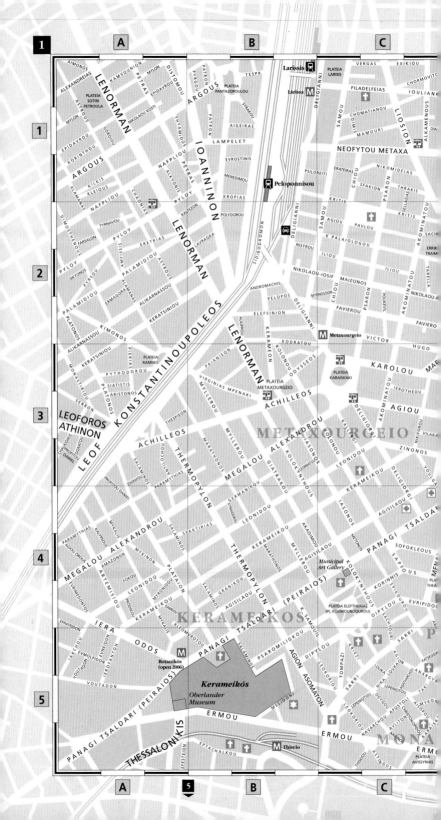

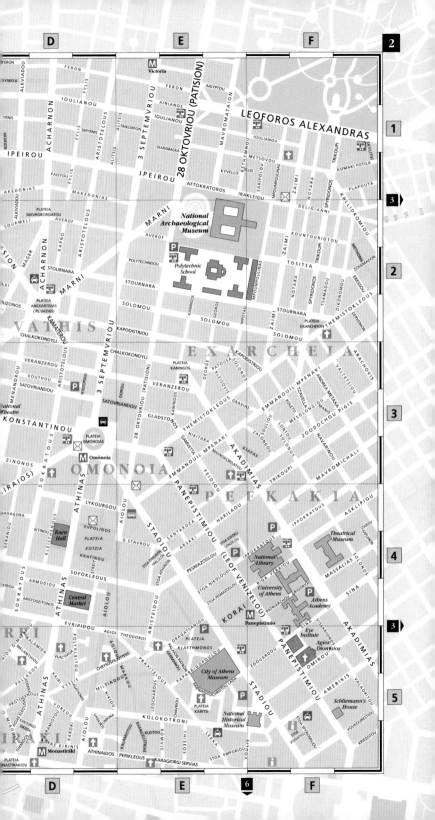

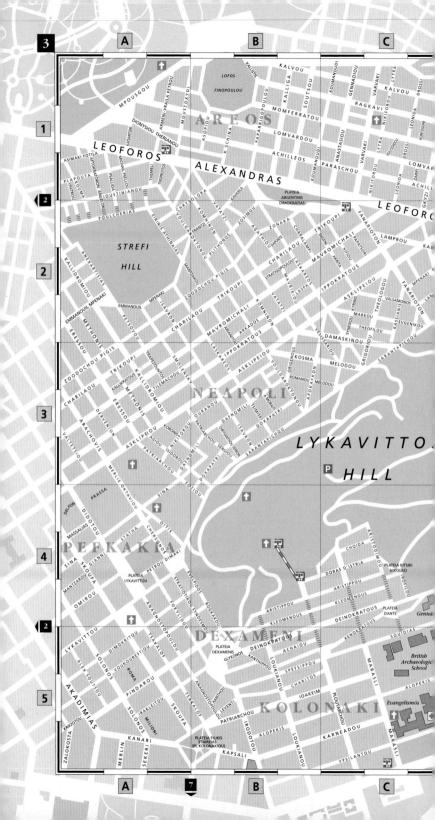

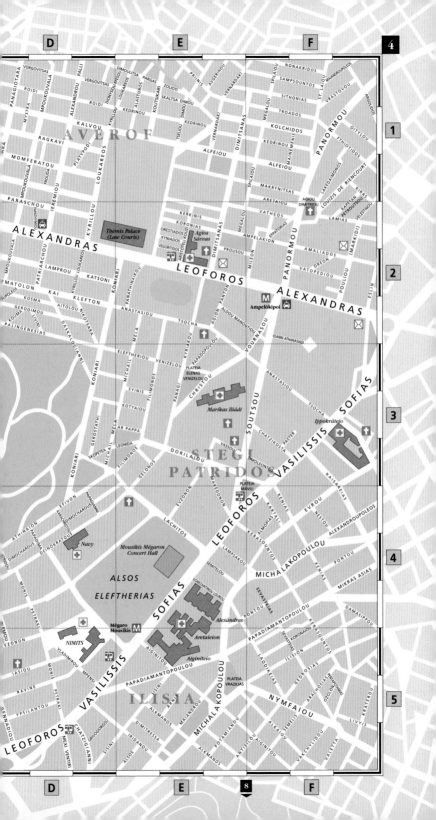

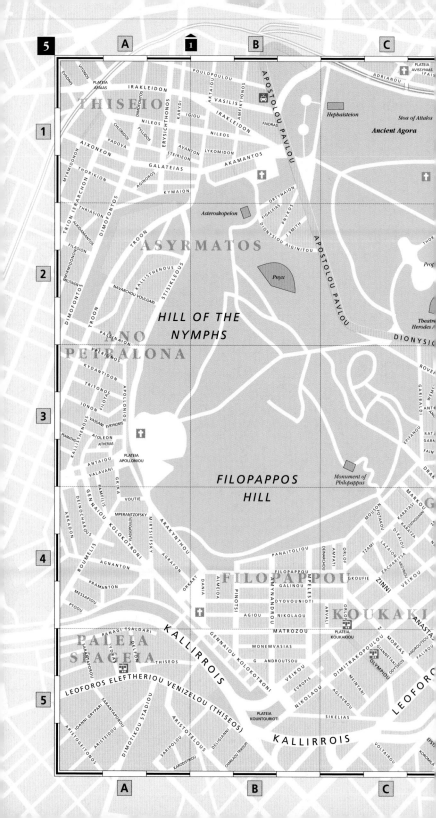

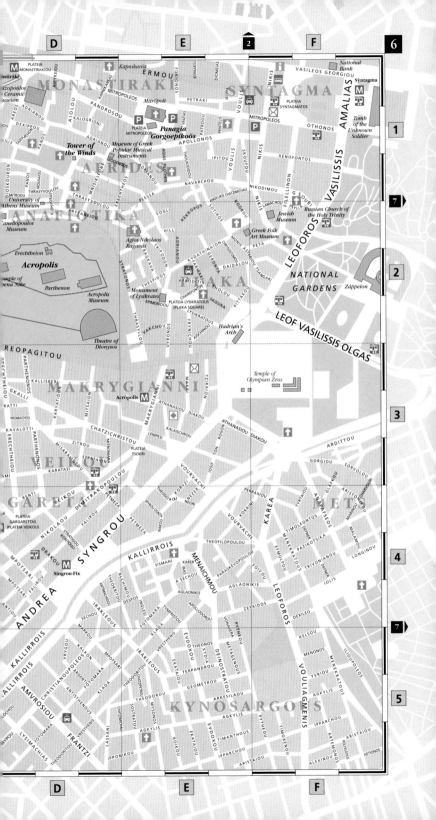

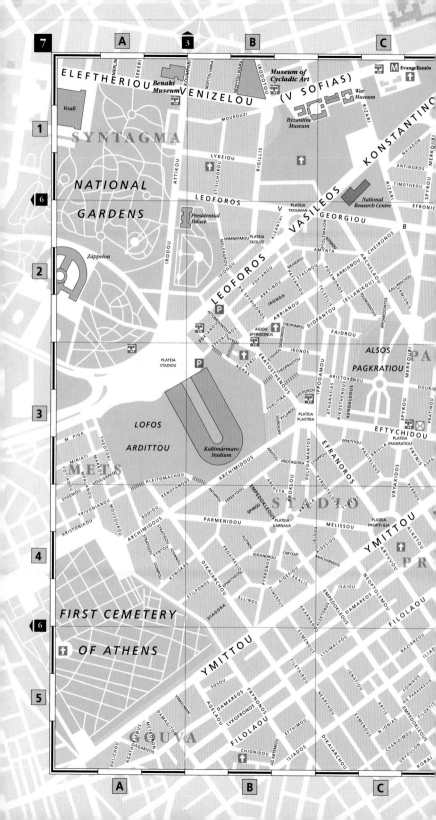

General Index

Acknowledgments

DORLING KINDERSLEY would like to thank the following people whose contributions and assistance have made the preparation of this book possible.

MAIN CONTRIBUTORS

MARC DUBIN is an American expatriate who divides his time between London and Sámos. Since 1978 he has travelled in every province of Greece. He has written or contributed to numerous guides to Greece.

JANE FOSTER is a travel writer currently based in Athens. She has travelled extensively through the Balkans and has written about Croatia, Slovenia, Bulgaria and Greece.

MIKE GERRARD is a travel writer and broadcaster who has written several guides to various parts of Greece, which he has been visiting annually since 1964.

ANDY HARRIS is a travel and food journalist based in Athens. He is the author of *A Taste of the Aegean*.

DEPUTY EDITORIAL DIRECTOR
Douglas Amrine

DEPUTY ART DIRECTOR
Gillian Allan

MANAGING EDITOR
Georgina Matthews

MANAGING ART EDITOR
Annette Jacobs

ADDITIONAL ILLUSTRATIONS

Richard Bonson, Louise Boulton, Gary Cross, Kevin Goold, Roger Hutchins, Claire Littlejohn.

DESIGN AND EDITORIAL ASSISTANCE

Hilary Bird, Elspeth Collier, Catherine Day, Jim Evoy, Emily Green, Emily Hatchwell, Leanne Hogbin, Kim Inglis, Lorien Kite, Esther Labi, Felicity Laughton, Andreas Michael, Rebecca Milner, Ella Milroy, Lisa Minsky, Robert Mitchell, Adam Moore, Jennifer Mussett, Tamsin Pender, Jake Reimann, Simon Ryder, Rita Selvaggio, Claire Stewart, Claire Tennant-Scull, Amanda Tomeh.

DORLING KINDERSLEY would also like to thank the following for their assistance: The Greek Wine Bureau, Odysea.

ADDITIONAL RESEARCH

Anna Antoniou, Garifalia Boussiopoulou, Anastasia Caramanis, Michele Crawford Magda Dimouti, Shirley Durant, Panos Gotsi, Zoi Groummouti, Peter Millett, Eva Petrou, Ellen Root, Tasos Schizas, Garifalia Tsiola, Veronica Wood.

ADDITIONAL PHOTOGRAPHY

Stephen Bere, Clive Streeter.

ARTWORK REFERENCE

Ideal Photo S.A., The Image Bank, Tony Stone Worldwide.

PHOTOGRAPHY PERMISSIONS

DORLING KINDERSLEY would like to thank the following for their assistance and kind permission to photograph at their establishments:

City of Athens Museum; Museum of Greek Folk Art, Athens; V Kyriazopoulos Ceramic Collection; National Gallery of Art, Athens; National War Museum, Athens; Nicholas P Goulandris Foundation Museum of Cycladic and Ancient Art, Athens; Theatrical Museum, Athens; University of Athens

Museum; Polygnotos Vagis Museum, Thassos. Also all other cathedrals, churches, museums, hotels, restaurants, shops, galleries, and sights too numerous to thank individually.

PICTURE CREDITS
t = top; tl = top left; tlc = top left centre; tc = top centre; trc = top right centre; tr = top right; cla = centre left above; ca = centre above; cra = centre right above; cl = centre left; c = centre; cr = centre right; clb = centre left below; cb = centre below; crb = centre right below; bl = bottom left; b = bottom; bc = bottom centre; bcl = bottom centre left; br = bottom right; bottom right above = bra; bottom right below = brb; d= detail.

Works of art have been reproduced with the permission of the following copyright holders: Vorres Museum *Water Nymph* (1995) by Apostolos Petridis 74t.

The publisher would like to thank the following individuals, companies and picture libraries for permission to reproduce their photographs:

AKG LONDON: 5tl, 37cr, 83 insert; British Museum 45b; Museum Narodowe, Warsaw 69br. ALAMY IMAGES: Robert Harding Picture Library 12-13. APERION: Kamarias Tsigamos 110cr. ATHENS INTERNATIONAL AIRPORT: 126cr, 126bl, 127cr, 128tl.

BENAKI MUSEUM: 15crb, 28cla, 28clb, 28b, 28t, 29c, 29crb, 29bl, 29t. BRIDGEMAN ART LIBRARY, LONDON/NEW YORK: Giraudon 45crb, 95bra; Giraudon/National Portrait Gallery London 73cra; Private Collection 10bl.

© THE BRITISH MUSEUM: 47br.

CENTRE FOR ASIA MINOR STUDIES: Museum of Greek Popular Musical Instruments, Fivos Anoyianakis Collection 54tl. CORBIS: Archivo Iconografico, S.A. 8; Thierry Orban 11rb; Gianni Dagli Orti 9bl; Gianni Dagli Orti 1; Kontos Yannis, /Sygma 9c.

EMPICS LTD: DPA 10c.

WERNER FORMAN ARCHIVE: 9br.

GETTY IMAGES: 11b, 11t; Aperion 76tl; Hulton Archive 10tr; Mike Hewitt/Allsport 112tr. NICHOLAS P GOULANDRIS FOUNDATION MUSEUM OF CYCLADIC AND ANCIENT GREEK ART: 15tr, 24tl, 24cl, 24c, 24br, 25cl, 25cr, 25t. GREEK FOLK ART MUSEUM: 60t and bl.

HUTCHISON LIBRARY: Hilly Janes 48tr.

IMAGESTATE/PICTOR: 49bl.

KOSTAS KONTOS: 64, 76tr, 77tl, 77cra, 77br, 111br, 112br, 121t, 127br, 137br.

MASTERFILE UK: Miles Ertman, 2-3. MUNICIPAL ART GALLERY OF ATHENS: Miss TK by Giannis Mitaraksis 38tl.

OLYMPIC AIRWAYS: 126t.

ROMYLOS PARISIS: 54bl. PICTURES COLOUR LIBRARY: Adina Tovy Amsel 82-83. POPPERFOTO: 10bc, 48bl.

SPATHARI MUSEUM OF SHADOW THEATRE: 75c. MARIA STEFOSSI: 110b. THEODOROS-PATROKLOS STELLAKIS: 78br. CARMEL STEWART: 95c.

TAP SERVICE ARCHAEOLOGICAL RECEIPTS FUND, HELLENIC REPUBLIC MINISTRY OF CULTURE: 1st Epharat of

Byzantine Antiquities 76cl, 77crb; A Epharat of Antiquities 44clb and br, 45tl and c , 46bl, 48cl, 49cr, 50tl and cl; Acropolis Museum 46tl, 46tl, 47tr, 47cl; B Epharat of Antiquities 32, 65b, 68, 69c, 70, 71cla, 71clb, 72c, b; Byzantine Museum, Athens 17, 76; Greek letter and Epharat of Antiquities 39c and bl, 40tl and bl, 41tl, ca, cb, b, 80, 81ca,cra,crb,bl,bc; Γ Epharat of Antiquities 38c and cb; Keramikos Archaeological Museum 39t, cr and br, 41cra; National Archaeological Museum, Athens 15tc, 18-19, 20-21, 49tl;

PETER WILSON: 42-43, 44cla, 50br, 56-57.

JACKET
Front – CORBIS: Bettmann br; James Davis/Eye Ubiquitous main; DK Images: Rob Reichenfeld bl; TAP Service Archaeological Receipts Fund, Hellenic Republic Ministry of Culture: A Epharat of Antiquities cl. Back – DK IMAGES: Rob Reichenfeld tr, bl. Spine – CORBIS: James Davis/Eye Ubiquitous.

All other images © Dorling Kindersley. For further information see: www.dkimages.com

Phrase Book

THERE IS NO universally accepted system for representing the modern Greek language in the Roman alphabet. The system of transliteration adopted in this guide is the one used by the Greek Government. Though not yet fully applied throughout Greece, most of the street and place names have been transliterated according to this system. For Classical names this guide uses the k, os, on and f spelling, in keeping with the modern system of transliteration. In a few cases, such as Socrates and Philopappus, the more familiar Latin form has been used. Classical names do not have accents. Where a well-known English form of a name exists, such as Athens or Corinth, this has been used. Variations in transliteration are given in the index.

GUIDELINES FOR PRONUNCIATION

The accent over Greek and transliterated words indicates the stressed syllable. In this guide the accent is not written over capital letters nor over monosyllables, except for question words and the conjunction ή (meaning "or"). In the right-hand "Pronunciation" column below, the syllable to stress is given in bold type.

On the following pages, the English is given in the left-hand column with the Greek and its transliteration in the middle column. The right-hand column provides a literal system of pronunciation and indicates the stressed syllable in bold.

THE GREEK ALPHABET

Α α	A a	**arm**
Β β	V v	**v**ote
Γ γ	G g	**y**ear (when followed by e and i sounds) **n**o (when followed by ξ or γ)
Δ δ	D d	**th**at
Ε ε	E e	**egg**
Ζ ζ	Z z	**zoo**
Η η	I i	bel**ie**ve
Θ θ	Th th	**th**ink
Ι ι	I i	bel**ie**ve
Κ κ	K k	**k**id
Λ λ	L l	**l**and
Μ μ	M m	**m**an
Ν ν	N n	**n**o
Ξ ξ	X x	ta**x**i
Ο ο	O o	f**o**x
Π π	P p	**p**ort
Ρ ρ	R r	**r**oom
Σ σ	S s	**s**orry (zero when followed by μ)
ς	s	(used at end of word)
Τ τ	T t	**t**ea
Υ υ	Y y	bel**ie**ve
Φ φ	F f	**f**ish
Χ χ	Ch ch	lo**ch** in most cases, but **h**e when followed by a, e or i sounds
Ψ ψ	Ps ps	ma**ps**
Ω ω	O o	f**o**x

COMBINATIONS OF LETTERS

In Greek there are two-letter vowels that are pronounced as one sound:

Αι αι	Ai ai	**egg**
Ει ει	Ei ei	bel**ie**ve
Οι οι	Oi oi	bel**ie**ve
Ου ου	Ou ou	l**u**te

There are also some two-letter consonants that are pronounced as one sound:

Μπ μπ	Mp mp	**b**ut, sometimes nu**mb**er in the middle of a word
Ντ ντ	Nt nt	**d**esk, sometimes u**nd**er in the middle of a word
Γκ γκ	Gk gk	**g**o, sometimes bi**ng**o in the middle of a word
Γξ γξ	nx	a**nx**iety
Τζ τζ	Tz tz	ha**nds**
Τσ τσ	Ts ts	i**t's**
Γγ γγ	Gg gg	bi**ng**o

IN AN EMERGENCY

Help!	Βοήθεια! Voitheia	vo-**ee**-theea
Stop!	Σταματήστε! Stamatiste	sta-ma-**tee**-steh
Call a doctor!	Φωνάξτε ένα γιατρό Fonáxte éna giatró	fo-**nak**-steh **e**-na ya-**tro**
Call an ambulance/ the police/the fire brigade!	Καλέστε το ασθενοφόρο/την αστυνομία/την πυροσβεστική Kaléste to asthenofóro/tin astynomía/tin pyrosvestikí	ka-**le**-steh to as-the-no-**fo**-ro/teen a-sti-no-**mia**/teen pee-ro-zve-stee-**kee**
Where is the nearest telephone/hospital/ pharmacy?	Πού είναι το πλησιέστερο τήλεφωνο/νοσοκο-μείο/φαρμακείο; Poú einai to plisiés-tero tiléfono/ nosoko-meio/farmakeío?	poo **ee**-ne to plee-see-**e**-ste-ro tee-le-pho-no/no-so-ko-mee-o/far-ma-kee-o?

COMMUNICATION ESSENTIALS

Yes	Ναι Nai	neh
No	Οχι Ochi	**o**-chee
Please	Παρακαλώ Parakaló	pa-ra-ka-**lo**
Thank you	Ευχαριστώ Efcharistó	ef-cha-ree-**sto**
You are welcome	Παρακαλώ Parakaló	pa-ra-ka-**lo**
OK/alright	Εντάξει Entáxei	en-**dak**-zee
Excuse me	Με συγχωρείτε Me synchoreíte	me seen-cho-ree-teh
Hello	Γειά σας Geiá sas	yeea sas
Goodbye	Αντίο Antío	an-**dee**-o
Good morning	Καλημέρα Kaliméra	ka-lee-**me**-ra
Good night	Καληνύχτα Kalinýchta	ka-lee-**neech**-ta
Morning	Πρωί Proí	pro-**ee**
Afternoon	Απόγευμα Apógevma	a-**po**-yev-ma
Evening	Βράδυ Vrádi	vrath-i
This morning	Σήμερα το πρωί Simera to proí	see-me-ra to pro-**ee**
Yesterday	Χθές Chthés	chthes
Today	Σήμερα Simera	see-me-ra
Tomorrow	Αύριο Avrio	**av**-ree-o
Here	Εδώ Edó	ed-**o**
There	Εκεί Ekeí	e-kee
What?	Τι; Tí?	tee?
Why?	Γιατί; Giatí?	ya-tee?
Where?	Πού; Poú?	poo?
How?	Πώς; Pós?	pos?
Wait!	Περίμενε! Perímene!	pe-ree-me-neh

USEFUL PHRASES

How are you?	Τί κάνεις; / Tí káneis?	tee ka-nees
Very well, thank you	Πολύ καλά, ευχαριστώ / Polý kalá, efcharistó	po-lee ka-la, ef-cha-ree-sto
How do you do?	Πώς είστε; / Pós eíste?	pos ees-te?
Pleased to meet you	Χαίρω πολύ / Chaíro polý	che-ro po-lee
What is your name?	Πώς λέγεστε; / Pós légeste?	pos le-ye-ste?
Where is/are...?	Πού είναι; / Poú eínai?	poo ee-ne?
How far is it to...?	Πόσο απέχει... ; / Póso apéchei...?	po-so a-pe-chee?
How do I get to...?	Πώς μπορώ να πάω.... ; / Pós mporó na páo...?	pos bo-ro-na pa-o?
Do you speak English?	Μιλάτε Αγγλικά; / Miláte Angliká?	mee-la-te an-glee-ka?
I understand	Καταλαβαίνω / Katalavaíno	ka-ta-la-ve-no
I don't understand	Δεν καταλαβαίνω / Den katalavaíno	then ka-ta-la-ve-no
Could you speak slowly?	Μιλάτε λίγο πιο αργά παρακαλώ; / Miláte ligo pio argá parakaló?	mee-la-te lee-go pyo ar-ga pa-ra-ka-lo?
I'm sorry	Με συγχωρείτε / Me synchoreíte	me seen-cho-ree teh
Does anyone have a key?	Έχει κανένας κλειδί; / Echei kanénas kleidí?	e-chee ka-ne-nas klee-dee?

USEFUL WORDS

big	Μεγάλο / Megálo	me-ga-lo
small	Μικρό / Mikró	mi-kro
hot	Ζεστό / Zestó	zes-to
cold	Κρύο / Krýo	kree-o
good	Καλό / Kaló	ka-lo
bad	Κακό / Kakó	ka-ko
enough	Αρκετά / Arketá	ar-ke-ta
well	Καλά / Kalá	ka-la
open	Ανοιχτά / Anoichtá	a-neech-ta
closed	Κλειστά / Kleistá	klee-sta
left	Αριστερά / Aristerá	a-ree-ste-ra
right	Δεξιά / Dexiá	dek-see-a
straight on	Ευθεία / Eftheía	ef-thee-a
between	Ανάμεσα / Μεταξύ / Anámesa / Metaxý	a-na-me-sa/met-tak-see
on the corner of.....	Στη γωνία του... / Sti gonía tou...	stee go-nee-a too
near	Κοντά / Kontá	kon-da
far	Μακριά / Makriá	ma-kree-a
up	Επάνω / Epáno	e-pa-no
down	Κάτω / Káto	ka-to
early	Νωρίς / Norís	no-rees
late	Αργά / Argá	ar-ga
entrance	Η είσοδος / I eisodos	ee ee-so-thos
exit	Η έξοδος / I éxodos	ee e-kso-dos
toilet	Οι τουαλέτες /WC / Oi toualétes / WC	ee-too-a-le-tes
occupied/engaged	Κατειλημμένη / Kateiliméni	ka-tee-lee-me-nee
unoccupied/vacant	Ελεύθερη / Eléftheri	e-lef-the-ree
free/no charge	Δωρεάν / Doreán	tho-re-an
in/out	Μέσα /Έξω / Mésa/ Exo	me-sa/ek-so

MAKING A TELEPHONE CALL

Where is the nearest public telephone ?	Πού βρίσκεται ο πλησιέστερος τηλεφωνικός θάλαμος; / Poú vrísketai o plisiésteros tilefonikós thálamos?	poo vrees-ke-teh o plee-see-e-ste-ros tee-le-fo-ni-kos tha-la-mos?
I would like to place a long-distance call	Θα ήθελα να κάνω ένα υπεραστικό τηλεφώνημα / Tha íthela na káno éna yperastikó tilefónima	tha ee-the-la na ka-no e-na ee-pe-ra-sti-ko tee-le-fo-nee-ma
I would like to reverse the charges	Θα ήθελα να χρεώσω το τηλεφώνημα στον παραλήπτη / Tha íthela na chreóso to tilefónima ston paralípti	tha ce-the-la na chre-o-so to tee-le-fo-nee-ma ston pa-ra-lep-tee
I will try again later	Θα ξανατηλεφωνήσω αργότερα / Tha xanatilefoníso argótera	tha ksa-na-tee-le-fo-ni-so ar-go-te-ra
Can I leave a message?	Μπορείτε να του αφήσετε ένα μήνυμα; / Mporeite na tou afisete éna mínyma?	bo-ree-te na too a-fee-se-teh e-na mee-nee-ma?
Could you speak up a little please?	Μιλάτε δυνατότερα, παρακαλώ; / Miláte dynatótera, parakaló	mee-la-teh dee-na-to-te-ra, pa-ra-ka-lo
Local call	Τοπικό τηλεφώνημα / Topikó tilefónima	to-pi-ko tee-le-fo-nee-ma
Hold on	Περιμένετε / Periménete	pe-ri-me-ne-teh
OTE telephone office	Ο ΟΤΕ / Το τηλεφωνείο / O OTE / To tilefoneío	o O-TE / To tee-le-fo-nee-o
Phone box/kiosk	Ο ΟΤΕ / Το tilefonefο / Ο τηλεφωνικός θάλαμος / Ο tilefonikós thálamos	o tee-le-fo-ni-kos tha-la-mos
Phone card	Η τηλεκάρτα / I tilekárta	ee tee-le-kar-ta

SHOPPING

How much does this cost?	Πόσο κάνει; / Póso kánei?	po-so ka-nee?
I would like.....	Θα ήθελα... / Tha íthela...	tha ee-the-la...
Do you have.....?	Έχετε...; / Echete...?	e-che-teh
I am just looking	Απλός κοιτάω / Aplós koitáo	a-plos kee-ta-o
Do you take credit cards/travellers' cheques?	Δέχεστε πιστωτικές κάρτες/travellers' cheques; / Décheste pistotikés kártes/travellers' cheques?	the-ches-teh pee-sto-tee-kes kar-tes/travellers' cheques?
What time do you open/close?	Ποτέ ανοίγετε/ κλείνετε; / Póte anoigete/ kleinete?	po-teh a-nee-ye-teh/ klee-ne-teh?
Can you ship this overseas?	Μπορείτε να το στείλετε στο εξωτερικό; / Mporeite na to steilete sto exoterikó?	bo-ree-teh na to stee-le-teh sto e-xo-te-ree ko?
This one	Αυτό εδώ / Aftó edó	af-to e-do
That one	Εκείνο / Ekeíno	e-kee-no

expensive	Ακριβό	a-kree-**vo**
	Akrivó	
cheap	Φθηνό	fthee-**no**
	Fthinó	
size	Το μέγεθος	to me-ge-thos
	To mégethos	
white	Λευκό	lef-**ko**
	Lefkó	
black	Μαύρο	**mav**-ro
	Mávro	
red	Κόκκινο	ko-kee-no
	Kókkino	
yellow	Κίτρινο	kee-tree-no
	Kítrino	
green	Πράσινο	pra-see-no
	Prásino	
blue	Μπλε	bleh
	Mple	

TYPES OF SHOP

antique shop	Μαγαζί με αντίκες	ma-ga-zee me an-dee-kes
	Magazi me antikes	
bakery	Ο φούρνος	o foor-nos
	O foúrnos	
bank	Η τράπεζα	ee tra-pe-za
	I trápeza	
bazaar	Το παζάρι	to pa-**za**-ree
	To pazári	
bookshop	Το βιβλιοπωλείο	to vee-vlee-o-po-lee-o
	To vivliopoleío	
butcher	Το κρεοπωλείο	to kre-o-po-**lee**-o
	To kreopoleío	
cake shop	Το ζαχαροπλαστείο	to za-cha-ro-pla-stee-o
	To zacharoplasteío	
cheese shop	Μαγαζί με αλλαντικά	ma-ga-zee me a-lan-dee-**ka**
	Magazi me allantiká	
	Πολυκάταστημα	
department store	Polykatástima	Po-lee-ka-**ta**-stee-ma
	Το ιχθυοπωλείο/	to eech-thee-o-po-lee-
fishmarket	ψαράδικο	o /psa-rá-dee-ko
	To ichthyopoleío/	
	psarádiko	
greengrocer	Το μανάβικο	to ma-**na**-vee-ko
	To manáviko	
hairdresser	Το κομμωτήριο	to ko-mo-tee-ree-o
	To kommotirio	
kiosk	Το περίπτερο	to pe-**reep**-te-ro
	To periptero	
leather shop	Μαγαζί με	ma-ga-zee me ther-
	δερμάτινα είδη	**ma**-tee-na ee-thee
	Magazi me dermátina eidi	
street market	Η λαϊκή αγορά	ee la-ee-**kee** a-go-**ra**
	I laïkí agorá	
newsagent	Ο εφημεριδοπώλης	O e-fee-mee-ree-tho-**po**-lees
	O efimeridopólis	
pharmacy	Το φαρμακείο	to far-ma-kee-o
	To farmakeío	
post office	Το ταχυδρομείο	to ta-chee-thro-mee-o
	To tachydromeio	
shoe shop	Κατάστημα	ka-**ta**-stee-ma ee-po-
	υποδημάτων	dee-**ma**-ton
	Katástima ypodimáton	
souvenir shop	Μαγαζί με "souvenir"	ma-ga-zee meh "souvenir"
	Magazi me "souvenir"	
supermarket	Σουπερμάρκετ/	"Supermarket"
	Υπεραγορά	/ ee-per-a-go-**ra**
	"Supermarket"/ Yperagorá	
tobacconist	Είδη καπνιστού	Ee-thee kap-nees too
	Eidi kapnistou	
travel agent	Το ταξειδιωτικό	to tak-see-thy-o-tee-**ko** gra-fee-o
	γραφείο	
	To taxeidiotikó grafeío	

SIGHTSEEING

tourist information	Ο ΕΟΤ	o E-OT
	O EOT	
tourist police	Η τουριστική	ee too-rees-tee-kee a-stee-no-mee-a
	αστυνομία	
	I touristiki astynomia	
archaeological	αρχαιολογικός	ar-che-o-lo-yee-kos
	archaiologikós	

art gallery	Η γκαλερί	ee ga-le-**ree**
	I gkalerí	
beach	Η παραλία	ee pa-ra-**lee**-a
	I paralia	
Byzantine	βυζαντινός	vee-zan-dee-**nos**
	vyzantinós	
castle	Το κάστρο	to **ka**-stro
	To kástro	
cathedral	Η μητρόπολη	ee mee-**tro**-po-lee
	I mitrópoli	
cave	Το σπήλαιο	to spee-le-o
	To spílaio	
church	Η εκκλησία	ee e-klee-**see**-a
	I ekklisia	
folk art	λαϊκή τέχνη	la-ee-**kee** tech-nee
	laïkí téchni	
fountain	Το συντριβάνι	to seen-dree-**va**-nee
	To syntriváni	
hill	Ο λόφος	o **lo**-fos
	O lófos	
historical	ιστορικός	ee-sto-ree-**kos**
	istorikós	
island	Το νησί	to nee-**see**
	To nisí	
lake	Η λίμνη	ee **leem**-nee
	I limni	
library	Η βιβλιοθήκη	ee veev-lee-o-**thee**-kee
	I vivliothiki	
mansion	Η έπαυλις	ee **e**-pav-lees
	I épavlis	
monastery	Μονή	mo-**ni**
	moní	
mountain	Το βουνό	to voo-**no**
	To vounó	
municipal	δημοτικός	thee-mo-tee-**kos**
	dimotikós	
museum	Το μουσείο	to moo-see-o
	To mouseío	
national	εθνικός	eth-nee-**kos**
	ethnikós	
park	Το πάρκο	to **par**-ko
	To párko	
garden	Ο κήπος	o **kee**-pos
	O kípos	
gorge	Το φαράγγι	to fa-**ran**-gee
	To farángi	
grave of.....	Ο τάφος του...	o **ta**-fos too...
	O táfos tou...	
river	Το ποτάμι	to po-**ta**-mee
	To potámi	
road	Ο δρόμος	o **thro**-mos
	O drómos	
saint	άγιος/άγιοι/αγία/	**a**-yee-os/a-yee-ee/a-yee-a/a-yee-es
	αγίες	
	ágios/ágioi/agia/agics	
spring	Η πηγή	ee pee-**yee**
	I pigí	
square	Η πλατεία	ee pla-**tee**-a
	I plateía	
stadium	Το στάδιο	to **sta**-thee-o
	To stádio	
statue	Το άγαλμα	to **a**-gal-ma
	To ágalma	
theatre	Το θέατρο	to the-**a**-tro
	To théatro	
town hall	Το δημαρχείο	To thee-mar-**chee**-o
	To dimarcheío	
closed on public holidays	κλειστό τις αργίες	klee-**sto** tees aryee-**es**
	kleistó tis argies	

TRANSPORT

When does the .... leave?	Πότε φεύγει το ....;	**po**-teh fev-yee to...?
	Póte févgei to...?	
Where is the bus stop?	Πού είναι η στάση του λεωφορείου;	poo **ee**-neh ee **sta**-see too le-o-fo-**ree**-oo?
	Poú eínai i stási tou leoforeiou?	
Is there a bus to..?	Υπάρχει λεωφορείο για....;	ee-**par**-chee le-o-fo-**ree**-o yia...?
	Ypárchei leoforeío gia...?	
ticket office	Εκδοτήρια εισιτηρίων	Ek-tho-**tee**-reea ee-see-tee-**ree**-on
	Ekdotíria eisitiríon	
return ticket	Εισιτήριο με επιστροφή	ee-see-**tee**-ree-o meh e-pee-stro-**fee**
	Eisitirio me epistrofi	
single journey	Απλό εισιτήριο	a-**plo** ee-see-**tee**-reeo
	Apló eisitirio	

bus station	Ο σταθμός λεωφορείων O stathmós leoforeíon	o stath-mos leo-fo-ree-on
bus ticket	Εισιτήριο λεωφορείου Eisitírio leoforeíou	ee-see-tee-ree-o leo-fo-ree-oo
trolley bus	Το τρόλλευ To tróley	to tro-le-ee
port	Το λιμάνι To limáni	to lee-ma-nee
train/metro	Το τρένο To tréno	to tre-no
railway station	σιδηροδρομικός σταθμός sidirodromikós stathmós	see-thee-ro-thro-mee-kos stath-mos
moped	Το μοτοποδήλατο / το μηχανάκι To motopodílato / To michanáki	to mo-to-po-thee-la-to/to mee-cha-na-kee
bicycle	Το ποδήλατο To podílato	to po-thee-la-to
taxi	Το ταξί To taxí	to tak-see
airport	Το αεροδρόμιο To aerodrómio	to a-e-ro-thro-mee-o
ferry	Το φερυμπότ To "ferry-boat"	to fe-ree-bot
hydrofoil	Το δελφίνι / Το υδροπτέρυγο To delfíni / To ydroptérygo	to del-fee-nee / To ee-throp-te-ree-go
catamaran	Το καταμαράν To Katamaran	to catamaran
for hire	Ενοικιάζονται Enoikiázontai	e-nee-kya-zon-deh

STAYING IN A HOTEL

Do you have a vacant room?	Έχετε δωμάτια; Échete domátia?	e-che-teh tho-ma-tee-a?
double room with double bed	Δίκλινο με διπλό κρεβάτι Díklino me dipló kreváti	thee-klee-no meh thee-plo kre-va-tee
twin room	Δίκλινο με μονά κρεβάτια Díklino me moná krevátia	thee-klee-no meh mo-na kre-vat-ya
single room	Μονόκλινο Monóklino	mo-no-klee-no
room with a bath	Δωμάτιο με μπάνιο Domátio me mpánio	tho-ma-tee-o meh ban-yo
shower	Το ντους To douz	to dooz
porter	Ο πορτιέρης O portiéris	o por-tye-rees
key	Το κλειδί To kleidí	to klee-dee
I have a reservation	Έχω κάνει κράτηση Echo káni krátisi	e-cho ka-nee kra-tee-see
room with a sea view/balcony	Δωμάτιο με θέα στη θάλασσα/μπαλκόνι Domátio me théa sti thálassa/mpalkóni	tho-ma-tee-o meh the-a stee tha-la-sa/bal-ko-nee
Does the price include breakfast?	Το πρωινό συμπεριλαμβάνεται στην τιμή; To proinó symperilamvánetai stin timí?	to pro-ee-no seem-be-ree-lam-va-ne-teh steen tee-mee?

EATING OUT

Have you got a table?	Έχετε τραπέζι; Échete trapézi?	e-che-te tra-pe-zee?
I want to reserve a table	Θέλω να κρατήσω ένα τραπέζι Thélo na kratíso éna trapézi	the-lo na kra-tee-so e-na tra-pe-zee
The bill, please	Τον λογαριασμό, παρακαλώ Ton logariazmó parakaló	ton lo-gar-yas-mo pa-ra-ka-lo
I am a vegetarian	Είμαι χορτοφάγος Eímai chortofágos	ee-meh chor-to-fa-gos
What is fresh today?	Τι φρέσκο έχετε σήμερα; Tí frésko échete símera?	tee fres-ko e-che-teh see-me-ra?

waiter/waitress	Κύριε / Γκαρσόν / Κυρία (female) Kýrie/Garson"/Kyría	Kee-ree-eh/Gar-son/Kee-ree-a
menu	Ο κατάλογος O katálogos	o ka-ta-lo-gos
cover charge	Το κουβέρ To "couvert"	to koo-ver
wine list	Ο κατάλογος με τα οινοπνευματώδη O katálogos me ta oinopnevmatódi	o ka-ta-lo-gos meh ta ee-no-pnev-ma-to-thee
glass	Το ποτήρι To potiri	to po-tee-ree
bottle	Το μπουκάλι To mpoukáli	to bou-ka-lee
knife	Το μαχαίρι To machairi	to ma-che-ree
fork	Το πηρούνι To piroúni	to pee-roo-nee
spoon	Το κουτάλι To koutáli	to koo-ta-lee
breakfast	Το πρωινό To proinó	to pro-ee-no
lunch	Το μεσημεριανό To mesimerianó	to me-see-mer-ya-no
dinner	Το δείπνο To deípno	to theep-no
main course	Το κυρίως γεύμα To kyrios gévma	to kee-ree-os yev-ma
starter/first course	Τα ορεκτικά Ta orektiká	ta o-rek-tee-ka
dessert	Το γλυκό To glykó	to ylee-ko
dish of the day	Το πιάτο της ημέρας To piáto tis iméras	to pya-to tees ee-me-ras
bar	Το μπαρ To "bar"	To bar
taverna	Η ταβέρνα I tavérna	ee ta-ver-na
café	Το καφενείο To kafeneío	to ka-fe-nee-o
fish taverna	Η ψαροταβέρνα I psarotavérna	ee psa-ro-ta-ver-na
grill house	Η ψησταριά I psistariá	ee psee-sta-rya
wine shop	Το οινοπωλείο To oinopoleío	to ee-no-po-lee-o
dairy shop	Το γαλακτοπωλείο To galaktopoleío	to ga-lak-to-po-lee-o
restaurant	Το εστιατόριο To estiatório	to e-stee-a-to-ree-o
ouzeri	Το ουζερί To ouzerí	to oo-ze-ree
meze shop	Το μεζεδοπωλείο To mezedopoleío	To me-ze-do-po-lee-o
take away kebabs	Το σουβλατζίδικο To souvlatzidiko	To soo-vlat-zee-dee-ko
rare	Ελάχιστα ψημένο Eláchista psiméno	e-lach-ees-ta psee-me-no
medium	Μέτρια ψημένο Métria psiméno	met-ree-a psee-me-no
well done	Καλοψημένο Kalopsiméno	ka-lo-psee-me-no

BASIC FOOD AND DRINK

coffee	Ο καφές O Kafés	o ka-fes
with milk	με γάλα me gála	me ga-la
black coffee	σκέτος skétos	ske-tos
without sugar	χωρίς ζάχαρη choris záchari	cho-rees za-cha-ree
medium sweet	μέτριος métrios	me-tree-os
very sweet	γλυκύς glykýs	glee-kees
tea	τσάι tsái	tsa-ee
hot chocolate	ζεστή σοκολάτα zesti sokoláta	ze-stee so-ko-la-ta
wine	κρασί krasí	kra-see
red	κόκκινο kókkino	ko-kee-no
white	λευκό lefkó	lef-ko
rosé	ροζέ rozé	ro-ze

raki	Το ρακί To raki	to ra-kee
ouzo	Το ούζο To oúzo	to oo-zo
retsina	Η ρετσίνα I retsína	ee ret-see-na
water	Το νερό To neró	to ne-ro
octopus	Το χταπόδι To chtapódi	to chta-po-dee
fish	Το ψάρι To psári	to psa-ree
cheese	Το τυρί To tyrí	to tee-ree
halloumi	Το χαλούμι To chaloúmi	to cha-loo-mee
feta	Η φέτα I féta	ee fe-ta
bread	Το ψωμί To psomí	to pso-mee
bean soup	Η φασολάδα I fasoláda	ee fa-so-la-da
houmous	Το χούμους To houmous	to choo-moos
halva	Ο χαλβάς O chalvás	o chal-vas
meat kebabs	Ο γύρος O gýros	o yee-ros
Turkish delight	Το λουκούμι To loukoúmi	to loo-koo-mee
baklava	Ο μπακλαβάς O mpaklavás	o bak-la-vas
klephtiko	Το κλέφτικο To kléftiko	to klef-tee-ko

NUMBERS

1	ένα éna	e-na
2	δύο dýo	thee-o
3	τρία tría	tree-a
4	τέσσερα téssera	te-se-ra
5	πέντε pénte	pen-deh
6	έξι éxi	ek-si
7	επτά eptá	ep-ta
8	οχτώ ochtó	och-to
9	εννέα ennéa	e-ne-a
10	δέκα déka	the-ka
11	έντεκα énteka	en-de-ka
12	δώδεκα dódeka	tho-the-ka
13	δεκατρία dekatría	de-ka-tree-a
14	δεκατέσσερα dekatéssera	the-ka-tes-se-ra
15	δεκαπέντε dekapénte	the-ka-pen-de
16	δεκαέξι dekaéxi	the-ka-ek-si
17	δεκαεπτά dekaeptá	the-ka-ep-ta
18	δεκαοχτώ dekaochtó	the-ka-och-to
19	δεκαεννέα dekaennéa	the-ka-e-ne-a
20	είκοσι eikosi	ee-ko-see
21	εικοσιένα eikosiéna	ee-ko-see-e-na
30	τριάντα triánta	tree-an-da
40	σαράντα saránta	sa-ran-da
50	πενήντα peninta	pe-neen-da
60	εξήντα exínta	ek-seen-da
70	εβδομήντα evdomínta	ev-tho-meen-da

80	ογδόντα ogdónta	og-thon-da
90	ενενήντα enenínta	e-ne-neen-da
100	εκατό ekató	e-ka-to
200	διακόσια diakósia	thya-kos-ya
1,000	χίλια chília	chee-ly-a
2,000	δύο χιλιάδες dýo chiliádes	thee-o cheel-ya-thes
1,000,000	ένα εκατομμύριο éna ekatommýrio	e-na e-ka-to-mee-ree-o

TIME, DAYS AND DATES

one minute	ένα λεπτό éna leptó	e-na lep-to
one hour	μία ώρα mía óra	mee-a o-ra
half an hour	μισή ώρα misí óra	mee-see o-ra
quarter of an hour	ένα τέταρτο éna tétarto	e-na te-tar-to
half past one	μία και μισή mía kai misí	mee-a keh mee-see
quarter past one	μία και τέταρτο mía kai tétarto	mee-a keh te-tar-to
ten past one	μία και δέκα mía kai déka	mee-a keh the-ka
quarter to two	δύο παρά τέταρτο dýo pará tétarto	thee-o pa-ra te-tar-to
ten to two	δύο παρά δέκα dýo pará déka	thee-o pa-ra the-ka
a day	μία μέρα mía méra	mee-a me-ra
a week	μία εβδομάδα mía evdomáda	mee-a ev-tho-ma-tha
a month	ένας μήνας énas mínas	e-nas mee-nas
a year	ένας χρόνος énas chrónos	e-nas chro-nos
Monday	Δευτέρα Deftéra	thef-te-ra
Tuesday	Τρίτη Tríti	tree-tee
Wednesday	Τετάρτη Tetárti	te-tar-tee
Thursday	Πέμπτη Pémpti	pemp-tee
Friday	Παρασκευή Paraskeví	pa-ras-ke-vee
Saturday	Σάββατο Sávvato	sa-va-to
Sunday	Κυριακή Kyriakí	keer-ee-a-kee
January	Ιανουάριος Ianouários	ee-a-noo-a-ree-os
February	Φεβρουάριος Fevrouários	fev-roo-a-ree-os
March	Μάρτιος Mártios	mar-tee-os
April	Απρίλιος Aprílios	a-pree-lee-os
May	Μάιος Máios	ma-ee-os
June	Ιούνιος Ioúnios	ee-oo-nee-os
July	Ιούλιος Ioúlios	ee-oo-lee-os
August	Αύγουστος Avgoustos	av-goo-stos
September	Σεπτέμβριος Septémvrios	sep-tem-vree-os
October	Οκτώβριος Októvrios	ok-to-vree-os
November	Νοέμβριος Noémvrios	no-em-vree-os
December	Δεκέμβριος Dekémvrios	the-kem-vree-os

ATHENS 2004 OLYMPIC DAILY COMPETITION SCHEDULE

SPORTS	VENUE	FRI 13/8	SAT 14/8	SUN 15/8	MON 16/8	TUE 17/8	WED 18/8	THU 19/8	FRI 20/8	SAT 21/8	SUN 22/8	MON 23/8	TUE 24/8	WED 25/8	THU 26/8	FRI 27/8	SAT 28/8	SUN 29/8
Opening/Closing Ceremonies	OCO																	
Archery	PS																	
Athletics	OCO																	
Badminton	GCO																	
Baseball	HOSC																	
Basketball	HOSC, OCO																	
Beach Volleyball	FCO																	
Boxing	PBH																	
Canoe/Kayak Flatwater Racing	SCH																	
Canoe/Kayak Slalom Racing	HOSC																	
Cycling Mountain Bike	MTB																	
Cycling Road	MTB																	
Cycling Track	OCO																	
Diving	OCO																	
Equestrian	EQU																	
Fencing	HOSC																	
Football (also at Pátra, Vólos, Thessaloníki and Irákleio (Crete))	KS																	
Gymnastics Artistic	OCO												Gala					
Gymnastics Rhythmic	GAI																	